Carl Horstmann

The Lives of Women Saints of our Contrie of England

also some other liues of holie women written by some of the auncient fathers (c.

1610-1615.)

Carl Horstmann

The Lives of Women Saints of our Contrie of England
also some other liues of holie women written by some of the auncient fathers (c. 1610-1615.)

ISBN/EAN: 9783337335687

Printed in Europe, USA, Canada, Australia, Japan

Cover: Foto ©Lupo / pixelio.de

More available books at **www.hansebooks.com**

THE LIVES
of
Women Saints of our Contrie of England,

ALSO

SOME OTHER LIUES OF HOLIE WOMEN
WRITTEN BY SOME OF THE
AUNCIENT FATHERS.

(C. 1610—1615.)

EDITED FOR THE FIRST TIME FROM MS. STOWE 949

BY

C. HORSTMANN.

LONDON:
PUBLISHED FOR THE EARLY ENGLISH TEXT SOCIETY
BY N. TRÜBNER & CO., 57 & 59, LUDGATE HILL.

MDCCCLXXXVI.

INTRODUCTION.

WHEN searching for Bokenham's second collection of lives of Saints which he mentions as his work in his *Mappula Angliae* (lately published in *Eng. Studien*, 1886), I found not it (it seems indeed to be lost), but the present collection which I had not before known of. This set of Female Saints' Lives is in a unique MS., MS. Stowe 949, in which, p. 1, the former owner has written 'Bibl. Thomae Astlei Arm.,' and then added: 'This MS. has not been printed, and the Lives in it are very different from those published in the *Britannia Sancta*: the following Lives abound with wonderful miracles and marvellous relations which are omitted in the printed works.' This MS., 8°, paper, numbering 357 pages, and containing only the present collection, is carefully written and executed, in a fine and legible hand, which has used italics in the titles, quotations, and proper names, and added marginal notes, headlines, and indexes. It is very correct, and might seem to be the author's own MS. but for a few mistakes which only a scribe could have made (f. i. p. 70, 12 'they for' instead of 'therfor') it was no doubt copied directly from the original MS., and is most likely the clean transcript from the author's draft. On account of this correctness, and the care taken in every detail, I have deemed it advisable to reprint the MS. as it is, retaining the same change of type, the same headings and marginal notes, and even the punctuation, which is correct, though deviating in some respects from the present mode, and which brings out the latinizing style of that period, with its intertwining of sentences by the frequent use of relative conjunctions. I have only removed some inconsistencies, added the quotation commas, used F instead of ff, and employed small capitals, instead of italics, in proper names. I have also added the references in marginal notes (in brackets) and footnotes.

Twice in the earlier English (and no other) literature, was an attempt made to put together the lives of female Saints: by Bokenham in verse, and in the present collection—a peculiar instance of the veneration which the weaker part of mankind, especially in its godlike members, enjoys in this island. But if Bokenham's collection is limited to some (13) of the most common Saints, the present collection takes a far wider range. It consists of two equal parts: (1) 'The lives of the women Saints of our contrie of England,' (2) 'Some other lives of holie women written by some of the auncient Fathers.' The first part is preceded by a long introduction, 'Some Notes before the liues,' on the questions why God has provided Saints, and why the Saints of Scotland and Ireland are numbered amongst the Saints of England in this collection and then treating of virginity by extracts from St. Cyprian and Ierome, and giving some specimens of true widowhood in St. Ierome's time (Marcella and Paula) and from the Bible (Iudith and Anna prophetissa).

I give here the list of the English female Saints of the 1st part, in the order of the MS., adding their anniversary, the date given to them by the author, and his source:—

INTRODUCTION. vii

1 S. Helena .... 18 Aug.	+ 326 from	' Baronius '*Ann. eccl.* iii. and iv.[1] (extracted).
2 S. Ursula .... 21 Oct.	c. 449 ,,	'Dr. Herm. Flien's'*Hist. S. Urs.*[2] (in Zach. Lippeloo *Vitae SS.*[3] iv. p. 745, Col. 1596.
3 S. Keyna .... 8 Oct.	c. 490 ,,	Capgrave *Nova. Leg. Angl.* 1516 (abr.).
4 S. Brigidae .... 1 Feb.	c. 518 or 521[4] } ,,	Lippeloo & Capgr. (abr.).
5 S. Dympna........ 15 May	c. 600 ,,	Martyrium b. Dympnae by 'Peter of Cambray' (in Lippeloo ii. p. 646).
6 S. Edburg ....(*a*) 12 Dec. (*b*) 15 June	c. 616 ,,	Capgrave[5] (abr.). (cf. Will. Malm. Reg. ii. 13.)
7 S. Eanswide...... 12 Sept.	c. 640 ,,	Capgrave (abr.).

---

[1] The life in Capgrave gives large verbal extracts from the *Hist. trium Regum* by John of Hildesheim.

[2] The exact title is: *Historia SS. Ursulae et Sociarum Virginum brevissime conscripta, cum annotationibus in quibus veritas eiusdem investigatur, Per R. D. Hermannum Fleien S. Theologiae Doctorem, S. Cuniberti Decanum, SS.que Virginum Coloniae Canonicum*. The same author is frequently referred to by Crombach, *S. Ursula vindicata*, Col. 1647. The English text is a verbal translation (but without the critical 'annotaciones'). The 'Bishop Lindan' quoted at the end, p. 39, is the well-known Lindan (1525-88) bishop of Roermond in 1562, and of Gand (Ghent) in 1588, who contributed the passage quoted to Baronius's *Martyrology*, 21 Oct. See also *Acta SS.* Bolland, 21 Oct.

[3] Res gestae illustratissimorum Martyrum, Confessorum atque S. Virginum . . ., eorum praecipue quae per R. P. L. Surium sex tomis comprehensae sunt & nunc restrictis verborum ambagibus, integra tamen historiarum serie ubique seruata, ad exactissimam doctissimi & praestantissimi viri D. Caes. Baronii Chronologiam digestae ac in quatuor Tomos distributae, Studio & labore F. Zach. Lippeloo, Carthusiae Coloniensis alumno, Col. apud Henr. Falkenburg, A.D. MDXCIII. (vol. 4: 1496); the 2 last vols. have also the title, *Vitae Sanctorum sive Res g. &c.* This collection was reprinted Col. 1604 and 1616. It contains most of the lives in Surius, in a somewhat abridged shape. The English author does not seem to have used Surius, or he would not have omitted St. Lioba (Surius: 28 Sept.). Surius contains the same English Saints as Lippeloo, except S. Walburge; with the text of Capgrave, a little modified.

[4] Lippeloo gives 521, Capgrave 518.

[5] He confounds her with S. Ethelburge, making her the daughter of Ethelbert and Berta.

INTRODUCTION.

8 S. Ethelburge (a)	11 Oct.	c. 640	from	Capgrave (abr.) (cf. Beda iv. 9).
(b) daughter of Ethelbert and Emma (cf. Beda ii. 11 ff.; Flor. Wig.)				
9 S. Sexburge	6 July.	640	,,	Capgrave (abr.).
10 S. Hilda	18 Nov.	c. 650	,,	Capgrave (from Beda iv. 23).
11 S. Ermenilde.....	3 Feb.	660	,,	Capgrave (abr.).
12 S. Werburge.....	3 Feb.	,,	,,	,,
13 S. Milburge	23 Feb.	c. 664	,,	,,
14 S. Mildrede.......	20 Feb.	c. ,,	,,	,,
15 S. Ebba............	25 Aug.	+ 683	,,	Capgrave.
16 Etheldred.........	23 June	c. 674	,,	'Beda' H. E. iv. 19 (and Capgrave).[1]
17 S. Kinesburge .. S. Kineswide ... S. Tibbe	6 March	c. 606	,,	Capgrave (cf. Math. Westm. a 705).
18 S. Ethelburge ... (wife of Ine)...	—	c. 690	,,	(Will. of Malm. R. i. 35-37, Higden Pol. p. 258.)
19 S. Hildelitha.....	24 March	c. 676	,,	Capgrave (abr.) (no Vita extant).
20 S. Cuthburge.....	31 Aug.	c. 690	,,	Capgrave.
21 S. Withburge....	8 Jul.	c. 650	,,	,, (no Vita ext.).
22 S. Inthware[2].....	?	c. 700	,,	,,
23 S. Frideswide....	19 Oct.	c. 740	,,	,,
24 S. Walburge......	25 Feb. (1 May)	c. 746	,,	Lippeloo ii. p. 397, 1 May (& Capgr.).[3]
25 S. Wenefride.....	3 Nov.	after 600, c. 800	,,	Lippeloo iv. p. 361 (& Capgrave).
26 S. Modwen	5 Jul.	c. 870	,,	Capgrave.
27 S. Ositha..........	7 Oct.	c. 880	,,	Capgrave & Lippeloo.
28 S. Maxentia	20 Nov. (24 Oct.)	?	,,	,, ,, ,,
29 S. Oswen (Osman)	9 Sept.	?	,,	Capgrave.
30 S. Elflede[4]	29 Oct.	c. 950	,,	,,

---

[1] What the English author adds at the end as taken from *The Catalogue of English Saintes*, is found in Capgrave.

[2] Iuthware in Capgrave. Nothing is known of this saint besides what Capgrave gives; cf. Rees's *Welsh Saints*, 321.

[3] Both abridged from the *Vita auct. Wolfhardo Presb.* (in *Act. SS. Boll.* 25 Feb. In Surius this life is wanting.

[4] Elfreda in *Brit. Sancta;* she was abbess of Romsey in Hampshire, and is mentioned by Will. Malm. Pont. 2.

31 S. Edith	16 Sept.	c. 980 from	Capgrave & Lippeloo (abr).	
32 S. Wulfhilde.....	9 Dec.	—	Capgrave.	
33 S. Margaret, Queen of Scotland	10 June	1100	,,	Capgrave (abr. in Lippeloo), abr.[1]
34 S. Mectilde	12 April	c. 1200	,,	Thomas Cantimpr. *de apibus*, lib. ii. cap. 1.

The 2nd part, p. 117 ff. contains lives from the Fathers, mostly in verbal translations:

1 S. Monica	4 May	(+ 387) trans. from	'S. August. *Confessiones.*'[2]	
2 S. Agnes	21 Jan.	(+ 304 or 305.	,,	'S. Ambros. *Serm.* 90.'
3 S. Gorgonia... ...	8 (Baron. 9) Dec.(+c.372)		,,	'S. Gregor.Naz.' her brother, *Or. fun.* 11 & 14.'
4 S. Nonna	5 Aug.	(+ 374)	,,	'S. Gregor.Naz.' her son, *Or. fun. in Caes. & in patrem.*'
5 S. Iulitta	30 May	+ c. 304	,,	'S. Basile' (*Homil. in mart. Iul.*)
6 A captive in Iberia	—	c. 327 (Baron.)	,,	'Rufinus, I. 10.'
7 S. Macrina	19 Jul.	+ 379	,,	'S. Gregor. of Nyssa, *Ep. ad Olympium.*'

Concluding with an admirable miracle of St. Macrina's grandfather.

The order of the English female Saints is chronological. The author may be said to represent fairly the hagiologic knowledge of his days. The time had arrived for digesting the vast materials: Lippomani

[1] At the end, p. 113, the English author mentions Hector Boece (+ 1536) *Chron. Scot.* (Paris 1526-7, and, increased by book 18 and 19, 1574). This was translated into Scotch verse by Stewart ab. 1530 (ed. in *Chron. & Mem.* by W. B. Turnbull, 3 vols. London, 1858), into prose by Bellenden 1530-3 (ed. Edinb. 1536, repr. 1821).

[2] The more special references I have given in the text.

(1551-60) and Surius (1570-75) had published their *Vitae Sanctorum;* Baronius had begun to sift the materials in his *Annales Ecclesiastici* (1588-1607, 12 vol.). Our author follows Baronius, not only in the life of St. Helen, which he extracted from the *Annales*, but, more frequently, in his chronology, for which he quotes both the *Annals* and the *Martyrology* (1586) of Baronius. But he already goes beyond this author in adopting, for his life of St. Ursula, the version of Herman Fleien [1] (ed. in Lippeloo, iv. 1596), who corrects Baronius, in fixing the slaughter of the holy virgins at the time that the Huns occupied Cologne. Sometimes he goes back to the original sources, as in the life of St. Etheldred, which he translates verbally from Bede (H. E. iv. 19): in St. Kinesburge he mentions Mathew of Westminster. But his chief source, besides Lippeloo (whom he consults in the few lives of English Saints contained in his collection)[2], is Capgrave's *Nova Legenda Angliae* (1516),[3] which collection comprises all the lives of our English author, in alphabetical order, except Dympna and Mechtilde, mostly in *verbal extracts* from the original *Vitae*. This was the only collection, then extant, which he could consult for his special purpose (English Saints). He follows Capgrave even in St. Hilda (with the account of Cædmon,[4] the Anglo-saxon

---

[1] His version rests on Galfridus Monmut., cf. *Act. SS. Boll.*, 21 Oct.
[2] Sometimes he combines the versions of Lippeloo and Capgrave, as in Brigid, where he gives the chronology of both ; in S. Walburg, where he uses the texts of both, and adds the miracles (om. in Capgr.) from Lippeloo.
[3] This collection exists in MS. in the York Minster libr., in Cott. Tib. E 1 (greatly injured by fire), and in MS. Tanner 15 (Bodl.). An abridged translation was published by Pynson in 1516. The entire work was printed in 1516 by Wynkyn de Worde. The introduction is also printed in *De Illustr. Henricis.*
[4] The tradition of Cædmon, it seems, was first revived by Capgrave

poet), when he might have gone back to Bede (H. E. iv. 23), whom however he does not even mention here. But he hardly ever translates Capgrave verbally: in most cases he more or less abridges him.

Though, strangely enough, he never mentions Capgrave's name, he seems to refer to his collection under the name of *The Catalogue of English Saints* (p. 70), as the account he gives there under this head is found in Capgrave.—The life of St. Dympna is a verbal translation of the *Vita* by Peter of Cambray (c. 1290), which he found in Lippeloo's collection. For St. Mechtilde he refers to 'a verie good Author that liued a litle after her, to weete, 1238.' In *Britannia Sancta* (under the 12th April, after Wilson's *Engl. Martyrology*) this author is 'Thomas Cantipratensis[1] in the 2nd book of the *Miracles of his own time*, chap. 10:' the passage is however found in the 2nd book of his *Bonum universale de apibus mysticis*, cap. 1, which was printed in 1597.[2]— It is not

and kept alive by our English author, till Junius took it up again and ascribed to Cædmon the poems now passing under his name.

[1] This Thomas de Cantimpré was born in 1201 (or 1186) at Lewis, not far from Bruxelles; was first an Augustin canon in the abbey of Cantimpré near Cambray, after 1232 a Dominican friar, studied in Cologne and Paris, and became prior at Louvain; he died in 1263 or 1280. He wrote, besides his book *de Apibus*, the lives of S. Christina mirabilis of Hasban, and of S. Mary of Oignon, English translations of which are extant in a MS. Douce (ed. by me in Anglia 1884).

[2] *Act. SS. Boll.* April 12, p. 65, remark about this Mechthildis: dicitur Vita eius extare MS. apud Robertum Bucklandium... Venit autem Alexander ad Claustrum Fonii, seu Fusniacum, in Landunensi episcopatu, secundo a Veruino oppido lapide, unde ad novem milliaria discedens Mathildis sancte vixit. Agunt etiam de ea et fratre Baptista Fulgosius lib. 4 factorum dictorumque memorabilium, cap. 4, et Andreas Eboreusis in suis exemplis, titulo de Paupertate. Non fit eius mentio in *Martyrol. Gallic. Saussaii*, neque arbitramur ullam venerationem Ecclesiasticam eidem concessam.—There is another Mechthildis mentioned in Trithemius (*Chron. Hirsaug.* ad. a. 1154), who coming from St. Alban's to Spannheim, lived there a recluse, and died in great reputation for sanctity in 1154; cf. A. Butler, *Lives of SS.* 10 April.

xii INTRODUCTION.

my present task [1] to follow up the original sources, or to give the development of each legend. More information of this kind will be found in *Britannia Sancta, or the Lives of the most celebrated British, English, Scottish, and Irish Saints*, London MDCCXLV. in 2 Parts (Jan.—June, July—Dec.) [2]; Alban Butler, *The Lives of the Fathers, Martyrs, and other principal Saints, compiled from Original Monuments and other authentic records*, 12 vol. Dubl. and Lond. 1833-8; Wm. Smith and Henry Wace, *A Dictionary of Christian Biography*, vol. 1—3 (A—M), London, J. Murray, 1877-82, and others.

The lives of the second part are verbally translated from the Fathers: in Nonna, the material is gathered from two funeral sermons of S. Gregorius Nazianzenus (*Or. fun. in patrem* and *Or. fun. in Caesarium fratrem*) and connected by the author's own narrative: an attempt which does not seem very successful. But it must be acknowledged that he has used not only Latin, but also Greek authors, and most likely, at least in part, translated the latter from the Greek texts.

There can be little doubt as to the author's date. He himself says (p. 7) that up to his time 400 years had elapsed since the conquest of Ireland by Henry II. (in

---

[1] Nor would it be easy to attempt that task, as the legendary and hagiologic part—not the least interesting—of English history has been blamably neglected up to the present; so much so that most of the original *Vitae* (from which Capgrave gives mere extracts) are still hidden in libraries. England has not done her duty in this regard.

[2] This book contains all the Saints of our Author, except Inthware and Oswen, and several besides: S. Ita (15 Jan.), Bathildes Queen (27 Jan.), Attracta (9 Feb.), Kennocha (13 March), Elgyve Queen (18 May), Buriene (29 May), Everildis (9 July), Lewine (24 July), Christiana (26 July), Alfreda (2 Aug.), Ebba (25 Aug.), Bega (6 Sept.), Lioba and Tetta (28 Sept.), Tecla (15 Oct.), Cyra (16 Oct.), Oda (27 Nov.), Christina (5 Dec.), most of them Irish and British Saints; besides numbering amongst the Saints Torgitha (26 Jan.), Earcongota (7 July), Milwyde (17 Jan.), as it does Cædmon (12 Feb.) and Richard Hampolle (29 Sept.) amongst the male Saints.

1172), and that St. Cyprian[1] lived above fourteen hundred years before his time. He quotes Bishop Lindan (p. 39), who, having been consecrated bishop of Roermond in 1562, became bishop of Gand (Ghent) in 1588, and died in the same year, and whose contributions to Baronius's *Martyrology* appeared with that work in 1586. He calls Herm. Fleien his contemporary, whose life of St. Ursula was published in Lippeloo *V. SS.* in 1596. He took his life of St. Maxentia from Thomas of Cantimpré's *Bonum de apibus*, which was printed in 1597. He uses Baronius, whose *Annales Eccl.*[2] appeared in 1588-1607 (1st edit.). So we come to the beginning of the 17th century. The character of the writing and the water-mark in the paper of the MS., as the Keeper of the MSS. in the British Museum kindly informs me, point to 1610-1615. So the book belongs to the time when Shakespeare's genius had reached its zenith. The author must be sought amongst the Roman Catholic theologians of Elizabeth's time. His name may perhaps be found amongst the eminent Romanists in Jos. Gillow's *A literary and biographical history or Bibliographical dictionary of the English Catholics from 1534 to the present time*, London and New York, 1885 ff. 2 vols. (in progress).

[1] This calculation is, however, not correct; he evidently does not know the date of Cyprian's death.
[2] He quotes tom. 3 and 4 of the *Ann. Eccl.*

[THE LIVES
OF WOMEN SAINTS OF OUR CONTRIE OF ENGLAND.

ALSO SOME OTHER LIUES OF HOLIE WOMEN WRITTEN BY SOME OF THE AUNCIENT FATHERS, Pag. 120 (MS. 175).]

Some Notes before the liues.

Why God hath prouided in his Christian Contries some famous Saintes aboue the common sorts.   Why God hath prouided Saints. [added by a later hand]

Faith decaying in the worlde, and Charitie becomming more and more colde, Christians commonlie thereuppon make small or verie base conceite of the vertue and force
4 of those vertues; obseruing as they imagine litle difference betweene naturall persuasion, and supernaturall instruction, betweene sensuall, worldlie, and humane loue, and betweene spirituall, heauenlie and diuine Charitie. Not-
8 withstanding as the admirable workes and benefits of nature are many, yet not obserued or dulie pondered, vntill by some speciall art and industrie they are proposed and proued, as the nature and vertues of herbes are not
12 knowne but by physicions, nor the precious earth of golde and siluer mines, but by the art of goulde-fyning, neither the secret effect and rare dignities of stones and pearles but by lapidaries, and so in other things; In like sort
16 gods grace and the workes thereof, the force of faith, the glorie of gods loue, are not ordinarilie considered or much

weighed, bicause they are vsuallie either not trulie present, but imagined; or if they be present, they are so confused with other drosse of sensuall affections and naturall imperfections, as that their light is much obscured, their operation blunted and dulled, and their dignitie vndiscerned. Wherefore when we may finde them pure and fined from such drossie desires, tried & cleane from such base affections, there may we beholde the beautie and glittering of those iewells, the worth of those gemmes, the admirable vertues and forces of their power. Then also may we know what a benefit it is to haue them, what riches to possesse them, what comfort to enioy them. For this cause hath our gracious God prouided some speciall Saintes in all sexes and estates, in all professions and callings, whereby all other of the same condition or qualitie, may learne the power of gods grace, the force of faith, the abilitie of charitie, when in the weakest sex, the yongest yeares, and in the greatest difficulties, as of kinglie honours, of princelie pleasures, of roiall riches, of youthfull concupiscence, of danger of dysgrace, pouertie, penurie, and death it self, they produce such potent effects, as to glorie in worldlie contempt, to choose pouertie for the greatest riches, obedience for Christs sake aboue any authoritie to command, spirituall solitarines before any pleasant temporall companie, payne for pleasure, fasting for feasting, penance for pastime. By which spectacle of so different deuotion in the same condition or sex, or such ods of vertue in equalitie or lesse abilitie of nature, they may playnlie perceyue their owne negligence, and accuse their coldenesse, and withall learne the value of true vertue, magnifie Christs grace & gracious gifts, quicken their sluggishnes, to be more trustfull in gods fauour and forces, more feruent in prayer for such help, more humble in seeing their farre distance from their like or more vnlike; they hauing made such a conquest of themselues and the worlde to which they feele themselues so inthralled, they hauing so armed

naturall imbecillitie with force of faith, when themselues
are yet so feeble and fainte in the same faith. / By such
greate lightes in moste ages, or at leaste by their memorable
4 acts and liues mercifullie conserued in moste contries, hath
god vsed graciouslie to open the eyes and awake the
drousines of his slacke people, to checke their coldenes, to
admonish their dull desires, that when they shall see or
8 reade how camells haue putt of their greate bunches, and
passed throughe the needles eye of Christs narrow way,
that is Princes and Potentates of the worlde haue contemned
so greate riches and honours for Christs loue and imita-
12 tion, and when they shall beholde fraile women to haue
taken vp so weightie and greate Crosses, and to haue
carried them so cheerfullie albeit deyntilie bredd and
brought vp, and inuited by the world to excellent aduance-
16 ments glorie and delightes; yet neglecting them all to
follow Christ; how many may be confounded that for
onelie mammocks and scrappes in comparison, neglect to
serue god or forgoe his seruice ? How many men may
20 blush at their more than womannish weaknes, that can
scarce beare any Crosse or verie small ones, when tender
ladies haue taken such strength and courage throughe loue
of their lord, to carrie so mightie burdens ? Who may not
24 be ashamed at the name of a man, that can not come nighe,
or at least dare not endeuour to contend in strength and
labour with a weake woman ? What inferiour person can
thinke they leaue or bestow much on Christ, when sondrie
28 Princes and greate states haue voluntarilie forsaken all their
substance and power for Christ Iesus ? What greate
matter to be abased and putt vnder foote, when supreme
commanders of Realmes subiect themselues and · be
32 obedient to their farre inferiour for their Sauiours sake, as
sondrie kings and queenes haue donne in this land, before
the Conquest ? Nay what indignitie is it, baser persons to
be proude of these worldlie things, and so greedilie to
36 hunger ·after them, so excellent personages glorying to

forgoe and despise them? Inferiours to strugle and striue for meaner dignities and honours, the higher estates casting away the cheefest so willinglie? Base conceite is it, which reputeth that greate which a noble mynde iudgeth contemptible, and vile is that spirit, who deiecteth his haught affection, to serue things farre inferiour to it self. / Neither lesse vaine is that harte, which neuer leaueth wooing and pursuing things whose nature is to be euer mutable, and whose benefits are neuer voyd of danger and sorrow. / Who loueth that which is nothing suteable to his loue? Reasonable loue is by nature to continue euer, why then shall it tye it self to that which by nature and of necessitie is corruptible, transitorie, and momentaneall? Much ignobilitie were it, for a potent and riche Prince, of goodlie & well featured personage, to cast his affection on a begger woman, for sterilitie vnfruitfull, for foule fauour and person vnamiable, and for condition and kinde as ignoble. Farre more indignitie is it, for our immortall soule to loue and serue dead bodies, for so worthie a substance to embrace fayer shyning shadowes, for a neuer decaying mynde to cast his whole hart on soone fading flowers; as indeede are all the graces of this bodie, all glorie and riches of this life, the Apostle saying: *The*

1 Cor: 7. *figure or shape of this world passeth away:* that is, the magnificence, pompe, pleasure and wealth of this visible world is but a figure and representation of the true magnificence, glorie, pleasure and substance in heauen our perpetuall contrie and fathers kingdome, which are vnspeakable and shall neuer alter, and which St PETER termeth, *the incorruptible, vndefiled, and neuer withering inheritance kept in heauen:* whereas all heere are cleane contrarie, corruptible sundrie wayes, as diuerslie defiling their possessors, and still decaying, neither is at all worthie of the name of inheritance, but for terme of life, and verie often not so long neither: so that all is but a glimse or light shew of the euerlasting and inexplicable glorie of

the saintes; nothing heere being stable, but varying and
changing euermore, vntill death comes, that sweepes away
goods, friends, pleasures, honors, powre and pompe, lands,
and life, all at a clappe, so cleane as if they had neuer
beene; the soule taken away and sent to giue his straight
accounte, for the vse of all those goods of his lord, lent
him, to repay him with gayne; his bodie tourned out to
feede the wormes, & all those foresayd things, bestowed
on other parties for them likewise to employ, and therefore
to render a like reckoning, they know not how soone. For
this cause in the forenamed place the Apostle aduiseth the
CORINTHIANS in this manner. *This therefore I say my
brethren, the time is short, wherefore it remayneth that those,
that be married, liue as if they were vnmaried; they that
weepe* (or haue cause of temporall sorrow) *be as if they wept
not*, (that is, not troubled but patient); *they that reioice*, (or
haue cause of secular gladnes), *be as not reioycing: they that
buy, let them be as if they possessed nothing; and they that
vse this worlde, be as if they vsed it not*, (that is, withoute
greate carking or care, and prepared straightwayes to leaue
them.) / If you would know the reason of this greate
counsaile, it was the wordes first mentioned, *bicause*
(sayth he) *the figure of this world passeth away: wherefore
I would haue you without solicitude*, to weete, of worldlie
things. In like sort holie IOB, long before, saw the
same of all these temporall things, saying: *Man borne of a* Job: 14:
*woman, and liuing a short time, is replenished with many
miseries, he sprouteth vp like vnto a flower, and is troden
downe, and flieth away like a shadow, and neuer abideth in
the same estate.* A man then is but of short continuance,
shooteth out like a fraile floure, and as soone allmoste as
the floure in the field, is troden on and mard by the
trauailers foote, or lickt vp by a beaste feeding on it, so is
our life and the glorie thereof often ended vnwares in our
freshest floure, and flourishing glorie, sometimes at our
first comming forth, and if some escape such mischance,

[SOME NOTES BEFORE THE LIUES:

by nature they soone fade, and wither away like drie
floures falling to the earth and neuer after appearing, and
others popping vp in their places: And humane glorie, be
it extended and sett out to the moste, as in Princes and 4
other greate Potentates flourishing in all sensible solace,
yet are they all subiect to those manifolde and sudden
oppressions, like floures, and last they all they can, yet
they passe away like a shadow, and all their pompe is 8
but a shew and base representation, or rather a shadow of
true happines in Christ, our Lordes euerlasting and
blissefull kingdome: for like a shadow, it is but a darke
resemblance of the thing shadowed, and after it leaueth no 12
signe of the partie or pageants there latelie appearing. If
the lord be thus fraile, what are the vassalls, & his seruants?
If man for whome these things are made and are prouided,
be thus momentaneall, so replenished with miseries, fading 16
like a floure, and comparable to a shadow, what are other
things withoute him, depending of others, as well as of himself, as honor, glorie, praise, pleasure and whatsoeuer els?
Riches are embeselled away by many slightes, inheritance 20
and lands lost by sundrie shifts, kings often expulsed out
of their dominions, and yet all these so stript out of their
temporalties, may in their persons remayne vnharmed:
strength likewise, beautie, fauour, health, and authoritie 24
perish often, the partie still lyuing: friends forsake vs often,
we loose our libertie, wife becomes vnfaithfull, husband vn-
kinde, children vnnaturall, seruants vndutifull, our sight
failes, our senses decay, memorie and witt faynteth, yet the 28
subiect continueth. Wherefore farre more mutable and
casuall are the things of this life, than the person lyuing;
they being more extrinsecall and lesse substantiall, more
accidentall than essentiall: Albeit in some sort, all these 32
mutations appertayning to the man, more or lesse afflict
him, as they concerne and affect him. All this being too
apparant to a considerate-faythfulle man or woman, now
beholde how prudently and prouidentlie Gods saintes and 36

true friends haue merchandised and made exceeding gayne and commoditie, in employing and putting them forth in gods affaires, not omitting the oportunitie of this gainfull markett. They therefore thoroughlie weighing the substance and qualitie of these corruptible commodities, and the incertayntie of future occasion, if they should neglect the present to employ them with profit, on the other side considering the greate Princes proclamation, who payeth so francklie for what we will sell him or exchange with him, saying; *Whosoeuer shall forsake brother, or sister,* Matt: 19. *father, or mother, wife or children, goods or lands for my sake, shall receiue an hundred folde, and life euerlasting:*. againe, *Blessed are the poore in spirit, for theirs is the* Matt: 5. *kingdome of heauen.* *Blessed are they that mourne* (that is for their owne sinnes, for the desire of heauen, for the greate ingratitude of men toward god, for the superaboundance of iniquitie reigning and such like holie respects) *for they shall be comforted by god:* and *Blessed are the mercifull* (that is, to all in miserie) *for they shall finde mercie at Gods hands:* and *Blessed are the cleane in hart, for they shall see God:* and that *Blessed are those that suffer persecution for righteousnes sake, for theirs is the kingdome of heauen:* Farder hearing proclaymed, how Virgins follow the lambe, singing a song that none els can [Apoc: 14.] sing, and to be briefe, that the paines and trauailes of this life are not worthie *of the future glorie, that shall be reuealed in vs:* and that, *you that haue left all and followed* Matt: 19. *me, at the resurrection when the Sonne of man shall sitt on the seate of his maiestie, you also shall sitt in seates iudging the twelue tribes of Israel:* and *whosoeuer forsaketh any friends or substance for my loue, shall haue an hundred folde, and life euerlasting,* like vnto which no eye hath seene, nor eare heard talke of, nor hart euer conceyued any ioy or glorie comparable. Heereuppon yong and olde, rich and poore, noble and ignoble, were inflamed with this loftie loue, so precious and well preferred in Christs kingdome;

hereuppon they gaue all they had, bodie and goods, hart
and mynde, to follow and please him, to buy this rich
margarite, to purchace this highe honour & inestimable
treasure. Noble virgins refused temporall husbands and 4
honours, gaue away their iewells to be poore in spirit, and
follow Christ, that they might sing that peculiar song of
virgins: thereuppon allso widows buried all carnall loue
with their first husbands, and deuoted themselues and that 8
they had to loue Christ onelie: Children forsooke their
carnall parents to imitate Christ gods onelie sonne: they
left their temporall possessions, to finde an eternall inheritance: others solde them and gaue them away to their 12
maisters poore seruants, and became of rich by birth
voluntarilie poore, to receiue them with farre exceeding
gaine in their rich contrie: nay more, not their goods
onelie, but themselues also they renounced ioyfullie, sub- 16
iecting their wills to others, and obeying them as parents,
for his loue, that being supreme lorde, became subiect to
earthlie parents, and temporall authoritie for them:
humbling themselues so for him to be exalted incom- 20
parablie better with him: They refused no paynes,
knowing their future rest should be proportionablie
farre excelling. They were well content to be esteemed
fooles of the worldes wisards, to be belyed for following 24
ẏ eternall truth, remembering their reward should be
therefore exceeding. They hungred and thirsted for
vertues and righteousnes sake, being assured on their
faithfull lordes worde, that they should be more happilie 28
filled. They mourned heere receyuing no worldlie comforte, that they might be withoute measure comforted in
endlesse blisse. They barred their eyes and eares, externall and internall senses, from foule or defiling obiects, 32
to keepe their hart cleane, thereby to become pure glasses
to receyue the surpassing light and sight of god. Others
did mightie works of mercie, feeding the hungrie, clothing
the naked, teaching the ignorant, comforting the afflicted, 36

and others of like charitable sorte, to procure themselues
abundant mercie with the Allmightie. Others gaue largelie
to the aduancing of Christs honour, to sette forth his
4 worship, in building Churches, religious houses, and the
like, to be repayed with gainfull interest in the land of the
liuing. In this manner they defeated theeues from preying
on their substance, preuented fortunes manifolde iniuries,
8 they preserued their beauties, strength and bodies from
endles corruption, bestowing them on him that could and
would repaire them by glorious immortalitie, far better
than he had first made them by naturall benignitie. / Thus
12 did they preuent all feare of losse of any thing, when they
solde them to the author of all things : for hauing deliuered
that they had to Christ, their vnderstanding, to know him,
their will, to loue him, their memorie to thinke of him,
16 their strength to serue him, their eyes to weepe and looke
after him, their eares to harken his commandements and
teachings, their tongue to speake and sing his praises, their
goods to releeue his pouertie in his members and friends,
20 what needed they to feare robbing, hauing left themselues
nothing; or losse of beautie, health and the like, hauing
resigned them allreadie to him, that can onelie securelie
keepe them, either to our longer vse and benefit heere, or
24 to our eternall and happie payment for them in his kingdome. Such were all saintes, and such these of our contrie,
whose memorable acts God hath preserued for our instruction in true christian loue, and incouraging towards such
28 perfection, so much the more forceiblie moouing, in that they
haue moste beene bredd in this land, where we our selues
haue beene borne, walked on this earth, on which we walke,
filled this ayer which we draw with their renowned fame,
32 sanctified it with their holie acts, blessed it with their
merits, magnified it with their miracles, and enriched it
with their sacred bones and bodies: More potent also are
they for their sex and number, who the weaker they were
36 by nature, so much more admirable to excell the perfecter

[SOME NOTES BEFORE THE LIUES:

sex by grace: And whereas by kinde they were more vnlike to attempt so heroicall workes, so much the more glorious is it, so many to haue performed them. But gods grace maketh litle difference of sexe: wherefore I may wish with S⸰ HIEROM, commending the like vertue of Ladies of Rome in his dayes, PAULA, EUSTOCHIUM, and BLESILLA, the religious mother, and two daughters, one a virgin, the last a wife, saying; *I would to god men would imitate the laudable liues of women, and that wrinkled olde age, would bestow what youth hath voluntarilie offered vnto god:* / By these now may we playnlie see the power of Christian vertue, the might of grace, the force of faith, when the weakest portions of nature by them are so inabled, to strong if not strange enterprises: that hence the slouth and pride of the perfecter sex may be more confounded, being so outgone by their inferiors, and the weaker also may be more emboldened and comforted in Christ, seeing their infirmitie made so potent by him, aboue sondrie by nature superiour: and that hence, all may humble themselues to him, who by the least can ouercome the greater, and abase the mightiest far vnder the weakest. / Embrace we their examples, sorrow we at our farre distance, and sighe we in parte after their resemblance. Their feruour inflame vs, their constancie confirme vs, their perseuerance crowne vs, which their suffrage obtayne vs. /

lib: 2: ep: 19

4

8

12

16

20

24

Of Scotch and Irish Saints. [added by a later hand]

2. *Why the Saintes of Scotland and Ireland, are numbered heerafter amongst the Saintes of England.* /   28

None may meruaile, why in the lyues following both saintes of Scotland and Ireland are numbered amongst English saintes: For first Scotland is part of this Ile, and in-deede in the time of the Saxons, the cheefe or best part thereof belonged to the kings of Northumberland. And   32

also Ireland, hath this foure hunderd yeares, belonged
to the crowne of England, as conquered by Henrie the
second, with leaue giuen him thereto by the Pope. But
especiallie for that in the Saxons time, that is, the yeare
664: as venerable BEDE recordeth in his Ecclesiasticall ll:3:ca:17.
historie, there was such friendship, sociotie, and familiarity
betweene the Religious of that contrie & England, that
gentlemen and others in greate aboundance went thither
to learne both religious life and good letters, all whome
they entertayned, maynteined, and taught moste liberallie;
of which was that famous man EGBERT, and sondrie others,
who what they had there industriouslie gotten, either vertue
or learning, they retourning home imparted it on their contrie. Againe for that S? MODWENNE whose life you haue
with others after, being an Irishe virgin, yet liued moste of
her life in England, and founded sondrie monasteries of
holie virgins in this land, at last bequeathing hir bodie to
England, althoughe dying in Ireland; and againe if mo
reasons were requisite, for that S? PATRIKE the Apostle
of Ireland, was borne in this Ile and Kingdome of
England. /

Bicause the liues following principallie concerne Virgins Of virgins
and widowes, I thought good to putt somewhat downe out & widows.
of ancient fathers of their excellencie and manners. / [added by a later hand]

3. *Of the dignitie of Virginitie out of S? Cyprian Bishop and Martyr, aboue fourteene hundred yeares since, in his booke, of the discipline and attire of Virgins.* /

'Virginnes (sayeth he) are the floure of the Churches [Cap. 4.]
seede, the honor and ornament of spirituall grace, the
moste towardlie impes, the intire and incorrupt worke of
praise and honor, the image of God, resembling our
lordes holines (who was a virgin) and the moste worthie
portion of Christ[1] flocke: By them and in them dooth the [1 r.Christs.]

glorious fertilitie of our mother the Church greatlie reioyce,
and aboundantlie flourish : and howe much the more in
number virgins augment and multiplie, so much the more
dooth our mothers comfort increase.'   4

And in the end after many instructions touching their
manners (whereof some we will add vnderneath) he
concludeth with singular commendation of virginitie
and earnest exhortation to virgins, to keepe carefullie,   8
their highe place to the end, saying,

[Cap. 12 ff.] 'The way to life is straight and narrow, and the path to
glorie hard and difficult : By this do the martyrs walke, by
this virgins and all iust persons. Beware the wide wayes,   12
for there are deadlie allurements, and mortall pleasures.
There dooth the diuell flatter to deceyue, smiles on you to
hurt you, allures you to kill you. The hundred folde
Matt : 13. increase of the good seede which our Sauiour mentioned,   16
is the fruite of martyrs, the second which is sixty folde, is
the fruite of virgins : and as the martyrs haue no cogitation
of fleshlie things nor the worlde, so in you must there be
none : for whose reward in glorie is next to theirs, let   20
your vertue of patience be likewise next. The ascending to greate things is not easie : for what payn is it,
how must we sweate, before we can climme to the toppe of
a hill? Much more haue we to labour and sweate to   24
ascend into heauen. If you consider the reward promised,
the payne is litle wherewith it is gotten. For immortalitie
is giuen to him or her that perseuereth to the end, perpetuall life is promised, a kingdome is by our Lord assured.   28
Keepe virgins, keepe safe I pray you, that which you haue
begunne, that which you are to be in tyme. A greate
reward is kept for you, a mightie price for vertue, the
highest payment for chastitie. Will you vnderstand what   32
euills continencie wanteth, and what commodities it con-
teyneth : *I will multiplie* (sayd God to the woman) *thy
griefes and sorrowes, with greate paine shalt thou beare thy
children, thou shalt be conuerted to thy husband, and he shall*   36

be thy lorde. You virgins are free from this sentence, you
feare not the sorrowes and paynfull trauailes of mothers,
you neede not be awfull of the griefes sustayned in childe-
bearing; neither is a mortall man your maister, but your
maister and head is Christ, as he is of men also: you are
now equall with them in freedome. Againe our Lord
sayd: *The children of this world marrie and are married,* [Luc: 20,36.]
but they that shall be partaker of the next world and of the
happie resurrection from death, shall neither marrie nor be
married, for they shall neuer dye being equall vnto Angells
and children of that immortall generation. That which
we are to be then, now you haue begunne to bee. You
allreadie haue the glorie of the resurrection; for you passe
throughe this worlde, withoute being polluted of the
worlde: You remayning chaste and virgins, you are presentlie equall vnto the Angels; onelie see you continue
your virginitie vnhurte, and as you haue begunne manfullie,
so perseuer constantlie. Neither lett your puritie seeke
the ornaments of apparrell, chaynes, or such materiall
iewells. But lett it onely procure the ornamentes of
manners and vertue. Let it looke vp towards god onely
and heauen, and the eyes being so well eleuated, let them
not deiect or abase themselues so much as to desire or
beholde carnall, worldlie or earthlie things. The first
commandement at the creation of the worlde, was to
increase and multiplie; but the second (at our regeneration
by Christ) persuadeth continencie. When the world was
rude and emptie, by fertilitie and generation multitude
was procured: but the world being now replenished, they
that can get chastitie and liue single like Eunuches, are
so spiritually gelded for the kingdome of heauen. Neither
doth our lord command this, but exhorteth vs thereto;
not laying on vs the yoke of necessitie, but profering it to
our free will and libertie. And whereas our Sauiour
witnesseth, that there are diuerse mansion-houses and
different places in his Fathers kingdome, and some best;

these best places are for you : / For subduing the desires of
the flesh, you shall haue the reward of this greater grace.
All by the sanctification of baptisme are admitted to a
diuine honour and calling, and made of the heauenlie
contrie: there they putt of their olde man by the grace of
the wholsome lauer, and being renewed with the holie
ghoste by this new natiuitie, are cleansed from the filth of
their olde vncleannesse: But to you there commeth
greater sanctitie and veritie by your regeneration in baptisme: for that you haue no desire of carnall or corporall
delightes, but onelie what appertayneth to vertue and
spirit, remayneth in you to be crowned. It is the voice
of the Apostle, whome our Lord called the vessell of
election, and whome he sent to preach the heauenlie commandements, who sayeth: *The first man is from the earth,
the second from heauen: like vnto him that is from the
earth are all that are earthlie, and like vnto him that is
from heauen, are all that are heauenlie: and as we haue
carried the image of him that is from the earth, so lett vs
carrie the image of him that is from heauen:* and this
image dooth virginitie beare, integritie, holynes, and veritie
carrie: They also that are myndefull of gods discipline,
keeping righteousnes with religion, being stable in faith,
humble in feare, stoute to all sufferance, milde to sustayne
iniuries, easie to shew mercie, and well agreeing in
fraternall veritie ; all which things you good virgins ought
to obserue, loue, and keepe, seing you attending on god
and his sonne Christ, do goe before others farre (throughe
your greater and better lotte) towards our Lord, vnto
whome you haue dedicated your selues; You that be elder
in yeares teache and gouerne the yonger, and you that be
inferiour to others in yeares serue and waite on them, and
incite your equalles; prouoke each other by mutuall incite-
ments, and with vertuous emulation, putt forward to
glorie: continue stoutlie, go forward spirituallie, and
obtayne your crowne happilie: onelie I pray remember vs

then, when virginitie in you shall beginne to be glorified.' /
All this S! Cyprian.

4. Touching Virgins behauiour out of the same place. /

After that he had in the beginning of his booke shewed how necessarie discipline (that is, watchfull custodie and gouernement of themselues) is in all sortes of Christians, yong and olde, to the end they may conserue vnto the end the puritie and holynesse receiued in Baptisme; then conuerting his speech to Virgins, he declareth that they haue more cause than others of such care, by how much more their glorie is greater amongst Christs seruants than others. For which respect also he protesteth that himself was more incited to write vnto them, to instruct and aduise them, that they who had dedicated themselues vnto Christ, and bidding adieu to all carnall concupiscence, had vowed themselues vnto god in bodie and mynde, may consummate & perfect their worke ordayned to a greate reward, and that they may not studie now to decke themselues, or please any other but their lord, of whome they expect the wages and payment for their virginitie: which was so renowned by gods angell in the Apocalypse, who sayd of them: *These are those that neuer were defiled with women, for they continued Virgins: These are those that follow the lamb, wheresoeuer he goeth.* The like excellencie he sheweth of women virgins after that. / Ca: 14.

5. Touching their attire and crucifying of bodilie delights. /

'Continencie and chastitie consisteth not in the onely integritie of flesh, but also in the modestie of attyring and decencie of dressing, that according to S! PAUL, the woman vnmaried be holie in bodie and spirit: The Apostle [Cap. 5 ff.]

[SOME NOTES BEFORE THE LIUES:

1 Cor: 7. instructeth and sayth: *The single person thinketh on the things pleasing our Lord, and how he or she may be acceptable in gods sight: the married man thinketh of worldlie matters, how he may please his wife, but the virgin or widow hath onely to thinke on our Lordes businesse, that she may be holie in bodie and soule.* A virgin must not onelie be so, but must also be knowne or deemed so of others; so that by her behauiour none may haue cause to doubte of her puritie. Let integritie of bodie prooue it self in all things, neither let apparrell defame the bodies riches. Why should she goe abrode trimme and tricked, as thoughe she had a husband or desired one? If thou be a virgin, rather feare to please men, neither desire thyne owne perill,
[? = þat.] thou that keepest thy self for god. They y̌¹ haue no husband, whome will they seeme to please? Let them continue pure not onelie in bodie but in soule also. It is not lawfull for a virgin to trimme herselfe to shew her beautie, or to glorie in her bodie, whereas they haue no greater combat to make than against their owne flesh, and their cheefe strugling should be to subdue their bodie.
Gal: 6. S? Paul crieth out with a loude voice saying *God forbid that I should glorie in any thing but in the Crosse of Christ, by whome the world is crucified vnto me and I to the world:*
[Gal: 5, 24.] for sayeth he, *they that are of Christ, crucifie their flesh with the vices and desires thereof.* Shall she then be founde in those delightes of the bodie, which she hath professed to renounce? If thou doost so, thou detectest thy self, to make shew of one thing, and yet indeede to affect an other: in so doing thou defilest thy self, who hast promised chastitie vndefiled. *Crie* (sayth our Lord to the
Esay: 40. Prophet Esay) *All flesh is hay and all the glorie thereof as the floure of the field: the hay or grasse withereth, and the floure fadeth, but the word of our Lord lasteth for euer.* It beseemeth no Christian much lesse a virgin to accounte of the bodies beautie, honour or brauerie, onelie they should desire the worde of god, and embrace the good things that

continue for euer. Or if thou wilt glorie in flesh, it must
be when it is afflicted or tormented in Christs confession,
when a woman is found more strong and valiant than the Nota.
4 men that torment her, when she endureth fire, crosses,
sword, or beastes to gett a crowne in heauen: those are
precious iewells of the flesh, those the best ornaments of
the bodie.
8 But there are some riche Virgins, who make shew thereof,
and contend that they may and must vse their goods. Let
such know first, that she is rich, who is rich in god, that
she is wealthie that is full of Christ, and that those are
12 true goods w*h*ich are spirituall, diuine, and heauenlie, which
can bring vs vnto god. But whatsoeuer is earthlie receyued of the worlde, and to abide onelie with the worlde,
must all be contemned as the worlde it self, which we haue
16 renounced with all the pompes and pleasures thereof, when
we came to Christ in Baptisme.. Well, thou art rich, and
thinkest thou mayst vse that, which God hath giuen thee.
Vse them in gods name, but on things not hurtfull, vse
20 them to good vses, vse them where god is pleased and
serued: Let the poore finde thee to be rich, let the needie
feele thee to be wealthie, giue thy patrimonie to god, that
thou mayest receiue it agayne with aboundant benefitt,
24 feede Christ therewith, that thou mayest carrie safelie the
glorie of virginitie, and by the prayers of many intreate to
attaine vnto thy lords rewardes. A greate patrimonie
vnlesse it be well spent and on good vses, is a greate
28 temptation, so that by his inheritance, he must rather
redeeme than augment his sinnes.'

6. *He reprooueth Virgins that were present at mariages.*

'Some Virgins are not ashamed to be at mariages, and in [Cap. 10.]
32 that libertie of wanton speeches, to talke with them, to
heare which is vndecent, to see what is dishonest, to speake

and to be present amongst filthie talking and drunken feasting, wherewith the fuell of lust is sett afire, the bride animated and much prouoked to suffer defiling, and the bridegroome to offer it. What place is there in mariages for her, whose mynde is not on mariage? Or can there be any delight there to her, whose vowes and purposes are so diuerse? What is seene there, what learnt, but wherewith a Virgin dooth much fainte from her purpose? When comming thither chaste, she departeth defiled, and albeit she remayne in bodie and hart stille a virgin, yet by her eyes and eares and tongue hath she diminished what she had.'/

Nota.

7. *Of the maners and demeanure of Virgins more particular out of S.{ Hierome, in his epistle to Demetrias*[1] *a moste noble Virgin of Rome, who hauing an husband prepared for her, refused to marrie, and to the good liking of her mother and grandmother vowed virginitie: and receiuing the holie veile of virginitie at the Bishops hands, liued so with others, albeit in her owne house: S.{ Hierome was requested by her mother and grandmother to instruct her, how she should liue according to her profession, which he doth in manner following, thoughe brieflie collected*

lib: 2:
ep: 18:

'First keepe thy hart with all carefull custodie, against all euill suggestions, intruded by Satan: and to that effect, often arme thy forehead, with the signe of the Crosse: that the slayer of the Aegyptians, and their first begotten, haue no power to hurte thine (that is, thy holie cogitations and purposes)../ After diligent guard of thy cogitations, thou must take on thee the armour of fasting, and so sing with holie DAUID, *I haue humbled my soule in fasting;* and that: *I haue eaten ashes as bread;* and that, *when they were troublesome vnto me, I putt on hayrcloth..*/ Yet thou must be moderate therein; for that thereby, often tender bodies

[1] In Migne P.C. tom. 32, p. 1115 ff.

are broken presentlie, so that they beginne to be sicke,
before they haue layd the foundation to holie life.. Chuse
men or mayd seruants, not by their fayre faces, but by their
4 faire and comelie manners. Let scurrill and wanton speach
or behauiour, neuer be permitted where thou art present : to
laughe or to prouoke laughter, leaue to secular persons,
grauitie best beseemeth thee.. Other affections and pertur-
8 bations, which as long as we liue in this fraile bodie, we
can not whollie cutt of, yet lett vs moderate them, and rule
them with reason. It is an humane infirmitie to be angrie,
but soone to end it, is the part of a Christian.. Giue not to
12 the riche nor to kinsfolke, but to the poore : be he priest
or kinsman to whome thou giuest, consider in him nothing
els but his pouertie.. From the time that thou wert con·
secrated vnto perpetuall virginitie, thy goods are not thine,
16 or rather they are thine, bicause they haue begunne to be
Christs.. Let others build churches, erect mightie pillers
therein, and guild the heads of them, or with various
worke of Iuory, siluer and precious stones garnish the
20 guilded Altars ; I doe not mislike nor reproue their worke,
let euerie one abound in his sense; but thou hast
an other purpose, to clothe Christ in his poore members, to *The best manner of almes :*
visite him in his sicke seruants, too feede him in his
24 hungrie ones, to lodge him in the harbourlesse, and *Nota.*
especiallie in the housholde of faith to feed *the Monasteries
of Virgins,* and to haue care of the seruants of god, and
poore in spirit, who day and night waite on thy lord, who
28 lyuing on earth imitate the conuersation of Angels, and
talke nothing but that appertayneth to the lauding of god :
who hauing foode and clothing, will haue no more ; at leaste
if they keepe their religious purpose. This haue I sayd
32 to thee, as a riche and noble virgin ; now to thee as a Virgin
onelie will I speake, not considering what is without thee,
but what is within thee. Besides the order of Psalmes
and prayers, which thou hast allwayes to recite, at the
36 third, sixt, and ninthe houre, at euening, midnight and *The Canonicall houres.*

c 2

morning, appointe certaine houres to thy self, wherein
thou maist learne and reade the holie scriptures, not to
the cloying, but to the delight and instruction of thy soule.
Haue allso at hand allwayes wolle or flax to spinne
yearne or thridd, or to winde vp what others haue spunne,
or ouersee what others doe: and if thou be so diuerslie
occupied, no day will seeme long vnto thee, thoughe it be the
longest of all sommer: And doing thus thou shalt saue thy
self and others; thou shalt be a mistresse of holie conuersation, and shalt make the chastitie of many virgins thine
owne gaine; the scripture saying: *The soule of the idle person is euer desiring one thing or other*: neither must you[1]
cease from working, bicause (thankes be to god) thou
needest nothing, but therefore must you labour with others,
that by occasion of working, you may thinke of nothing but
what pleaseth god. And I will tell you in simplicitie, that
albeit you had giuen all you haue to the poore; yet nothing
is more precious to Christs sight, than what you make
with your owne handes, either for your owne vse, or for
example to the rest of the Virgins.'/

In the end he aduiseth her verie earnestlie to beware of
heretiks venemous doctrine, and for safetie against them,
to adhere to the faith of the Romane Churche, and
Apostolike chaier./

8. *Of Virgins liuing in Monasteries the sayd S.* Hierome writeth to a Virgin thus: li: 2: ep: 9:*

'If any carpe thee for that thou art a Christian and a
Virgin, care not: if they speake hardlie of thee for that
thou hast left thy mother to goe liue in a monasterie with
Virgins, be not grieued; for such detraction is thy commendation: when straite life is reproued in a mayde of
god, not wantonnes, that crueltie towards thy self is true
pietie.'

He also commendeth holie MARCELLA, a famous Ladie of ROME, both for nobilitie, learning and holynes, for that by her example, many monasteries of Virgins and monks were founded at ROME: so that monasticall profession, which before-time had there beene of litle request, then began to be of greate reputation, and embraced of many.

lib: 3: ep: in Epithaph: Marcellæ:

He commended to the forenamed rich virgin DEMETRIAS, as the especiall kinde of almes and charitie, to relieue the monasteries of Virgins, and other religious persons the seruants of god and poore in spirit, who day and night serue our Lord, and lyuing on earth imitate the Angells conuersation, who talke nothing but what belongeth to the praise of god, who hauing foode and cloathing, esteeme them selues riche, and require nothing more: these be his wordes of them, related before.

He there also mentioneth, that there were women Anchorets, as men, who beside the religious women that lyued in monasteries, lyued alone in contemplation and penance: of which two sorts he sayeth much question was, which was the moste perfect state of those two: which doubte he resolueth, saying: that the Anachoreticall was the moste perfect, yet withall moste dangerous, especiallie in women./

9. *Of widowes liuing in Monasteries in S.* Hieroms time./

He relateth in the Epitaph or life of holie MARCELLA widow, how she being a moste noble and vertuous ladie at ROME, and interteyning in her house S. ATHANASIUS and afterward PETER his successour bishops of ALEXANDRIA driuen thence by the Arrian heretickes, and learning of them the manner of S. ANTONIES life then lyuing, and the orders of the monasteries of PACHUMIUS in THEBAIS, and the discipline of Virgins, and widows liuing religious there, she began to practise the same manner of life, and was not ashamed, to professe that publicklie, which she knew pleased Christ: Her example, SOPHRONIA and others

lib: 3 ep.

of S. Marcella widowe.

followed: and whereas she was the first noble woman that
tooke on her monasticall profession, yet afterward by her
imitation, multitudes of noble personages, men and women,
followed that profession, and it became glorious by her
deuoute enterprise, which no greate person before durst
take in hand. At the same time when ROME was sacked
and rifled, and the inhabitants putt to the sword, by the
barbarous Gothes, her house also, albeit poore and out of
the Cittie was rigged by them, and she beaten to confesse
what golde she had: when indeede her poore attire, might
easilie haue instructed them of her voluntarie pouertie.
And whereas her vertue deserued to be reserued aliue,
when the Barbarians had brought her to Sr PAULES
Church, there to be safe; she burst into greate ioy
and thankes vnto god, that had preserued her disciple
PRINCIPIA a Virgin from the violence of the barbarians
defiling, and that that captiuitie and sacke had not made
her poore, but found her so voluntarilie become poore before,
that she then wanted daylie foode, and yet being filled
with Christ, did not feele or greeue at hunger./

Of S^t
Paula
widow:

10. At the same time almoste, her friend and fellow for
nobilitie and vertue PAULA, a rare widdowe, left ROME,
her greate friends & children, went into PALESTINE, S^t
HIEROME being her companion and guide, and after she
had religiouslie visited and adored all the holie places of
fame in all that contrie, where our Sauiour had lyued, and
his olde Prophets, and new Apostles: after that when she
had visited all the Armies of monks in ÆGIPT, seene the
moste famous Confessours of them, the MACABIJ, ARSENIJ,
SERAPIONS, ISODORUS, and others of greate renowne for that
holie profession, and had cast her self at their feete for
their blessing, had beheld their celles, and liberallie bestowed on them, she retourned to HIERUSALEM: where
hauing curiouslie and deuoutlie visited and adored all the
worthie places there, she went to BETHLEEM, where our
Sauiour was borne so poore, aud where she settled herself;

building lodgings to entertayne pilgrimes in the place
where her Lord coulde finde no lodging fitt for man, when
he came in to this worlde: There she erected allso two
4 monasteries, one for men, which Sr Hierom did gouerne,
the other for herself and a number of Virgins, which she
had gathered together in one spirite and purpose to waite
on Christ, which her self did rule: whose vertue in part
8 I thought good brieflie to sett downe, as also the order of
her monasterie, out of the same Father Sr Hierom, in her
life: He first calleth god to witnesse, that he addeth or
amplifieth nothing, as praysers vse commonlie, but that he
12 diminisheth rather, the greatnes of her vertue, it seemeth
so exceeding.

'Her humilitie was such, that being amongst multitudes Her vertues:
of virgins with her, both in apparrell, speeche, and gate, [Vita Paulæ
16 she seemed the basest and lowest of all; so that if you Cap. 6.]
had not knowen her, you would haue deemed her the least
and lowest, not the cheefe: From the death of her husband,
she would neuer eate with men, thoughe he were an holie
20 man or bishop: Her bed was the hard grounde, with a
litle haire-cloth vnder her, wherewithall night by night
she powred oute aboundance of teares, wherewith she bewayled small faltes as thoughe she had beene guiltie of
24 greate crimes: And I reproouing her, telling her that she
must keepe her eyes to reade holie bookes, she answered;
'That face must be fyled with weeping, that against gods
commandement, hath often beene braued with paynting:
28 the bodie that hath taken greate delighte, must be much
afflicted: long laughing must be punished with continuall
wayling, soft linnen and precious silke garments must be
recompenced with roughe haire-cloth': None was more milde
32 and courteous than shee: her chastitie was such that slan-
derous tongues could finde no matter of calumniation in
her: onelie her liberalitie to the poore passed; in so much
that she would borrow at vsurie, that she might denie none
36 that needed or asked: And when I would (god forgiue me)

finde some falte with her therefore, telling her that she
should so releeue other, that she oppressed not her self;
she with few wordes answered, 'God is my witnes, I doe it
onelie for his sake, and this is my desire and wishe, that I
may dye a begger, and not leaue my daughter one pennie
of monnye, and that I may for pouertie be shrowded in a
sheete of an other bodies': adding withall; 'If I aske
euerie one, at leaste many will giue me, but if I giue not to
these poore soules, and they dye in their necessitie, of
whome shall their life be required?' And thus feruent in
faith, and whollie vnited vnto Christ in pouertie of spirite,
she bestowed all he had giuen her on him, obtayning her
desire, that is to dye indebted: yet her daughter trusteth
in Christ, in time to ouercome it.. And whereas no Saints
want enuious enemies, as our Sauiour had store, and I
wished her to depart thence for a time, she answered: 'You
say well, if Satan, did not fight against gods seruants
euerie-where, and did not ariue first at euerie place, whether
good folkes shall flie. Neither will the loue of these holie
places permitt me to leaue them, neither can I finde
BETHLEEM other-where: why rather shall not I conquer
enuie with patience, pride with humilitie, and to him, that
will strike me on one eare, tourne the other; ouercoming
(as the Apostle teacheth) euill with good': And so with
diuerse sentences of scripture would she teache and exhort
her self, how god tempteth and trieth his seruants loue, by
permitting such aduersaries, and how the iniurie of the
outward man, is the healing of the inward man and
spirit. / &c.'/

The order of her monasterie.
[Vita Paulæ Cap. 8.]

Touching the order of her monasterie it was thus:
'She hauing gathered many virgins in one, of the best,
meane, and lowest sorte out of diuerse prouinces, destributed them into three companies: yet so that albeit they
wrought and did eate apart, yet at prayers and psa'modie
they all mett: After *Alleluia* was cried or song aloude,
which was the signe to call them together, none might sitt

still, but away they must come presentlie, and they that
were neerest and came first stayed for the rest, and her
self would commonlie be first; that so by her example and
4 for shame, she might prouoke others to be dilligent, not
by feare. In the morning, at the third houre, sixt, ninthe,
euen and midnight, they sang in order the psalter; neither
was it lawfull for any of the sisters, to be ignorant of the
8 psalmes, or to passe any day without learning some thing
of the holie scriptures. On the sunday onelie did they goe
forth to the Church, aboute which they all dwelt; and then
did euerie companie follow their owne mother or guardian:
12 In like manner they retourned: That donne, they applied
their appointed worke dilligentlie, which was, to make
either themselues or others, garments and cloathing. If
she were of nobilitie, she was not permitted to haue for
16 companion of her owne and olde acquaintance, leste remembering her olde actions, she might renew talke and conceite
of her childish and former follie passed in the worlde:
Their apparrell was all alike: They vsed linnen onelie to
20 wipe their handes: they were so barred from companie of
men, that Eunuchs could not haue accesse to them; and
this was, least bad tongues should haue any occasion of
backbyting, whose delight is, doing ill themselues, to bite
24 vertuous persons: If any were slow in comming to prayer,
or at her worke, PAULA their gouernesse amended them
diuerslie: if the mayd were chollericke, she would with
faire and milde speach allure her to doe better: if she
28 were patient she would reproue her; None might possesse
any thing priuate beside their meate and apparrell. If any
iarred betweene themselues, she would with gentle speach
make them friends: the wanton or kicking flesh of yong
32 maydes, she would represse with often or double fastings;
choosing rather that they should feele their stomacke
ake, than their mynde. If any did trimme herself somewhat curiouslie, with bended browes, and sower lookes,
36 she would rebuke her, saying withall; 'the featnesse and

finenesse of the bodie or attire, is the fouling, and defiling
of the soule': she taught them farther, that a foule or
wanton worde, might neuer issue out of a virgins mouth,
for that by such signes, a leacherous mynde is discouered; 4
and by the exteriour shape, the inward man is shewed. If
any were too talkatiue, and delighted to braule or quarrell
with her fellowes; if being admonished againe and againe,
she would not amend, she putt her last and behinde all the 8
rest, and made her pray without the dore of the Oratorie,
neither let her feede with others, but apart to eate by herself, that whome chyding would not helpe, shame and con-
fusion might. She was meruailous carefull and officious 12
aboute her sicke sisters, prouiding plentifullie whatsoeuer
they needed; moreouer would make them eate flesh, but to
her self being sicke, she was still rigorous, hardlie admitting
a litle wine, with her water-meates.' 16

11. *Of the excellencie of true widdowed and of true widowes
conuersation.*

Ep: 1 : ca: 5.   Saint PAULE to holie TIMOTHIE Bishop of EPHESUS
writing, willeth him to honour those that be true widowes, 20
of whome after he addeth this comfortable speeche, *She
that is a true widdow and desolate let her trust in God, and
persist in prayer and obsecrations to him, day and nighte.*
[Hom. in Tim. 1, 5, 5.] On this place S⸰ CHRYSOSTOME writeth thus; *She that* 24
whollie casteth of, secular life, and dooth persist in widdowed
A true widdow: *is a true widdow, who trusteth in God as is meete, and day
and night is earnestlie attending on prayer and calling vpon*
[Hom. in Tim. 1, 5, 3.] *God:* And somewhat before he sayeth; *Bicause to be* 28
*withoute a husband is counted a reprochefull thing to many,
therefore is the Bishop willed by the Apostle, to reuerence
and honour her the more, as also for her worthinesse,* that is
for deseruing praise for her chastitie, by accompanying it 32
with sondrie other vertues: as by lyuing withoute quarrells

with others, by continuall occupation in godlie businesse, by attending still on god himself: Of them also the same Apostle sayd to the CORYNTHIANS: *I say to those that are unmaried and widowes, it is good for them to continue so as my self doe: And againe: The vnmarried woman and virgin thinketh of things belonging vnto God, that she may be holie in bodie and spirit, but the married woman mindeth worldlie matters, and how to please her husband: Wherefore this single state is best, and yieldeth oportunitie to serue god withoute impediment, althoughe I enforce none theretoo, but they that freelie doe choose that course, doe best.* Of them (whome St HIEROME calleth the second degree of chastitie, as St PAULE also signifieth heere, ioyning them next to virgins) two examples recorded in the holie scripture, both confirmeth their worthines and expresseth their manner of life, by which they attayned to that excellencie: The first is IUDITH, that famous widdow of the olde testament, by whome onelie god ouerthrew HOLOFERNES that proud and terrible captaine with all his ASSYRIAN hoste: Her life is described thus in the booke of IUDITH: IUDITH being left widdow, made her self a secret chamber or closet in the vpper part of her house, where with her mayds she remayned shutt: on her bodie and loines she ware a smocke of haire, and she fasted all the dayes of her life, except the holie and festiuall dayes: she was verie beautifull and left verie riche, and verie famous euerie-where, or that she feared god exceedinglie, in so much that none could nor did speake any euill of her: So the scripture: / This woman was so strong in faith and courageous in spirit, that when mens hartes quailed, she was not amazed, nay animated them, being almoste in despayer: That which none could imagine or hope for, that did she enterprise and bring to passe, being instructed and armed by god aboue nature and reason, exalted the true faith and worship of god, proued her chaste vertue to the sauegard of herself and her Cittie, yea and her whole

margin: Thus St Chrysostome.
1 Cor: ca: 7.
Iudiths vertue and conuersation.
ca: 8:

contrie; and to the prouocation of others to emulate chastitie and holie life. Of her sayeth S.̇ HIEROME to a
Ep. 19. li: 2: vertuous ladie and widow called FURIA, inciting her to her more comfort in her like purpose: *We reade* (sayeth he) *how Iudith wasted with fasting, and vnhansome for her mourning attire, in that manner not to haue bewailed her husband departed, but with that roughnes and austeritie of bodie prepared her self against the comming of her spirituall husband: Her right hand do I beholde with a sword in it, and all bloudie, killing and taking away the head of Holofernes, out of the midst of her enemies: a woman vanquisheth many men, chastitie murdereth lust, and returning home she changeth her apparrell, casting of her late brauerie, and taketh to her, her conquering course, and simple weede againe, which were more pure and precious, than all the decking of the worlde.* / Thus S.̇ HIEROM:

Luc: 2: The second famous widdow renowned by the Gospell was
Annes vertue and behauiour. ANNA the Prophetesse, the daughter of PHANUEL of the tribe of ASER: who after that she had beene a wife seuen yeares from her virginitie became a widdow, and so remayned eightie and fower yeares: who neuer went from the Church, but day and night by fasting and prayer serued god: She for this vertue, deserued to meete the Sauiour of the worlde being presented in the Temple, confessing him openlie, whome few ells knew; and so became a prophet of Christ then an infant; and by that her chaste and religious life deserued her name ANNA, which signifieth 'spirituall grace,' and to be the daughter of PHANUELL, which signifieth 'the face of god,' and to be numbered of
li. 2: ep: 10: the tribe of ASER. which signifieth 'rich and blessed,' as S.̇ HIEROME writeth in the place aforesayd. / And as true widdowed before declared is of rare dignitie and power,
false wyddowed. as hath beene shewed, so false widdowed, that is, which liueth so more freelie to take her pleasure and to follow the worlde, is likewise more dishonorable: wherefore the
1: Tim: c: 5: Apostle in the place first alledged sayeth: *The widdow*

which liueth in delightes, liuing is dead: that is, she is voide of spirituall life, and liuelie workes of grace, destitute of gods quickening presence and fauour : / Wherefore the
4 Apostle did chasten his bodie, and bring it into subiection, least sauing others, him self might become a reprobate, and giuing his beaste the reynes, he might carrie his rider hedlong to perdition : For this cause the two famous
8 widdowes IUDITH and ANNE beforesayd, putt their bodies to paynfull exercises, and did not cherish them with carnall comfortes : They shunned worldly companie, and shutt them selues vp, either by solitarie abode at home, or much
12 conuersing with god at the Temple; auoyding externall societie, to be internall secret with their lord : talking to him by prayer, or listening to his talke, by holie reading and secret inspiration. Thus they became familiar with
16 god, honorable to good and greate men, potent in spirit, mightie in faith, moste gratefull to their lorde, and greatlie able to benefit others. Such were MARCELLA and PAULA Romane widdowes, of whome you haue heard greate
20 things, and such were these holie widdows whose liues follow together with virgins./

They all pray for vs, that we may obtaine part of that their pure spirite, that their holie purpose may incense
24 others to follow their steppes, that we may euer enioy their happie companie in heauen.

THE LIVES

OF THE MOSTE FAMOUS WOMEN SAINTS WHICH HAUE BEENE WITHIN THE ILES OF ENGLAND AND IRELAND OUT OF THE BEST AUTHORS. 4

The life of holie Helena Mother to Constantine the greate and first Christian Emperour
Out of Baronius[1] *: she died about the yeare of our Lord* 326:

Constantius CLORUS a famous Captaine of the ROMANES 8 being sent into BRITANNIE (now ENGLAND) in the time of AURELIAN the Emperour to compose and order some troubles then raised in this Prouince, being intertayned there with his Armie by Prince COELUS, who had one onelic 12 daughter named HELENA, a beautifull Ladie and well nurtured, he tooke such liking to this yong damsell that he vouchsafed her for his wife; and on her he begott CONSTANTINE, the first founder of Christian peace and libertie 16 vniuersallie, the builder and enricher of Churches throughe the worlde. CONSTANTIUS her husband being afterward CÆSAR and Emperour, MAXIMIANUS HERCULEUS and DIOCLETIAN giuing vp the Empire vnto her husband CONSTANTIUS 20 and MAXIMIANUS-GALERIUS, he being made Emperour of the West, GALERIUS of the East; HERCULIUS caused him to putte away HELENA by letter of diuorce, as thoughe she were base and vnworthie of so greate a prince, being no Romane, 24 but an externe and a Barbarian, by nation and the Romanes estimation: and that donne, he gaue him to wife THEODORA his daughter in law, by whome he had many sonnes and daughters. Notwithstanding all these children, 28 CONSTANTINUS his onelie sonne by HELENA, being a braue prince euerie way liked him best; so that dying at YORKE in BRITANNIE, and CONSTANTINUS being come to him before

Her contrie, father and husband:

She was diu· reed from her husband.

[1] See Baronius, *Annal. Eccl.* tom. 3 & 4; a. 306—326.

his death he gaue him the Emperiall Ensignes, and caused the Romane hoste to elect and proclayme him his successour. He was then thirtie yeares of age and somewhat more, and
4 allbeit he was a greate fauourer and friend of Christians then, imitating his fathers vertue therein, and his mothers pietie, of whome he was instructed in the faith, yet he lyued a good while after the Gentills manner of super-
8 stition, sacrifycing to the gods; and after many Edicts, and other benefits donne vnto the Christians, being a *Catechumene*, or learner of the faith, by the space of sixteene yeares, throughe worldlie feare or fauour of the
12 Romanes, yielding vnto them, the renewing of the solemne diuination by beastes bowells and sacrifices, God punished him, by permitting him to fall into crueltie against his owne bowells; that is, to kill his eldest sonne CRISPUS,
16 that was a moste excellent prince, and had beene CÆSAR some yeares, which he had by his first wife MINERUINA; and on false surmise that he would haue beene naught with his mother in law FAUSTA daughter to HERCULEUS Em-
20 perour, in his rage he slew him: Whereat his mother HELENA tooke such griefe, that she would not be comforted: Whereuppon he after vnderstanding, thoughe too late, that CRISPUS his sonne was innocent, and that it was
24 rather FAUSTA his wifes false suggestion and accusation, for that she loued CRISPUS, and would haue enioyed his like loue, but he would not defile his fathers bed, for which refusall, she fayned her owne falte on the chaste yong
28 prince; wherefore he was so pittifullie slayne: when I say CONSTANTINE vnderstood this troth, he raging a-new, althoughe more iustlie against FAUSTA his wife, he slew her: For appeasing of gods wrath against him self in this
32 manner and other-wayes threatened, in the nineteenth yeare of hys reigne he was baptized at ROME by Pope SILUESTER, and soone after, he with his mother HELENA were present in the ROMANE Councell holden by the sayd
36 Pope, wherein diuerse heresies were condemned. The

[margin: Constantius made Constantine Empereour at Yorke.]

[margin: Gods punishment of Constantine for condescending to much to Idolaters.]

[margin: Helenas griefe:]

[margin: Constantines penance and baptisme.]

Iewes seeing Christianitie, to wax daylie so in credit aboue humane expectation, that of them many conuerted vnto Christ, the rest disdayning thereat, vsing diuerse contumelies and iniuries to their fellowes that had forsaken them, and presumptuouslie preferring their owne blyndnes before Christian light, solicited the Emperour CONSTANTINE and his mother from their faith, offerring to proue vnto them, by disputing the matter with the doctors of Christianitie that they were deluded. Thereuppon HELLENA with her sonne, willed them to come to ROME, the learnedest of them, where with SILUESTER, and other Bishops they might discusse the cause: They came they contended, and both by scriptures and miracles they were confounded, putt to silence, and by publicke Edict forbidd to iniurie any wayes their fellow Hebrues conuerted, vnder paine of death. Afterward the holie Queene to giue god thanks, for his greate benefits bestowed on her self, her sonne, and his glorious children, that were now Cesars, and to obtaine his perpetuall grace and fauour towards them, throughe singular deuotion, albeit verie olde, yet as speedilie as if she had beene verie yong, she went vnto the holie land: Where after that she had visited all places of religious fame and note verie curiouslie, and had fullfilled that saying of holie Dauid, *We will adore in the place, where his feete stood,* according as she had beene by diuine vision and reuelation instructed, she seeketh out the holie Crosse of Christ, which by aduise and counsell taken with the moste learned and vertuous Christians and the moste skillfull of IEWES RABBINES, she learnt to be neere the place, where our Lord was buried: for that it was an aunciente vse, to burie the instruments of malefactors executed neere where the parties therewith punished were buried. Digging therefore aboute the Sepulcher, by helpe of her souldiors and the Cittisens, at last they founde three Crosses, and three or foure nailes: but yet vncertaine which was the wholsome Crosse, and which the theeues: God that had

The Iewes chalenge of disputation with Christians.

Her pilgrimage to Hierusalem and other holie places.

She sought the Crosse by diuine reuelation.

inspired the holie Princesse to seeke it, suggested also to
her mynde how to trie it ; Wherefore she called for a dead
bodie, which being brought her, they touched the corps
with one first, then with an other, and yet nothing was
donne : but when the true Crosse touched the dead bodie, *The miraculous discerning the true Crosse of Christ.*
life entred into it, and it rose vp aliue to the glorie of
Christ and the admiration of all the beholders : And
forthwith it was reuerenced with due honour and placed in
a sumptuous Church built by her in the place of our Lordes
passion, which glittered with golden Altars, and guilded
roofes: the crosse being kept in a secret holie place, which
the bishop of HIERUSALEM euerie yeare at Ester doth take
forth, and propose it to the people to be adored : But *A continuall miracle.*
which is moste admirable, of that greatest part remayning
there (for some part was sent to her sonne to CONSTANTI-
NOPLE) faithfull people that came on pilgrimage thither
for deuotion, beseeching some peeces of the Bishop in
reward of their long iournie, and they being granted, by
gods diuine power, it is nothing diminished, and by a
perpetuall miracle daylie so diminished, yet as it were
growing againe, is indeed still repaired : It is diuided to
allmoste innumerable receyuers of it daylie, yet still whole
to those that adore it, and all this inconsumptible in- *All this of the Crosse hath*
tegritie hath it by the bloud of that flesh, that dying on *S.t Paulinus.*
it, yet did not corrupt. The nailes wherewith our Lord *Of the foure*
was crucified, were thus disposed : Of one, CONSTANTINE *nailes.*
had a bridle made him for his more protection in the
warres against his enemies : an other HELENA putte into
a riche golden diademe which she sent to CONSTANTINE
also : The third the pittifull Ladie cast into the Adriaticke sea, when she retourned out of the East : For
knowing how innumerable people, had beene drowned,
throughe greate rage and trouble of those seas ; she
pittying mens destruction, and trusting in our Lords
mercie that thereby the furie of those waters would quaile,
she commanded one to be putte into it, and therevpon that

sea became moste calme and quiet. Whereuppon vnto this day (sayeth S⁺ GREGORIE of TOURS) the seamen doe reuerence that sea as sanctified, and when they enter into it, they therefore fast and pray and laude our Lord. Beside the foresayd deuoute workes donne at HIERUSALEM, the holie Empresse built other goodlie churches worthie of her estate, as at the manger and denne of our Lords natiuitie at BETHLEEM a magnificent Church couered with golde and siluer: an other at the Sepulcher of our Sauiour, the fourth in the honour of the holie Crosse, the fift in the denne where our Sauiour consecrated his Apostles and disciples with the secret mysteries: the sixt in the toppe of Mounte Oliuett, where our lord ascended into heauen, and where his footesteps remayned visible to all men, and not to be defaced or couered: but whatsoeuer was layed thereon, pauement or els, it was presentlie cast of by diuine and inuisible power, and from thence vpward vnto heauen, directlie as our Sauiour ascended, the church could not be couered by any roofe or ornament, but it would still be dissolued, and the way of our Lords Ascention euermore be open. No lesse singular declaration of her religious mynde, did she shew at HIERUSALEM, to the lyuing Temples of Christ, to weete to the holie virgins consecrated vnto god: whome she inuited to dinner and did so deuoutlie intertaine, that she thought it an vnworthie thing, to vse her mayds seruices to waite on them, but she herself being girded like a wayting mayd, with her owne handes serued them their meate and their drinke, and powred them water to wash their handes: so did the Queene of the worlde and mother of the Emperour make her self a seruant and handmayd of the handmaides of Christ. After this, she visited other places of the Easte with Princelie munificence, bestowing infinite gifts on Citties as she past and persons that came vnto her: and on the militarie orders, as she went, she powred out her bountifullnes with full hand: What she gaue to the

Marginalia:
- Other chi rches built by her.
- This hath S⁺ Hierome, S⁺ Paulinus, and Seuerus.
- Her humble seruice of the holie virgins:
- Her other lornies and munificent workes:

poore and needie, to the distressed and desolate persons, can not be numbered. For to some she gaue greate store of monnye, to others apparrell in greate plentie: some she 4 sett out of prison and fetters; others she let free from their miserable moyling and digging in the mines: many oppressed by fraude, and iniuried she deliuered; and many that were exiled, graciouslie she vouchsafed to call home, 8 to their beloued contrie. And allthoughe she was thus noblie beneficiall to men, neuerthelesse was she studious of religious pietie towards god: For what Church soeuer she entred into, albeit in litle townes, she enriched it with 12 braue furnitures, or with other liberalitie she proued to them her benignitie. Neither did she omitt to conuerse often with the common sort and multitude, to the end that by all sorte of vertuous offices and godlie duties of life, 16 she might make knowne her true deuotion, and worship towards god. In this iournie and pilgrimage did our holie HELENE, leaue a noble monument of her pietie at DREPANUM in BITHINIA, for her religion to S.t LUCIAN there 20 latelie martyred, whose body being afterward cast into the sea, delphins did on their backes, bring it to the shore: the fresh fame of which miracle, and the martyr then sounding all-aboute, she much deuoted towards holie 24 martyrs, vnderstanding his bodie to be but baselie buried, built him a moste sumptuous Church, and moreouer inlarged the towne, and made it a Cittie; fencing it with strong walls, and calling the inhabitants thereaboute to 28 come and dwell there: Whereuppon it tooke a new name, and was thenceforth called HELENOPOLIS. And that which fardered much her princelie mynde and munificent pietie, her sonne CONSTANTINE gaue her leaue, to vse his treasure 32 as she thought good, and to dispense it to her good lyking, thereby to make her more renowned and admirable. When she was come backe to ROME, the part of the holie Crosse which she brought with her from HIERUSALEM, with the 36 title of the same Crosse, whereon was written by PILATE;

Her benignitie toward the poore and miserable persons.

Her religious pietie to holie Churches.

Her munificence toward S.t Lucian Martyr.

Drepanum called Helenopolis: that is He cuns Cittie.

JESUS OF NAZARETH KING OF THE IEWES; one of the
nailes, with other reliques, she placed religiouslie in the
Church called of her name *Helen*, otherwise of *Holie*
Crosse in Hierusalem.¹ She being fowre score yeares olde,
and feeling her end to approche, she made her will giuing
to her deere sonne and her nephews what she had, and
giuing him, being then still attendant on her, and holding
her by the hand, many good exhortations to lyue religiouslie, after all she blessed him, and so departed this
life, to liue with the Angells and god in heauen for euer,
and her bodie was buried at ROME./

Her age and death.

*The historie and martyrdome of S! Vrsula and her fellow
Virgins gathered moste exactlie and brieflie by* HER-
MANNUS FLIEN *Doctor of Diuinitie and Deane of
S! Cunibert, and Canon of the holie Virgins in Colen,
in our age: They suffered about the yere of our
Lorde* 449:

When the Romane Empire did much decline and allmoste
fall, what throughe the tyrannie of Princes possessing it,
and barbarians breaking in on euerie side, and what
throughe the defection of many good Christians, that
pulled their neckes out of the yoke of that hard seruitude,
at the same time the Brittans in like sort were continuallie vexed and wasted by the fierce incursions of the
PICTES and SCOTTES. And albeit the Romane power there
did often vanquish and putt to flight those hostile forces,
and so defended the prouince some-while; notwithstanding
whereas the Romane forces did daylie diminishe, and
became weaker, and the Romane Legion which was sent to
help the Brittans left the land, dyuerse of the Brittish
nobilitie accompanying them, amongst whome was
CONANUS of good stocke and reputation in his nation; who
passing the seas landed in ARMORICA of FRANCE now called

¹ The name of the church was "Jerusalem"; cf. Baron. a. 324, CVI.

BRITTANIE, and began to setle themselues there, and to
erect a kingdome. Hereupon the poore Brittans remayning at home, becomming whollie destitute of all ayd
4 against those PICTISH aduersaries, they were enforced to
hire the ANGLES and SAXONS barbarous people also to come
and defend them and their contrie. As these matters were
thus in doing or not long before, CONANUS that was by
8 the captaine of the legion made cheefe or gouernour of
that new kingdome of French BRITTANIE, sendeth Embassadors into greate BRITTANIE vnto DIONOTHE king,
requesting him to grante him his daughter VRSULA to *Vrsula with hir virgins*
12 wife and fellow in his kingdome, and to the rest of his *required to wife.*
souldiors, other virgins in mariage: for it was thought
that this new kingdome would not be stable and firme for
long continuance, vnlesse they had wiues of their owne
16 nation./ DIONOTHE as yet liuing was a man of greate
name and authoritie, and from his infancie a christian, as
the other BRITTANS were. His daughter VRSULA was likewise a seruant of Christ, and beside so affected vnto
20 chastitie and the loue of virginitie, that to these mariages,
albeit with a king, she was rather haled perforce than
voluntarilie assenting. Now were the Englishe nation
that had beene called hither for defence of the contrie, so
24 delighted with the fertilitie of the land, that breaking
their league and friendship with the BRITTANS vnder
pretence of defalte of their stipends and pension not payed,
and ioyning handes with the PICTES, with vnited forces,
28 they runne, as BEDE affirmeth, on publike and priuate
buildings, ruining all: The priestes were slaine euerie- *The Saxons*
where at the Altar, the bishops with their people were *rage against the Brittans.*
hewed in peeces, and burnt withoute all distinction or
32 respect of their dignitie and honour, neither was there
any to be founde that would burie them so cruellie
murdered. The BRITTANS being pressed with this slaughter,
and withall preparing the dispatch and sending away of
36 this new spouse, greate multitudes as well of Ecclesi-

Many left Brittanie with Vrsula.

asticall men as lay men, seeking to flie this calamitie, ioyned themselues in the iournie with this ladie and her companie. Taking then the sea towards ARMORICA, presentlie there ariseth a cruell tempest, that disperseth the Nauie: wherein others perishing by shipwracke, the holie virgin VRSULA, with her eleuen thousand companions (reserued all for the crowne of martyrdome) after many perills and long ranging; in fine by the RHENE they arriued at COLEN AGRIPPINA, which at that time was beseeged or rather holden by the HUNNES, a barbarous nation, fleshlie and enemie to Christianitie. These HUNNES then beholding the excellent beautie and comlinesse of these women, as they themselues were moste prone to leacherous lust, so did they incite these virgins to the like; wooing them moste egerlie to haue their pleasures of them. But holie VRSULA, no lesse glorious for the claritie of vertue and virginitie, than for hir nobilitie of birth, instructed all her companie with so sound admonitions of

Their martyrdome.

pietie and Christianitie, that they all chose constantlie to suffer death, rather than with detriment of their faith and chastitie, to yield vnto the Barbarians fleshlie desire. Thereat the HUNNES, that could not stay in that place ong, moued with a greate rage, in barbarous cruell manner kill the whole companie. The Inhabitants of COLEN, when the Barbarians were remooued thence, came oute, gathered vp the holie bodies, and religiouslie buried them in the places where they suffered, doing them such honour, as was due to holie martyrs: For not long after in the places where many bodies lay together, they builded

The Church of the holie Virgins.

Churches, of which, that which is called the Church of the holie Virgins, they haue allwayes had it in such reuerence, that they neuer buried any other bodie there. In which place also, in the yeare of our Lord 922: HERMANNUS the first of that name Archbishop of COLEN founded a Colledge of holie Virgins and of Canons, endowing it accordinglie, whose successors increased that religious office and worship

by godlie zeale, bestowing no small riches and benefitts to
the honour of god omnipotent and his holie virgins.

The ground or earth of that Church will receiue no
other bodie, no not the corps of yong infants newlie
baptized, but as it were vomiting them vp againe in the
night, they will be cast vp aboue grounde, and not be
conteyned within it, as hath often beene tried. / BISHOP
LINDAN.

*The life of holie Keyna Virgin; who flourished about the
years of our Lord: 490: /*

Holie KEYNA virgin was daughter to one BRAGHANE a
litle king of the Brittans of BRECHNOCH territorie. He [Her happie kinred.]
is sayd to haue had twelue sonnes and as many daughters,
all of greate pietie: his eldest sonne was St CANOCH,
his eldest daughter named GLADE was mother to S.^{t}
CADOKE, his second daughter was mother to MELABIUS, S.^{t}
DAUIDS father bishop of MENEUIA: And our KEYNA,
before she was borne, being in her mothers bellie, had her
future holinesse foresignified: For her mother in a vision,
beheld her wombe replenished with myrrhe and baulme,
and her papps to shine with heauenlie light: moreouer
she thought she brought forth a snow-white doue.
This virgin when she was of yeares fitt for marriage, and
desired to wife of many, despised carnall bed, and consecrated herself to our Lord by vow of perpetuall
chastitie: whereupon in their tongue she is called
KEYNWIRE, that is ' KEYN the virgin.' / Afterward she
leauing her Contrie, the more freelie to serue god remote
from the worlde, she passed ouer the SEUERNE, and came
into a wood that was so infested with serpents, that man
nor beaste before her, durst not enter into it for feare of
death: But she armed with greate faith entered boldlie
into that woode, and with her prayers slew all those

Serpents turned into stours. serpents, and vipers, and turned them into stones; but in such sorte, that being stones, they retayned the perfect shape of their former serpentine kinde. After that she had long conuersed there in greate perfection and by her example had drawne many to the loue of god, she retourned into her contrie; where on a certaine litle hill she serued God with all deuotion, still cladd in hayre and lying on the grounde. Drawing neere her end in her *An Angell appeareth vnto her.* sleepe she beheld an Angell to strippe her out of her hayrecloth, and to putt on her a singular white vesture, and a garment of scarlett wrought with golde; who sayd vnto her withall: 'Be in redinesse to go with vs, that we may bring thee into the kingdome of thy father': after that, she hastening hence, her nephew St CADOKE was present with her, and assisting her in her passage, she departed vnto our Sauiour Christ, the viijth of October, *Her bodie dead is very odoriferous.* her sacred bodie leauing a moste fragrant sweet sauour to those that were aboute it, to their greate delighte and comforte./

The life of S^t: Brigide Virgin who disceased about the yeare of our Lord 518: or 521:

One DUBTACUS an Irishe man of the prouince of LEINSTRE boughte a captiue mayd named BROSECH of good conuersation and behauiour. Her maister being enamoured greatlie with her violentlie oppressed her: whereof she conceyuing, her mistresse grew into greate furie against her, not abyding that she should remayne in the house. Thereupon she was solde to a certaine magician; with whome her time comming she was deliuered of a daughter which was this BRIGIDE: who as often as she eate of the magician her maisters meate, she by vomite cast it vp *Her yong puritie and charitie.* againe; which he aduisedlie considering, perceiued the yong mayd to be moste pure and to good for his

vnworthines. Wherefore he sett her free, and restored her
to her father; where lyuing she was of such profuse
charitie towards the poore, that all whatsoeuer she could
4 gett, she bestowed on them. When she was mariageable,
and vehementlie vrged by her friends to take an husband,
she earnestlie besought our lord to send her some deformitie, whereby men might cease to loue her, or to request
8 her to wife. Her petition was heard, and her eye burst. *She asketh deformitie to keepe her Virginitie.*
Then taking with her three other maydes for companions,
she went vnto Bishop MACHILLA, that was disciple to S^t
PATRICKE; of whome she tooke the holie veile of virginitie;
12 and that men might know how greatelie her vow pleased
god, by meruailous miracle she touching the wooden foote
of the Altar with her hand as the Bishop was reading
holie prayers ouer her, forthwith the drie wood became *The vow of Virginitie honored with double miracle.*
16 flourishing and greene, neuer after corrupting, and as
soone as she had receiued the holie veile, her eye that was
burst and ran like water, was perfectlie cured. Her
singular holines god testified by sundrie miracles, she *Miracles donne by her.*
20 healing diuerse leapers with onelie holie water. A certaine
woman one day brought the holie virgin a present of
aples; at the same moment there stood poore leaprous
men that asked an almes of the virgin, she therefore bad
24 the aples to be giuen to those poore soules. The woman *A punishment of one hindering a worke of mercie.*
would not, but tooke them to herself, saying that she
brought them not for the leaprous persons, but for the virgin
and her fellow virgins. Holie BRIGIDE being moued at
28 the euill mynde of the woman, sayd vnto her: 'bicause thou
wouldest hinder this worke of mercie, know that thy trees
are condemned to perpetuall barrennes': the woman went
her way, and founde her wordes too true, neuer after
32 hauing fruite of them. An other woman, hauing a sonne *She made an Infant tell who was his father*
by false play, no lesse impudentlie than wickedlie, falslie
affirmed, that she had conceiued that sonne of BISHOP
BROONE; holie BRIGIDE causing the woman to be brought
36 to her, made the signe of the holie Crosse on her mouthe,

and presentlie the head and tongue of the impudent
woman did greatlie swell : She likewise signing the
Infants tongue sayd withall to him ; 'My litle babe, who is
thy father?' A strange worke of god, who once of olde 4
made BALAAMS asse to speake, the childe answered and
sayd: 'Bishop BROONE is not my father, but that vile fellow,'
(noting one) 'which sitteth amongst the basest sort of the
people.' The daughter of a certayne greate Prince had 8
vowed virginitie, yet her father enforced her to marrie:
when all costlie prouision for the marriage was redie, and
the day of the wedding at hand, the virgin by gods
inspiration fledd vnto holie BRIGID; whome her father 12
pursued presentlie, with a greate troope of horsmen : the
sainte then made her accustomed signe of the Crosse on the
earth, and therewith so repressed their force, that they
could not goe one steppe farther, and by the same signe, 16
brought the father to better mynde; and obtayned that
the virgin performed her vow to god, by consecrating
her self to him, as she wished. One time she receiuing the
blessed Sacrament at the Bishops hand, she saw in the 20
chalice which the deacon had in his hand, the shadow of
a goate ; wherewith she being moued, refused to drinke
thereof, and tolde the Bishop the cause. He called his
deacon to him, and mildlie exhorted him to confesse his 24
secret falte ; thereat he being confounded, confessed that
he had stollen a goate ; for which crime he hauing beene
penitent, and making satisfaction, the deformed shape
neuer appeared after in the chalice. A certaine noble 28
woman of SCOTLAND had a daughter which had beene mute
from her natiuitie; the mother brought her to BRIGIDE,
who taking her by the hand, asked her if for the loue of
Christ, she would keepe her self chaste perpetuallie : see 32
a wonder: She presentlie hauing her tongue losed, did
answer that she would moste promptlie doe, whatsoeuer she
would will her. / Others moe I omitte for breuitie. Wher-
fore the blessed virgin knowing her end to be come, called 36

She defendeth a Virgin from mariage.

one of her schollers to her, and signified vnto her, that she
must passe hence and leaue them: the which day assigned
being come, she yielded her blessed spirit vnto her Lord;
4 the yeare of our Lord: 521:

*The life and martyrdome of holie Dympna a kings daughter
of Ireland out of her acts written by Peter of Cambray:*[1]
She liued about the yeare of our Lord: 600:

8 **There** was in Ireland a Pagane King verie renowned for
greate power and much wealth, for vaine religion and rare
deuotion toward his Idoles. This man begatt on his wife,
whome he deerelie loued for her peerlesse beautie, a daugh-
12 ter for comelinesse comparable to her mother, for meritts
and name called DYMPNA, which signifieth 'worthie': She being
princelie brought vp in her fathers house, when she had
passed her childehood, by gods supernall illumination, she
16 began to despise princes riot, and all sortes of pleasures,
and at last being secretlie baptized, gaue her self vnto
Christ, and by vow of perpetuall chastitie dedicated her Her vowe of
bodie and mynde to serue him. The Queene her mother   Virginitie.
20 dying about the same time, and her father immoderatlie
lamenting her decease, by counsell of his nobles, he
thought best to match his fayre daughter with some king
fitt for her: but when after earnest serch none could be
24 founde, whome they iudged worthie of her, some wicked
counsellers thinke her fitt for none so much, as for the
father himself to take to wife: which when he had heard,
the diuell desiring to reduce the virgin to profane Idolatrie
28 againe, so inflamed the kings hart with incestuous loue, Her fathers
that presentlie he began to wooe her with flattering and incestuous
faire promises, offering her all glorie, riches and honour, if loue of her.
she would be his wife. The virgin of Christ answered
32 him playnlie, that she would neuer consent to that impietie;
adding that by no law nor righte, the daughter might

[1] See Act. SS. Bolland. 15 May, p. 478, ff.

defile her fathers beadd, nor by such shamefull wickednes
staine and infame all her stocke and posteritie for euer.
He still more eagerlie soliciting her, and she the more
vehementlie repelling him, in fine he fell into choler, and 4
tolde her if she would not yielde with faire meanes, she
should be compelled: Whereuppon she craued fortie dayes

Her holie prudence. respite, and withall required new garments and ornament
of iewells and other precious things wherewith to make 8
her self more gratefull to her father, as she pretended; but
indeede to auoyde his incestuous furie. All that being
granted moste gladlie, that while she crieth to her
Sauiour moste instantlie for help and deliuerie. At that 12

Gerebern an holie Priest. time was there a priest of famous holines and learning
named GEREBERN in Ireland, who secretlie laboured moste
seriouslie to conuert soules vnto god, who had often heard
the Queenes confession that was dead, and had baptized 16
DYMPNA, and communicated her and her mother with the
bread of heauen. For this priest did she send secretlie,
who vnderstanding her danger, and seing her many teares,
wherewith she besought his assistance and help, his prayers 20
and aduise, counselled her to flie thence priuilie, and in
pouertie to follow poore Christ into a strange contrie.

She flieth out of her contrie; and her life. Thereupon withoute delay, at the next oportunitie, taking
GEREBERNE with her, and her fathers iester with his wife 24
for safer passing vnder colour of them, hauing a ship
prepared and prosperous weather, she came to ANTWERP,
where staying a while and ill brooking secular noise, and
worldlie companie of the towne, they determyned to seeke 28
some solitarie place to liue in. Taking therefore their
iournie thence, after that they had passed throughe wooddie
and wilde places, they came to a village named GHELE,
where there was one Church dedicated to St MARTIN, and 32
where at this day the holie virgins bodie lieth. Not far
from that Church in a place called ZAMMALE did they build
them a house, that there remote from all secular tumult in
sweete contemplation of heauenlie things, they might serue 36

god, where after that they had liued in prayer and fasting three moneths, they were founde. For as soone as her father vnderstood of her departure, he rent his garments
4 for sorrow, and when he had sought her euerie-where in Ireland and could not fynde her, he tooke shippe and came to ANTWERP, where staying he sent messengers euerie way to harken after her: of which some comming to WESTERLE
8 and lodging there, when they came to pay for their charges, and offered their contrie monie, the hoste thinking no harme, sayd he had of their coyne, but could not tell the value thereof. Whereupon the guests demanding of him
12 where he had that monie, he sayd 'of a certaine Virgin a stranger that dwelt thereby in the desert, who still sent that kinde of coine, to buye her self and those with her victuals.' Vpon these speeches the messengers conceiued
16 greate hope of their purpose, and being brought to the place, they perceyued it was she. Then posted they to the father at ANTWERP; who ioyfullie hearing that tydings, forthwith came with his retinue to the place, where fynding
20 her, but her colour empayred with fasting, he burning notwithstanding with lust towards her, first assalted her with faire wordes, saying. 'O myne owne and onelie daughter DYMPNA, my loue, my desire and ioye, what neede
24 vrged thee to despise thy roiall dignitie and natiue soilo, to forgett naturall loue, and to forsake thy father to adhere to this decrepit olde priest, as his daughter, and to obey his sowre precepts with all alacritie? Why contemnest thou
28 the kings Courte, being the onelie heire to the Crowne of Ireland? Follow my counsell, and retourne with me; if thou wilt assent vnto me, I will sett on thy head the kinglie diademe, and exalte thee aboue all Princes of my
32 realme; nay more I will builde thee a Temple of white marble, and an Image of fine golde will I erect therein to thine honour, which shall be wrought moste curiouslie, and glitter with precious stones of inestimable price; so that
36 thou shalt be adored as a goddesse of all men.' When the

Marginal note: She is descried and found out and tempted by her father.

virgin would haue answered him hereto, GEREBERN preuented her, reprouing the king verie sharplie, calling him a moste abhominable and horrible man, that would seeke to defile his owne daughter, whereas the moste impure whoore- 4
maisters that were, detested that wickednes. The holie man also admonished the virgin, neuer to yield to the king in that villanie, leste she incurred the eternall kings displeasure, whose sweetnes she had allreadie begunne to 8
taste. The king and his nobles about him being highlie offended at that admonition of GEREBERN, cried out that he was worthie of death, and remouing him from the Virgins companie, they missused him with sundrie des- 12
pites, and in conclusion with violent hands slew him: and thus the glorious martyr gayned the crowne of blisse prepared for gods faithfull witnesses. Then the king againe retourning to the virgin, vrged her afresh to yield 16
to his desire, saying, 'O my daughter why sufferest thou thy father to be so plunged in sorrowes? Why doost thou not pittie him? why despisest thou him that loueth thee: harken vnto me and thou shalt want nothing; nay thy 20
name shall be renowned in all my kingdome amongst the sacred goddesses.' Then the zealous virgin of god answered with indignation, saying. 'Vnhappie tyrant, why seekest thou by deceitfull promises to putte me from my purpose 24
of chastitie? Thinkest thou wretch that I will euer forsake my vowe, and offend my onelie louer Christ by polluting my bodie? I despise all thy roiall delightes from my hart, and for the promises of my Lord ÍESUS, 28
which surpasse all desire, I wish and long for them with all my affections: and to be accounted a goddesse I vtterlie refuse, and to haue an Image erected vnto me, I make no reckoning: wherefore henceforth vse no such speeches to 32
me.' The king raging at these wordes and full of con-cupiscence, furiouslie sayd vnto her. 'See thou prouoke vs no farther, thou malicious queane, and presentlie fullfill our commandement, and sacrifice vnto our gods, or els 36

kings daughters shall learne by thy payne not to contradict
their fathers will.' To that the virgin replied, 'Cruell *Her courageous con-*
tyrant for what cause didst thou kill the notable priest *stancie and martyrdome,*
4 of god guiltie of no fault? Thou shalt not escape the
iudgement of god omnipotent; I detest thy gods and
goddesses, as false mawmets, and I committe my self
whollie to my Lord Iesus: He is my despoused husband,
8 he is my glorie, my health and my desire: all the paines
that thou canst lay on me, I will ioyfullie sustayne them
for my Lord.' The king being madd at this, commanded
her to be beheadded: but when none was to be founde that
12 would execute that cruell sentence, he himself forgetting
all roiall clemencie or fatherlie pittie, with his own sword
cutt of her head: and then retourning home, he left the
holie bodies to be deuoured by the foules of the ayre, and
16 the beastes of the fielde; and after they had beene there
some dayes vntouched, they were buried by those that
dwelt by in a certaine hole not far of. That village GHELE
had then but few inhabitants, all the houses there not
20 exceeding fifteene, and those inuironed with woods, sixe
miles compasse. Many yeares after, when this village was *Ghele becometh*
greatlie peopled, and for store of dwellers verie famous, *famous for miraculous*
by reason of wonderfull cures there wrought, the cleargie *cures by these Saints.*
24 and laitie assembling themselues, at the place where these
saintes were buried, they began to seeke for the bodies;
where beholde the admirable worke of god. For digging
they founde two coffins, more white than snow, and cutt
28 out of stone made by Angells hands: then pulling them *They had toombs or*
out with ease and viewing them, they could finde no signe *coffins made by Angelli-*
of peecing, but all whole of one substance and stone, yet *call hands.*
the bodies within: whereat admiring they well perceiued
32 those toombes not to haue beene mens workes but of
Angells, and by the cleare whitenes, they gathered the
Saintes chastitie. The fame of these wonders and miracles,
were brought to the towne of SANTEN on RHENE; the
36 Inhabitants thereof vnder colour of pilgrimage went

thither, and spying their oportunitie in waggons prepared, they stale away the coffins and reliques. But when
the dwellers of GHELE vnderstood the matter, with all
speede they poste after them, who being much terrified   4
with the noise of the multitudine pursuing them, they
brake one of the Coffins, and tooke with them the Reliques,
and the other which was of the virgin DYMPNA, they left
in the way behinde them : They escaping safe to their towne   8
SANTEN with GEREBERNS reliques, the people thereof receiued them with honourable deuotion of hymnes and
lightes. The men of GHELE fynding the wholle coffine,
would haue carried it backe; but they could not mooue the   12
bodie out of the place, as thoughe it had bene rooted within
the earth : They then not knowing what to doe, one night
a certaine olde woman, was admonished in her sleepe to
take a yong calfe that she had in her stable, to fasten it to   16
her litle cart or drey, and then to goe where the holie
Coffine was, and so carrie it backe whence it was brought,
which others could not, their sinnes letting them to accomplish that worke. The morrow therefore she did as she   20
was bidden, and comming to the place to carrie the holie
burden in that manner, and praying the men that kept the
bodie, to help place the Coffine in her cart, they scorned
her, deeming her half madd, and some reiected her. After   24
much importunitie they being content to trie, when they
putt their hands to lift it into that cart, it resisted not,
but verie lightly yielded, and was with greate ease placed
therein, and with exceeding ioy so carried backe to their   28
Churche : where by her merits, innumerable miracles are
daylie wrought. Afterward the best of the Inhabitants
there, placed the holie corpes in a chest of golde and siluer,
richlie sett with precious stones. Wherefore the Bishop   32
of CAMBRAY, coming thither with a greate companie of the
common people, he translated the bodie out of the former
tombe of stone, into this new one made of golde, siluer,
and precious stones : And opening the coffine, the bishop   36

found in the brest of the Virgins bodie, a red stone, hauing   A miraculous stone
this inscription, 'DYMPNA'; there is no doubte but it was   found in her brest.
putt there by gods Angell, that by it, her martyrdome
4 might be notified to all men. That translation was made
with greate solemnitie the fifteenth of May, on which also
the festiuitie of her martyrdome was instituted, albeit she
suffered the thirtethe of the same moneth. Possessed per-   Mircoles.
8 sons brought to her shrine at GHELE are daylie deliuered;
and diuerse other benefits donne to deuoute persons seeking
her help: And for as much, as it would be ouerlong to
rehearse the wonderfull miracles, which our Lord Iesus
12 hath vouchsafed to worke by this glorious virgin and
martyrs merits and intercession, for breuitie they are
omitted. /

The life of S! Edburge Virgin and Abbesse: She flourished
16 *in the yeares of Christ: 616 :*

Edburge daughter vnto holie king ETHELBERT and
BERTA his Queene, the first Christian Princes of England and
Kent, after by her fathers and mothers example, she had
20 giuen her name vnto Christ, and was baptized, day and
night she attended on prayer, and praysing of god, whollie
burning with the loue of the heauenlie HIERUSALEM, and
her beloueds presenco Christ IESUS: For better prepara-
24 tion of her self to that happines, she forsooke the worlde,
entered into the monasterie of her Neece S! MILDRED there   She entered into a monasterie and subiected
in TENET Isle, humblie subiecting herself to be gouerned   herself to her yonger and neece.
by her yonger far, for his loue that for her had beene
28 obedient vnto death. She more and more kindling her
heauenlie loue there by spirituall exercises; when S! MIL-
DRED was dead that gouerned the Abbey, she was enforced
to take the regiment vpon her, being chosen Abbesse.
32 Lord how wiselie and couragiouslie, did she saile throughe
the flouds and tossings of this worlde, guiding her self and

others towards the port of happie rest, comforting her hart with diuine studies, fencing and garnishing her soule with diuine contemplation and prayer, despising all the ioyes of this life as durt; and thus after many conflicts and tentations, she by happie decease arriued at heauen, and enioyed the ioyfull presence of Christ, which she long had sighed for, the xiij*th* of December, shyning after her death with

Her miracles:

greate miracles: For when a certaine Priest of that monasterie throughe secular greatnes, neglected the place & her

A negligent Priest punished sore:

reliques, not vsing that care and reuerence which was due, and being in a vision often admonished of his faulte, yet regarded nothing, one night he was taken by two blacke villaines before the Church doore, and by them was beaten and tormented cruellie, and with their nailes his eyes were pulled oute: Then seemed the holie sainte to arise and come from her sepulcher, and to deliuer him so beaten and made blinde out of their handes, she saying to those tormenters of him withall: 'Away and let my priest alone you vile wretches,' and from that houre was he euer after blinde. An other being infamed to haue committed a theft, and admonished too restore that which he had stollen, he rashlie desirous to purge himself before men, not fearing Gods knowledge of his contrarie hart, with

A dredfull vengeance on one for swearing:

execration sayed: 'If I haue committed this theft wherewith I am charged, I pray god and the holie virgin EDBURGE, before whome I stand, that I neuer go oute of this place aliue.' He had no sooner spake the worde, but at his fundament he voided out his entrailes, and withall his life: so that as he vnhappilie wished with false hart, he indeede and deseruedlie, departed not thence with his life. In the yeare of our Redemption: 1085: her bodie and S*t* MILDREDS, were translated by S*t* LANFRANK, Archbishop of CANTERBURIE, out of the Ile of TENET, vnto the Church of S*t* GREGORIE, which he had repayred and enriched at Canterburie a litle before.

*An other S*t* Edburga.*

There was an other EDBURGE Virgin and Abbesse,

daughter to king ADULPHE in Hamshire at WINCHESTER, about the yeare: 860: she was of renowned holines also, as of greate fame in those partes, but her particular life, I could not see.

The life of S! Eanswide Virgin and Abbesse, she flourished in the yeare: 640 : /

Eanswide daughter to king EDBALD, and EMME his Queene, who reigned in Kent, neece to EDBURGE the sainte before: She renouncing the world from her infancie, and bearing in her hart the purpose of religious and perpetuall Virginitie; notwithstanding when she was ripe for marriage, her father laboured her with much intreatie to marrie. The saintlie virgin, no lesse wiselie to satiafie her father, than godlilie for sauegard of her holie purpose, answered him in this manner. 'Moste deere father if you can prouide me an husband immortall, whose death may not grieue me, and whose loue shall be constant and stable, whose issue and fruite may not perish and so afflict, whose societie shall be voide of all brauling and discontentments, whome louing I shall still remayne chaste, and touching him shall not be defiled, and enioying shall continue a virgin, then will I accept of your offer; but if there be no such to be founde beside my heauenlie lord and loue Christ whose marriage hath all these conditions in surpassing manner and excellencie, then I beseeche you haue me excused, if for so far better a condition I refuse a worse: and grante me an Oratorie where I may liue with him and serue him.' The father being conuinced with the forceible reason, and wise discourse of his daughter yielded to her request, and built her a Church and a monasterie in the honor of S! PETER, in a place called FOLKAM neere the sea and remote from the concourse and trouble of men. Where in her regular habit, adorning her virginall chastitie

A worthie wise answer of the difference betwene spirituall mariage and carnal.

with other vertues and vertuous excrcises, she serued our
Lord many yeares, and after rested in him the twelfth of
September./

*The life of St Ethelburge Virgin and Abbesse: She liued 4
aboute the yeare: 640:*

Sainte ETHELBURGE sister to St ERKENWALD Bishop of
London, was daughter to one OFFA, a moste noble Prince
albeit an infidell, who ruled in the prouince of LINDSEIE, 8
and had his mansion-house at the village of SALINGTON.
This holie mayde from her prime age, abhorred the delights
of the flesh, and the allurements of the worlde; yet for her

*Her afflic-
tion by her
father.*

more probation, she found her father a moste cruell perse- 12
cuter and enemie of her faithfull mynde and endeuours;
yet in fine, by her vertue and patience, by her faith and
pietie towards god for him, she did not onelie preserue her
owne feruour and deuotion, but warmed her colde father, 16
and of a persecuter made him a professor of Christ: But
before she reaped that croppe of her labours with ioy, she
sowed in sorrowe: For he vrging her to marrie a mortall
man, that had chosen Christ that neuer dieth, and had 20
betrothed her self to him, the father not enduring her
refusall, vexed her not a litle nor a litle space. Wherefore
to saue her self from dangers iustlie feared, she taking one
companion with her, fledd away, thinking to passe ouer the 24
sea, and there to lyue to her beloued Christ in monasticall
profession. But her brother ERKENWALD liking better, that
she should take that religious course heere at home, pro-

*Hildelitha
her learned
and vertuous
teacher.*

uided for her a spirituall teacher named HILDELITHA, a 28
woman as well excellentlie learned in the liberall sciences,
as verie expert, in skill of religious discipline and life; and

*The Monas-
tery of Bark-
ing founded.*

building them a monasterie at BARKING in ESSEX (which
then was in an other kings dominion, being seauen in all, 32
and that at once) placed them there with other virgins.
This virgin in short time surpassed all others farre in all

vertue and holynes, and at last was chosen mother or Abbesse of them all. She subdued her bodie to her spirit by fastings, watchings, and praying, day and night seruing the Allmightie. She preached and exhorted her Sisters without ceasing to all contempt of this worlde, teaching them to abhorre the vanitie and corruption thereof; and this principallie in the time of the plague: whereby diuerse of them being taken out of this life, she would be at their graues praying for them, when others were fast asleepe. In which holie offices she with her sisters being studiouslie occupied, God did often comfort them with heauenlie consolations of celestiall lights; whereby he did as it were inuite them vnto their heauenlie home and contrie. One of the sisters named TORGITHA, that had beene wasted by nyne yeares sicknes, in a vision of a glorious bedd carried vp into heauen, in triumphant manner, vnderstood that her mother ETHELBURGE was shortlie to leaue this life, for attayning of a better, which indeede so fell oute: But afterward she did requite TORGITHA with like charitie, for when she dyed ETHELBURGE appeared vnto her and tolde her she was come to fetch her to heauenlie ioyes; whereat TORGITHA yielding her moste hartie thankes, withall yielded vp her religious spirite. This monasterie did god meruailouslie protect from the furie of the Danes: for they burning and spoyling all where they went, comming to this monasterie, at euerie gate or entrie, they found fierce wilde beastes, readie to inuade them, yea running vpon them; here a wolfe, there a beare, at an other place a lion, as it were watching and warding their church and house. The Barbarians that came to frighte others, being herewith frighted, whereas before they thought imperiouslie to goe where they list, now desire to enter into the church not as enemies in hostile manner, but as friends and in peace, not to spoile but to giue, and to make their offerings to god: which they performing, the beastes resisted them not, but departed.

Her charitie toward her sick sisters and dead:

A vision:

A miraculous protection of that monasterie.

An other Ethelburge

There was an other ETHELBURGE Queene, wife to holie ding EDWINE, and daughter to holie ETHELBERT king of Kent, who after her husband EDWINE, the first Christian king of Northumberland was slaine, she fledd thence, and came backe into her contrie Kent: where forsaking the worlde she receiued the holie veile of chastitie and was consecrated vnto God by S? HONORIUS Archbishop of Canterburie in a monasterie which she built at a place called LIMING, where in holines seruing god, she was mother of many holie virgins and widdowes, that did imitate her religious purpose and profession. /

She taketh the holie veile.

The life of S? Sexburge Queene and Abbesse: She liued in the yeare of our Lord: 640:

Sexburge daughter to ANNA king of the East Angles, was married to ERCOMBERT king of Kent, by whome she had two sonnes EGBERT and LOTHARIE, and two daughters of greate holynes, to woete ERMELINDE, who was married to WULFERE king of midle-England, by whome she had S?: WERBURGE virgin; and ERKENGODA, who went beyond the seas, to professe her self a religious woman, and there in the monasterie of BRIGA, shined with greate holinesse and many miracles. The good mother of these good children and Queene SEXBURGE, so laboured her husband by her singular zeale and vertuous studie, that Idolatrie was whollie rooted out of his realme; for what his predecessours permitted or left as not able conuenientlie to extirpate, that this king did by the religious industrie of this his faithfull Queene perfectlie abandon, building Churches and monasteries in greate store. And as she was so carefull of all her subiects saluation, so much more of her childrens vertuous education, teaching them with all reuerence to feare and serue god. She caused her husband so earnestlie to command Lentfast and abstinence to be

Her holie daughters.

Her husbands noble acts by her meanes:

observed, that the violaters incurred seuere punishment.
Her husband deceasing she cast away all the pompe and rioting of the worlde, and tooke the religious habit of pro-
4 fessed chastitie and sanctimonie in the Abbie of ELIE, subiecting her self for Christs sake vnto her sister Sᵗ ETHELDRED or AUDRIE Abbesse then, and founder of that Nonnerie. There liued she in all vertuous labour,
8 washing away the staynes of secular pleasures with flouds of teares, and with the fire of diuine loue consuming them; emulating her sisters holynes, in all humilitie, continencie and deuotion, and after her death she was chosen to rule
12 the house: which she performed in such sort, that whereas she was greatest of all, yet she by singular humilitie abased her self vnder euerie one, seruing them with all dutie and officiousnes, whose superiour she was by office. In fine
16 when she was fraught with vertues and yeares, she passed hence vnto Christ her loue and bridegroome. Her daughter ERKENGODE before her death, being by god admonished of her end, went to all her sisters, especiallie the grauest and
20 those that were of moste perfection, commending her passage vnto their charitable assistance and prayers. The night following she was called hence to our Lord, and honoured with Angellicall songues; her bodie yielding
24 a moste fragrant odour, meruailous pleasant and delectable to all aboute it; a greate token of her ghostlie suauitie, in gods sense and his Angells; and seauen yeares after being founde incorrupt.—In the same partes beyond the sea, were
28 these consecrated virgins also SETHRITH daughter vnto the wife of King¹ ANNA, and ETHELBURGE his owne daughter, both hyding themselues in that same monasterie of BRIGA, from the sighte and companie of the infectious worlde.
28 Where in tyme both became Abbesses after other, and when they had absolued their time of mortalitie allowed them to worke their saluation in religious profession, they departed in the peace of Christ and rested in him.

Side notes:
She entered into the Abbie of Elie.
Her religious humilitie and vertue.
Erkengodes saintlinesse.
Her end.
Sethrith and Ethelburge two other.
[¹ MS. orig. Queene.]

The life of holie Hilda Virgin and Abbesse: she liued about the yeare, 650:

Hilda was daughter to HEREBIKE king EDWINE the saintes nephew: who when she had leadd thirtie three yeares in the worlde, being then desirous to follow Christ in more perfection, purposed to passe ouer into France, and there in the monasterie of CALE with her sister [1]HERESWIDE to yield herself vnder regulare discipline: but by persuasion of holie Aydan Bishop, she accompanyed with some other fellowes, first ledd monasticall life, neere aboute the riuer of WIER in NORTHUMBERLAND: After that she became Abbesse in the nonrie called HERTHEIE; where BEGA the spouse of Christ is sayed to haue taken the profession and religious habite, at the hands and consecration of holie AIDAN, first of all women in NORTHUMBERLAND. This HILDA, AYDAN did often visite and carefullie instruct: Whence she becomming a mistresse of vertues, did likewise endow the monasterie of STRENESHALCH otherwise WHITBY, with the same vertues and regular doctrine. She was of so greate wisedome, that not onelie those of the meaner sort, but kings and Princes would come to her for counsell and aduice, which they found of her moste rare. She caused her subiects to applie the reading and studie of holie scriptures so earnestlie, and to busie themselues in workes of righteousnes so industriouslie, that fiue of them became moste worthie Bishops, to weete BOSA, ACCA, OSTFORUS, IOHN, and WILFRIDE; who all were men of rare merit and holynes. All called her mother for her singular pietie and excellent grace: whereby verie trulie was fullfilled in her the vision which her mother BREGUSWIDE had; which was this. She seeking verie carefullie her husband that was in banishment with CERDIKE king of the BRITTANS, and not fynding him, she thought she found vnder her coate a moste riche tablet or ouche, whose bright-

Marginalia:
[1] Mother to Adulph king of the East Angles (*so the MS.*).
Bega the first professed Nonne in Northumberland:
Her rare wisedome.
Her mothers vision of her.

nes did illumine and adorne all England. In that monasterie
of Whitbye, there were such aboundance of serpents, what
throughe the thicknes of bushes, and the wildernesse of the
woods, that the virgins durst not peepe out of their Cells,
or goe to draw water: but by her prayers she obtayned of
god, that they might be tourned into stones; yet so as the Serpents
turned into
shape of serpents still remayned; which to this day, the Stones:
stones of that place do declare, as eye-witnesses haue
testified. Moreouer a greate number of birds alighting
in her fields of corne, and deuouring it shrewdlie, she commanded her seruant to penne them vp all within a litle Birds ad-
mirablie
place: afterward she letting them goe abrode, fynding one vsed:
of them to be dead that while, restored the bird to life,
and let it flie after the others. One CEDMON there was, who Cedmon a
diuine Poet
a litle before in his dreame, was taught by God poetrie in in English
admirablie
the English tongue onelie, and for holie matters, whome made.
she persuaded to forsake the worlde and to enter into
Religion. This man became a sacred Poet in this manner.
He being one day at a feast or bankett with diuerse others,
all present were in their turne to sing to the harpe, and to
make some rimes: He perceyuing the instrument to
approche towards him, and that he must sing which he
could not, for shame sloncke out of the place; and being
out thence he fell asleepe; when one appearing vnto him,
gaue him the gift to make rymes, and withall bad him
sing: which he long refusing at last yielded as it were
perforce, and did sing moste cunninglie, more than he euer
thought he could haue donne: From that time he composed
sundrie poems, but voide of all friuolous matter or superfluous, and full of all pietie and religion, in such patheticall
sorte that diuerse were moued to forsake the world by
hearing and reading them, and inflamed in the loue of
celestiall blisse: And in this deuoute kinde or vaine, none
was comparable to him. Stories of the scriptures giuen
him in English (for he was alltogether vnlearned) or other See what
poetrie is to
deuoute sentences, he would straitewayes tourne them into be wished:

moste sweete English verse or metre: as of the creation of
the worlde, of the beginning of man, and allmoste of all
the stories in Genesis, he made excellent poemes, and
moste deuoute: Likewise of the Incarnation, Passion,
resurrection, and Ascension of our Sauiour, of the last
iudgement, of the paines of hell and ioyes of heauen, and
the like; in all which he sought to excite and moue them
to the loue of god and hatred of sinne: He was an humble
and religious person, vehement against wicked liuers, and in
this manner singing vnto god euermore, at last ended his
life with praising god also. This sweete Poete, for religious
profession was a plant of holie HILDAS setting. She (that
her vertue might be perfected by infirmitie) sixe yeares
before her death was continuallie sicke, in which she
yielded vnto god hartie thankes, as well for infirmitie as
health, and publikelie and priuatelie instructed her flocke
moste diligentlie in health to serue god moste stud'ouslie
and in sicknes to giue him thankes moste hartilie; and in
such vertuous exercises passing her dayes vntill she was
sixtie and sixe yeares olde, then she left this miserie, and
by Angells handes was carried to Christ in heauen. /

The life of S͟t Ermenilde Queene that liued in the yeare: 660:

This Queene ERMENILDE was daughter to ERCOMBERT king
of Kent and S͟t SEXBURGE: She was a mother to all in
any kinde of necessitie or miserie, thoroughe christian
compassion desiring and studying to helpe all. She being
giuen to wife to WULFERE king of midle-England, by her

Her zeale of Gods glorie. zeale and religious industrie, no meane was omitted, to
bring that people to the knowledge and fauour of Christ.
Whereby you may coniecture, what fruite ensued of that
trauaile to the people, what glorie of god, what benefitt
to her self. When her husband was dead, by whose help
she wrought that former promotion of gods glorie, she

ceased not in an other kinde to edifie all, that was by
example: teaching them to contemne the worlde, and moste
feruentlie to runne towards heauen. For with her
4 daughter WERBURGE (whose life followeth) she forsooke
the glorie and vaine pompe of this life, and entred into the
monasterie of ELIE, where her mother SEXBURGE was, but
her sister AUDRIE Abbesse, and tooke the religious habit
8 and profession of monasticall life; there heaping vertues
vpon vertues, good workes vpon good workes, vntill being
riche with holie merits, and adorned with graces fitt to
occurre and meete her beloued bridegroome IESUS,
12 she was sent for home vnto his kingdome, to raigne
with him for euer; for hauing serued and obeyed heere
a while for his sake in religious discipline and chaste
humiliation.

O what a glorious societie, the grandmother mother and neece, all religious together and Saints: and the Abbesse Aunt and a Sainte.

16 *The life of S! Werburye daughter to the former Ermenilde: with whome she liued in religion, and continued a perpetuall holie Virgin. /*

Werburge descended by her mother ERMENILDE of the
20 famous and saintlie kings ETHELBERT of KENT, and ANNA
of EAST ANGLES, and daughter to king WULFERE of
MERCIA, louing Christ aboue all earthlie Princes and delightes of the worlde, entered into the Abbie of ELIE with
24 her mother: where vnder her Aunte ETHELDRED or
AUDRIE, she receiued the monasticall weede. There she
excelled all in humilitie, wherefore god in this life exalted
her aboue all. For when her father WULFERE was dead,
28 and his brother her vnckle ETHELRED reigned in MERCIA,
she was made cheofe or supreme gouernesse of all the
monasteries of Nonnes in all midle-England: For she surpassed in all holie exercises of vertue, conuersing in spirit
32 with the Angells and saintes in heauen, thoughe in bodie
she was in earth. This virgin abyding one time at a
mansion-house of theirs at WEDUNE neere NORTHAMPTON,

greate flockes of wilde geese deuoured her fieldes. She
being aduertised thereof, by one of her people, commanded
him to driue them vp into a house and keepe them there:
A strange thing it is to tell. The partie did simplie her
commandment, and the geese are driuen before him, as if
they had no wings; so that he pend them all fast in a
house of the holie virgins. The next day she lett them
lose, and permitted them to departe, withall commanding
them to retourne no more thither. And whereas one had
stollen away one of the companie; the rest being dismissed,
neuer left crying and flying aboute the house, vntill their
fellow taken away was restored to them. Her heardman
became an Anchoret, for loue of better conforming himself
to Christ crucified; whose name was ALNOTHE. He hauing
serued god in that manner some time was by gods secret
permission martyred by theeues. The holie virgin departing
hence chose to be buried in the Abbey of HAMBURGE: but
when she was dead, her bodie was carried to the Church of
TRIKINGHAM; where with the gates fast locked, she was
kept and watched verie carefullie, rather curiouslie: But
see a wonder. The watchmen fell all into a deepe sleepe,
and they of HAMBURGE came for the bodie, all the gates of
the monasterie and Church of their owne accorde, withoute
mens hands opened vnto them, so that withoute resistance,
but with greate ioy they tooke away the sacred bodie, and
interred it, as she dying required: where God testifyed her
holines by innumerable miracles. / Nine yeares after,
her corps was taken vp, and founde moste incorrupt; her
face most white, her garments cleane, her cheekes ruddie,
so that God thereby was greatlie glorified in his virgin.

The life of S. Milburge Virgin: she liued about the years of Christ: 664:

This holie virgin by her mother DOMPNEUA descended of
holie king ETHELBERT, had for her father MORWALD one of

king PENDA his sonnes, and king after him in a parte of
MERCIA: yet a Pagan as his father had beene when he
liued. She had two other sisters, MILDREDE and MILGITH,
4 the first of which was as famous a sainte as her self, as in
her life shall appeare. Her father being a Pagane had this
dreame. He thought two ghastlie and fierie dogges sett vpon *A vision.*
him to kill him; by whome he being greatlie endangered,
8 beholde a venerable personage in countenance and his haire *The description of S!*
poulled in forme of a crowne all aboute by his eares came *Peter, and*
and rescued him, deliuering him out of their iawes with a *of the power in him:*
goulden keye which he had in his hand. At the verie same
12 time was one EDFRIDE a Priest of Northhumberland commanded by god to goe into MERCIA, to conuert the king
thereof, and his people vnto Christ: who comming as he
had beene appointed, by happe then lodged at the house of
16 one of the kings seruants: who being delighted greatlie with
this vertuous Priests demeanure, brought him to the king,
being then verie anxious and troubled aboute his dreame,
like as IOSEPH was to PHARAO to expounde his hidden
20 visions: which he did moste fittlie, declaring to the king *The exposition.*
how that those moste cruell and gastlye doggs which
inuaded him, were the fierce and raging diuells that sought
by all their power to destroy him, being as he was,
24 destitute of the sauing faith of Christ: and that the
reuerend person, that saued him out of their iawes was
S!: PETER the Porter of heauen, and Christs vicar on
earth, who hath granted him power of bynding and losing:
28 All which the good Priest explicating at large, the king
beleeued, and builded to S!: PETER a churche endowing it
with greate riches and possessions. Afterward king *Her father is conuerted.*
MERWALD and his Queene DOMPNEUA incensed with greate *after he and her mother*
32 loue of extraordinarie puritie, by mutuall consent, liued *liue chaste.*
all their life chaste, without companie keeping as man and
wife: And the queene founding herself a monasterie in the
honour of the Blessed Virgin Marie, with diuerse virgins
36 which she gathered together, in greate holynes gouerned

THE LIFE OF St MILBURGE.

that sacred familie : Whome her eldest daughter MILBURGE with seauentie other virgins did happilie succeede : but she building an other monasterie called WIMNICA (after WENLOKE) liued there with her holie societie. A certaine kings sonne was extremelie in loue with her, and purposed for satisfying his foule affection, by force to take her: which she vnderstanding fledd from thence, and passed ouer the riuer of CORF. The impure louer pursued after her, but when he came to the said riuer of CORF, it as it were disdayning that he should passe throughe it self suddenlie swelled in such sort, that he could not follow her. Whereat this yong man being confounded and amazed, gaue ouer his purpose./ MILBURGE one day learning, that exceeding multitudes of wilde geese did deuoure the corne of her fieldes, thereuppon she in the name of god commanded them to come no more to indamage her so, and to spoile her fieldes. They presentlie depart, and neuer after lighted there, or if for wearinesse they happened to rest themselues a while there, they touched nothing, and quicklie departed; and this did all that kinde of foule. A poore widdow hauing lost her sonne by death, came to the holie virgin, importunatelie beseeching her to helpe her sonne and herself, being then desolate of her comfort. When she could not auoide her instant petition, she prayed to god for her, and as she lay prostrate praying, fire seemed to fall from heauen vpon her, and to burne her being all rounde aboute couered withall: whereat one of her sisters being terrified, cried to her to gett away : whereat the fire vanished away, and the dead person reuiued. Dying she bequeathed her sisters to God and his holie mother Marie, and so left this life the six and twentith day of May./

A miraculous protection.

Wilde geese obey her.

Her potent prayers.

The life of holie Mildrede Virgin, Sister to the former Sainte. /

Mildred was daughter to Queene DOMPNEUA, and sister
4 to MILDURGE, as is sayd before, who had also a brother named
MEREFIN an holie Childe : She was sent by her mother ouer
into France to the Abbey of CALUM, there to be instructed
in holie conuersation and vertuous studies, allbeit she was
8 in secular habit: notwithstanding she so profited in
vertue, that she excelled all the other sacred virgins in
humilitie and pitie. The diuell enuying her happie progresse, inflamed a verie noble yong gentleman and kinseman
12 to the ladie Abbesse to loue her exceedinglie, and to desire
her in marriage ; and for greater probation of her chastitie,
faith and patience, the Abbesse her self for her carnall
kinsmans sake, both against her owne purpose, and vow,
16 and of this holie virgin that had dedicated herself to god
by purpose of perpetuall chastitie, persuaded her to assent
to marrie him that loued her so deerlie. MILDRED not
lyking in any case to forgoe her holie course, and to retourne
20 to the worlde, the Abbesse vrged her moste vehementlie,
and by incredible afflictions would compell her : / The constant virgin nothing changed from her former resolution, for
all that : the wicked Abbesse raging at her in her furie, did
24 cast the pure virgin into a burning ouen or furnace, shut-
ting the mouth thereof fast, that no breath thereof mighte
issue out, and so kept her three whole houres. She then
retourning and thynking that the virgin was consumed to
28 ashes, fyndeth her perfectlie sounde and singing thus :
*Lord thou hast examined me by fire, and yet no iniquitie
is found in me.* All the sisters seing her so vntouched
greatlie admired her, and all that heard thereof reuerenced
32 MILDRED exceedinglie. But the badd Abbesse nothing
moued with this miracle, assalteth her with new torments,
beating and bouncing her without all measure, but without

*Her proba-
tion for her
chastitie.*

effect: for the sacred Virgin was vnmoueable being builded
on a firme Rocke. The distressed virgin certifying her
mother of her estate, besought her to help her, which she
neglected not. For by a slight being gott out of the
monasterie, she was conueyed safe away and brought into
England; bringing with her certaine precious reliques, as a
naile wherewith our Sauiour was nailed to the Crosse, and
some other which she had procured and gotten with greate
pryce. As she descended from the shippe to the land, and

A stone retayned the print of her feete; with other miracles.
sett her feete on a certaine square stone, the printe of her
feete remayned on it moste liuelie, she not thinking any
thing; so God working to the glorie of his handmayd; and
more than that, the dust that was scrapen of thence being
dronken did cure sundrie diseases. The same stone moste
miraculouslie being pulled, would yield like a bowe, and
being let goe it would leape backe to his former place. The
people much moued at these miracles, built in that place an
oratorie, in memorie of the holie virgin; where they

She receiueth the religious vell e.
kept the foresaid meruailous stone: And Archbishop
THEODORE then ruling the Sea of CANTERBURIE came
thither, and gaue MILDRED accompanied with seauentie
other Virgins the habit of religious profession, and she
with her mothers consent was consecrated Abbesse by the
same Bishop. Heere therefore the holie virgin dooth not so
much command, as by example prouoke her sisters to all
good workes, by humilitie abasing herself vnder all, that by

Miracles:
office and worthinesse excelled all. She praying one night,
the diuell putt out her candle, but the Angell of god came
to the rescue, chased away Satan, and restored her light
for to reade withall. And as she was once praying with
teares, the holie Ghoste in forme of a doue appeared sitting
on her head, and clapping his wings for ioy and applause.
She shined with miracles both lyuing and dead, and that
manifoldlie. This monasterie in TENET was burnt with all
the religious sisters in it by the Danish furie. S⸱: EDBURGA
her Aunt, succeeded her in the regiment, as before is men-

tioned in her life. Long after EMMA mother to king
EDWARD the Confessour, being vniustlie accused and therevpon spoiled of all her substance, was thereby much afflicted
4 and deiected in mynde: This Sainte then appeared vnto
her, comforted her, and by her help the king her sonne was
mooued towards her, and restored her to her former dignitie.
An other once sleeping in her Church, she appeared to him,
8 and gaue him a blow on the eare, saying, 'Vnderstand fellow
that this place is an Oratorie to pray in, not a Dormitorie
to sleepe in,' and so vanished awaye. /

The life of holie Ebba Virgin and Albesse: who died the
12 *yeare: 683:*

Ebba daughter to ETHELFRIDE king of Northumberland
and sister to Sainte OSWALD and OSWIE kings also, seeing
in those dayes that it was accounted a cheefe signe of a Note the
true signe of
16 noble minde, and verie vsuall then for noble personages, to a noble
minde.
forsake the worlde, and in religious habit, humblie to follow
Christ in monasticall obedience, vnder one father or Abbot
if they were men, or vnder one mother or Abbesse, if they
20 were women: she burning with like holie zeale, and religiouslie emulating the vertue of such, in the floure of her
youth contemned the kingdome of this worlde, and all the
glorie thereof for the loue of Christ the sonne of god,
24 entered into religion, and tooke the veile of a holie virgin,
at the handes of FINANE Bishop of LINDISFARNE, which is
neere Scotland now. Notwithstanding she being afterward
importunatelie desired to wife by AADAN king of Scotts,
28 she fledd to saue her self vnto Mount COLUDE; where
COLDINGHAM is and was so called after that. The king
pursuing her with tyrannicall intemperance, the sea by
Gods commandement arose in defence of his spouse and
32 three dayes together it enuironed the hill, so that he was
putt by his desire. In that desert place, did she afterward

leade her life, moste soberlie, iustlie, and holilie, and in
fine died. An other monasterie of women did she build
vpon the Riuer DORWENT, which of her name was called
EBBECESTRE, her brother king OSWAY allowing the cost and　4
charges thereto. In the desert of COLUDE, she founded a
monasterie of men and women, one dwelling neere the
other, which she ruled. Her disciple was Queene and virgin
ETHELRED or AUDRIE, the glorie of ELIE Island. St CUTH-　8
BERT lyuing not farre of visited her often, abyding some
dayes in counselling and comforting her and hers with
wholsom and heauenlie documents. For all that by the
diuells secret working (vnknowne to the holie Abbesse) and　12
by gods secret permission (that posteritie mighte learne

How perillous for men and women allthoughe holie to liue together

how perillous it is for men and women, thoughe religious to
be familiar or dwell so neere) those habitations neere eache
other, which were built for prayer, holie reading and other　16
ghostlie exercises, were tourned into places of feasting,
tatling and wanton sporting. For which grieuous crimes,
one of the monckes being a verie vertuous man, and
watching in prayers (whose name was ADAMNANUS) his other　20
fellowes then watching in ill occupations, or sleeping on
both eares drousilie had reuealed vnto him, that ere long,
that greate monasterie, which for the greatnes thereof was
called a Towne, should be all consumed by fire, and made　24
vtterlie desert: Which punishment came iust so to passe:
But for the vertue of the holie Abbesse, which was nothing
witting thereof, it was deferred vntill she was dead. By
which example is it made moste apparent, how perillous the　28
cohabitation of women and men is, allthough they be holie,

Gods terrible Iudgement.

and what miseries ensue thereby: by which also euerie one
may learne, how terrible god is in his counsells, that
whome he made begin in spirit, for their negligence and　32
want of due custodie, chaste feare and watchfullnes, he
permitted to end, and perhaps to perish in flesh. The
holie mother EBBA, after that she was full of vertues and
yeares, departed out of thys life, the yeare of our　36

Redemption: 683: resting euerlastinglie with Christ, and shyning with miracles here on earthe./

The life of S! Etheldred or Audrie Queene and Virgin: out of venerable Bede.¹ / She flourished in the yeare: 674: [¹Hist. eccl. 4, 19.]

'**Etheldred** or AUDRIE was daughter to ANNA king of the EAST ANGLES (which were the people of SUFFOLKE, NORTHFOLKE and CAMBRIDGESHIRE) a verie religious man, and moste notable in mynde and worke. She was first giuen to wife to one TONBERT Prince of the people of the fennes neere by, then called Giruij, who dying verie soone, she was giuen to ECGFRIDE, king of the English beyond Humber: with whome lyuing twelue yeares, she was glorious for contynuing in perpetuall virginitie, which she conserued, as Bishop WILFRIDE of blessed memorie tolde me asking him the question, for that some did doubt of it, who sayd that himself was a moste assured witnesse of her virginitie: in so much that king ECGFRIDE promised him greate summes and possessions, if he could persuade the Queene to vse matrimoniall companie with him: which he did, for that he knew the Queene loued holie WILFRIDE, none like. Neither may we distrust, but that this may be donne in our age; whereas in the next age before many did the like, as vndoubted histories do witnes: which they performed by the grace and gift of god, that promised to remayne with vs to the end of the worlde. And gods miraculous working that made her flesh not to corrupt after death, was assured token and proofe, that she had continued incorrupt and vndefiled by mans touch. She lyuing a long while with the king, as is sayd, did often and moste ernestlie beseeche him to permitte her to forgoe the cares of the world, and in a monasterie to serue Christ her Lord onelie: which after much adoe, when she had

She being married yet continued a virgin.

Note.

She forsooke the worlde and tooke the holie veile of St Wilfride.	obtayned, she entered into the monasterie of EBBA aforesayd, who was the Aunt of her husband ECGFRIDE. In that Abbie situated in the place called the towne of COLUDE, she receiued the religious veile and weede, at the 4 handes of the aforenamed WILFRID. After a yeare compleate, she became Abbesse in the region or territorie called
Elie monasterie founded.	ELGE, (now ELIE): where building a monasterie of virgins, dedicated to god, this their mother and virgin began to be 8 a patterne and document of heauenlie conuersation and a
Her vertues.	leader to eternall life. Of whome they relate, that from the first entrance into the monasterie, she neuer would vse
Clothing without linnen.	lynnen cloathes, but onelie wollen, and verie seeldome hotte 12 bathes, vnlesse towards greate solemnities, as Ester, Pentecost and Epiphanie, and then would she wash her self last, after she had with her seruants attended on her
Abstinence.	fellow virgins, while they washed. Sieldome did she feede 16 aboue once a day, vnlesse on greate solemnities or when sicknes or such like necessitie vrged her. From the time of mattins or night-meeting vntill day, would she continue in the Church at prayer. They report also that by the 20
Prophecie.	spirite of Prophecie, she foretolde the plague whereof she her self should dye, and also how manie of her monasterie should dye by the same pestilence, which openlie she pronounced, all being present. She was taken hence seuen 24 yeares after she had beene Abbesse, all her companie being
Her death and translation.	aboute her; and as she commanded, she was buried in the midst of her fellowes departed as her turne came, and that in a woodden coffine. For successour in that office of 28 Abbesse she left SEXBURGE her sister, who had beene wife to ERCOMBERT king of Kent. After that she had beene buried sixteene yeares, her sister SEXBURGE tooke vp her bodie, and purposed to translate her bones into the Church 32 within a new coffine. Whereuppon she commanded some of the brethern to go seeke a stone, whereof they might make her a Coffine: They taking boate (for that ELIE is naturallie enuironed with waters and fennes) came to a certaine 36

desolate litle Cittie called GRANDECESTER then, (now
GRANTOME,) where withoute the walles of the towne they   *A miraculous coffine.*
found a coffine of white marble, verie finelie made, with
the couer of the same stone lying on it; whereby perceyuing that god had prospered their iournie, they giuing
thankes brought it to the monasterie. And when the   *Her body incorrupt*
bodie of this holie virgin and spouse of Christ was taken   *after 16 yeares.*
vp into the lighte, it was founde moste incorrupt, as if she
had beene buried that day: so did holie WILFRID, with
many other that knew the thing, giue testimonie: And of
more certaine knowledge was CINIFRID the physicion, wont
to tell; who being present both at her departure, and when   *Cinifrid the physicion his report and eye witness.*
she was taken vp, sayd that when she lay sicke, she had a
greate swelling vnder her arme pitte, 'and they willed me
(said he) to cutte the swelling, and so to lett out the ille
humour in it; which when I had donne, she seemed two
dayes after to me somewhat amended, so that many hoped
she would recouer; but the third day, being againe pressed
with her former griefes, she was also sodainlie taken out
of the worlde, changing all paine and death into perpetuall
health and life: And when after so many yeares, her
bones were to be eleuated out of her sepulchre, and a
pauilion being spreadd ouer head, all the congregation of
religious brothers and sisters stood aboute singing, the men
on the one side, the women on the other, and the Abbesse
with some few were entred into the Sepulcher, to take vp
the bones, soddainlie we heard the Abbesse within crie
with cleare and open voice: 'Our Lords name be glorified';
and after a litle while they called me into the Pauilion,
opening the dore thereof to me, where being entered I
beheld the bodie of the holie virgin of god, now taken vp,
and layd in a bed, seeming as if she were asleepe; and remouing the couering on her face, they shewed me also the
wounde, which by my incision had beene made, but now
cured and whole, in so much that (verie meruailouslie) for
the wide and gaping wounde that I made, and wherewith

she was buried, there was onelie now remayning and to be seene, a verie fine signe and small marke of the scarre or wound healed.' Moreouer all the lynnen clothes, wherein the bodie was wrapt, appeared intire, incorrupt, and so new, as thoughe that verie daye, they had beene putt aboute her chaste bodie. They report farder, that when she was afflicted with that swelling, and with paine of her cheeke and necke, she did much delight in that kinde of infirmitie, and vsed to say : 'I know well that I am deseruedlie vexed with this payne of my necke, for that (I remember) being a yong wench, I wore thereon superfluous weightes, of iewells and tablets. And I beleeue that they for[1] the supernall pietie of god, would haue me grieued in my necke, that thereby I may be absolued from the falte of superfluous leuitie, whiles now I endure in my necke rednes and burning of swelling, for my golde and precious stones, then and after worne thereon.' By the touching of those clothes of hers, were diuells expelled from possessed bodies, and diuerse infirmities were cured likewise. Againe the coffine wherein she first lay, hath (as is related) cured some of their sore eyes. For putting their heads to it, and praying withall, they haue some beene deliuered of their paine, others of their dymnesse of sight. Taking vp therefore the bodie, and putting new garments on it, they brought it into the Churche, they placed it in the new stone coffine, founde as was sayd before, where it is at this day in greate veneration and honour : And it was a meruaile to see, how fitte that coffine of white marble was for her, as if it had beene framed of purpose for her, and the place cutt for the head seuerallie was made so iust for her[1] head as could be deuised. This Elie was belonging to the prouince or territorie of the East Angles of whome she was by birth : wherefore this seruant of Christ desired to haue her monasterie there, within her natiue contrie.'
Thus far S[t] Bede.

The Catalogue of English saintes, hath this more not to

be neglected. When she was maried to her first husband
Prince Toubert, and was in her mariage bed chamber,
knowing that her husband would quicklie follow after, and
4 fearing leste she might be putt from her holie purpose of
perpetuall chastitie, she betooke her self to earnest prayer
with teares beseeching god to protect her, and yielding
her self whollie into his mightie and mercifull handes,
8 withall came the Prince, and looking into the chamber, he
espieth it all light and flaming like fier; wherefore retiring
backe through admiration and feare, he called to her and
sayd, 'Thinke not good Ladie that I will abuse thee, for thy
12 Lord is thy protector.'

*The life of holie Kinesburge Queene and Abbesse, Kineswide
and Tibbe. Mathew Westminster calleth the two first
Kinesdride and Kineswithe. They flourished aboute*
16 *the yeare 666 : /*

Kinesburge and KINESWIDE were daughters to PENDA,
a Pagan thoughe king of MERCIA, holie shootes of a dead
stocke or truncke, and not they onelie but three or fowre
20 sonnes also kings succeeding him; whereof PEADA was the   See an holie companie.
eldest and first christian king of that realme, WULFHERE
the second and father to holie WEBBURGE virgin, the third
MERWALD father to holie MILBURGE, the fourth ETHELRED,
24 all moste christian and good Princes. KINESBURGE being
ioyned in matrimonie, yet she soone forsooke her kinglie
marriage bed, for single and chaste life. For getting her
king and husbands consent, they with mutuall deuotion,   Her husband and her
28 did after attend vpon Christ lyuing as brother and sister,   mutuall consent to
seruing in spirite not in fleshe. She withall did take the   liue chaste.
holie veile and entered into religious profession there
consecrated vnto Christ: which she performing, forthwith
32 Dukes and Princes daughters flocke vnto her, desiring to
follow her in religious life vnder her teaching and gouernement, whome she receyuing, as she was her self a glasse or
myrrour of all holynesse, so did she frame and instruct

them, teaching them to loue Christ in perfect manner.
Her monasterie was at the first in a place called DORMUNDS,
but afterwards it was called CASTER, two miles from PETER-
BOROUGH, where the sixt day of march, the solemne memorie 4
of these holie virgins was wont to be celebrated. This
holie womans famous actes as of diuerse others, the barbarous
furie of the Danes did abolish, burning all such monuments:
wherefore this litle must serue, to coniecture the rest by. 8

Kineswides vertue. Her sister KINESWIDE being yong, and beholding her
glorious behauiour and gouernment of the virgins of
Christ, was not a litle kindled to imitate that puritie and
perfection of seruing Christ: whereupon when she was 12
mariageable, and desired to wife by OFFA king of the East
Angles, she wishing rather to conserue her virginitie chaste
vnto Christ, was by her brethren, what by promises and
threats, much pressed and vrged to yield to that offer. / 16
What refuge could this deuoute virgin of Christ haue for
her saueguard? Trulie she could deuise none better, than
to flye vnto the virgin of virgins, the mother of Christ:
wherefore with ernest prayers and many teares, she be- 20
seecheth her to helpe and to giue counsell what too doe. /
The pittifull mother was readie at her chaste suppliants

[1 MS. petition.] humble petition,[1] appeared vnto her in greate light and
OurB.Ladies counsell vnto her. glorie, and comforting her, sayd, 'My aduise and wholsome 24
counsaile is, that you keepe your self a virgin perpetuallie:
for nothing is more healthfull or profitable, than to remayne in that puritie wherein you were borne. Nothing
Note. is more excellent, than to haue my sonne for husband: 28
Nothing more blessed and happie, than not to know the
euils of corruption in this life, and in heauen to receiue the
crowne of incorruption.' KINESWIDE the virgin answered
with teares: 'But, O Ladie what shall I doe, seeing all my 32
kinne and friends haue opposed themselues against me,
being so affected, and wage warre vpon me therefore?
Deliuer me therefore O Ladie from the mire that I doe not
sticke fast in it, and preserue me from the snares, that are 36

layed to intrappe me.' Then sayd the mother of god to
her, 'Do not weepe neither be dismayed, I will pray my
sonne to helpe and keepe thee, and he shall speedilie, I
4 doubt not, saue thee': and with that, she vanished away.
The virgin being therewith encouraged, confidentlie sent
the king this message: 'I beseeche you by the dreadfull
name of Christ, doe not offer me any more force, vrge me
8 not from Christ, I am his spouse, wherefore beware you
iniurie not him, by iniurying me.' OFFA receyuing that
message, did moste willinglie giue ouer his suite, ceasing
to molest the virgin, and giuing her freedome to doe as
12 pleased her. Nay more, he perceyuing such puritie and
strange contempt of the worlde with all his delightes in so
tender a mayd, was much moued with remorse, and con- The king Offa is confounded to consider himself so inthralled to the vanitie of founded and conuerted to
16 the worlde, and a seruant of his temporall kingdome, she imitate her forsaking
with so sublime and noble mynde despising them all: the worlde.
Hereupon and through her holie persuasion, he changed
his loue to better, despised all earthlie delightes, likewise
20 forsooke his kingdome and contrie, for the loue of his
celestiall king and contrie, went to ROME with KENRED
king of the MERCIANS, and there became a monke; so dying
to the glorie and delight of this life, that he might lyue
24 and enioye more happilie eternall comforte and kingdome.
And KINESWIDE the holie virgin entred into her sister
KINESBURGES monasterie, and there in all spirituall watchfullnes, expected the comming of Christ her beloued in
28 maiestie, prepared to meete him: and so dying was buried
in the same place. /

The kinswoman of these two glorious women, whose S! Tibbe.
name was TIBBE lyued many yeares, recluse, or anacho-
32 reticall life, and that in greate holines, and after died, and
was buried in the same monasterie with them.

*Of holie Ethelburge Queene and after a Nonne, who
flourished in the yeare* 690 : /

Ethelburge a woman of noble linage and wife to INE
or INAS, king of the West Saxons, the founder of GLASTEN-
BURIE, and first bestower of Peter pence vpon the sea
Apostolike. She was rather more noble of Christian mynde,
than by corporall natiuitie, lyuing in pleasures and lothing
them, aloft and moste highe in the worlde, yet hartilie
despising it: in so much that she sought to abandon it
whollie, and to hide and abiect her self for the loue of
Christ in a monasterie: But as she desired that for herself like a good woman, so did she wishe and labour to
make her husband partaker of the like perfection, like a
moste louing wife. Wherefore she was ernest in hand
with him a long time, to persuade him to forsake the
worlde, but could not by any meanes bring her purpose to
passe, till on a time the king and she lodging at a mannor
place in the contrie she wonne him by this wise deuice.
After that all prouision had beene made there for the
receyuing of them and their trayne in moste sumptuous
manner that might be, as well in rich furniture of housholde, as also in costlie viands, and all other things
needfull or that might serue for pleasure, and soiourning
there a while, they were thence departed, the Queene
ETHELBURGE caused the keeper of that house to remoue all
bedding, hangings, and other furniture appertayning to the
beautifying of the house, and in place thereof, to bring
ordure, straw and such like filth, as well in the chambers
and hall, as into all the houses of office: and that donne
to lay a sowe with piggs in the place, where before the
kings bed had stood. Hereuppon when she had intelligence that euerie thing was ordered according to her
appoyntment, she persuaded the king to retourne thither
againe, feyning occasions greate and necessarie. After he

Inas his liberalitie towards the Church:

She persuaded her husband to forsake the world, and her wise deuice thereto.

was retourned to the place, which before seemed a palace
of pleasure, and now founde it in such a filthie state, as
might lothe the stomacke of the beholder, she then tooke
4 occasion thereof to persuade him to the consideration of
the vaine pleasures of this worlde, which in a moment
tourned to naught, together with the corruption of the
flesh, being a filthie lumpe of claye, after it should once be
8 dissolued by death hourelie to be feared: And in fine,
where before she had spent much labour to moue him to
renounce the worlde thoughe all in vaine, yet now the
beholding of that change in his pleasant pallace, wherein *Good sights*
12 so late he had taken so greate delighte, wrought such an *moue more than words,*
alteration in his mynde, that her wordes lastlie tooke effect: *but moste both together.*
So that he resigned the kingdome to his cousin ETHELARD,
and went himself to ROME as a poore pilgrime, and there *Inas left his*
16 ended his life. Thus was this greate king after the con- *kingdome and went to Rome.*
quest of the Southsaxons, and many valiant actes, better
conquered by his godlie wife from the worlde, than he had
reigned in the worlde, she alone gayning more to Christ,
20 than he had wonne on the earth, she subduing the subduer
of men, to follow Christ, he onelie subiecting inferiour
men to an other thoughe greater man: And which was
moste of all, she gayned him from the middst of all power
24 and pleasures, whereby moe conquerours and worthies
perishe than by the sworde. And when she had thus
offerred her beloued husband to Christ, she her self made
oblation of her self in the Abbie of Barking, becomming a *She be-*
28 Nonne and after Abbesse, and lastlie ended her mortall *cometh a Nonne.*
course with a better hope With what feruour trow you,
did she follow Christ in religion that in the worlde was so
potent in spirite? how swiftlie did she runne when she
32 was disburdened and free from all worldlie impediments,
that amidst them ran so fast? that was able not onelie to
disoumber her self from so weightie and manie allurements,
but to hale her husband out of them to follow Christ, the
36 supreme king of kings, in humilitie, abiection, and pouertie

heere, that in his kingdome where he reigneth in glorie,
they might enioye him more highlie, gloriouslie and
richlie. /

*The life of Hildelitha Virgin and second Abbesse of
Barking; aboute the yeare: 676:*

Whereas many histories of the noble actes of English
saintes, were burnt in the Danish incursions, they setting
fire on all bookes they could meete with, and whereas the
holie bishops DUNSTANE, ETHELWOLDE, and ELPHEGUS, haue
giuen singular testimonie of this virgins holynes, declaring
her greate worthines and venerable renowne, albeit her
particular actes and memorable recordes did perish with
many others, yet their generall commendation and reuerend memorie of her, may giue greate coniecture of her
notable life and rare vertues, such wise and perfect men
not easilie giuing termes or names, but according to the iust
value and qualities of the things named or commended. She
succeeded next in the regiment of the Nonnerie of Barking
to holie ETHELBURGE, the first foundresse thereof, after
whome also she is accounted second in holines. Three
blynde women on a time came to this monasterie, to beseeche the helpe and patronage of three holie virgins there
deceased, and famous for holines, to weete, ETHELBURGE,
HILDELITHA and WULFHILD, by which three saints, the
faithfull blynde persons were cured, but euerie one by diuerse
of them. This monasterie is knowne to be the treasure as
it were of so many saintes, that many times the heauens
haue appeared open ouer it, to declare before-hand, what
glorie the bodies there should in time possesse, by shewing
the claritie and brightnes of the soules then presentlie
reigning in heauen. Moreouer in the time when S.[t] EDMOND
the king of the East Angles was martyred, was this holie
familie, the daughters with their mother or Abbesse, all

Barking Abbie the treasurie of manie Saintes.

burnt by the Danes, the virgin mother comforting and
encouraging her fellow virgins, in the midst of the flames
and moulten leadd running on them, constantlie to expect *All martyred at once.*
by short patience, the palme and crowne both of virginitie
and martyrdome presentlie to ensue. /

*The life of S^t. Cuthburge Queene and Virgin: aboute
the yeare: 690. /*

8 **Cuthburge** daughter vnto KENREDE of the bloud royall
of Westsaxons, from her yong yeares soughte to please
Christ: At the fame of whoso vertue and beautie, many
kings and nobles were inflamed with her loue: but she
delighting in the spirituall embracings and loue of Christ
auoided the sight of men. Notwithstanding ALFRIDE king
of NORTHUMBERS sent Embassadours to her brother king
INAS, requesting her to wife; her brother proposed to her
king ALFRIDES request, to which the holie virgin answered
and sayd. 'My Lord and good brother INAS, if I may be
permitted to lyue to my owne lyking, I will neuer marie
mortall man, but adhere to Christ alone: but if I be compelled, I can not resist your power: yet I trust in my
Lord, that allthoughe I be deliuered to a man, Christ will
deliuer his spouse and preserue her vndefiled.' For all
that, she was betrothed to king ALFRIDE and married,
and when she was come to her wedding bed chamber
conuerting her self with her whole hart to her Lorde, she
prayed saying. 'O my Lord thou knowest that I haue
chosen thee onelie for my loue and husband, to thee haue
I vowed my self from my youth, thee haue I liked aboue
all things; Wherefore sweete Lord keepe safe that which is
thine: defend thy portion and vouchsafe me to be tearmed
thy spouse; powre into the harte of my earthlie husband
thy good spirite, whereby he may despise the allurements
of the flesh and world, and assent vnto me, in this purpose

of chastitie': And when she was alone with the king in
his chamber, she talketh to him in this manner. 'My Lord
and my king, I beseeche thee doe not despise the godlie
counsell of thy handmayd. This world passeth away, and 4
all the delightes and desires thereof, why then should we
loue that which shall vanish away so cleane and quicklie,
as if it had not beene. And whereas they that sowe in
flesh shall reape onelie corruption, but they that sow in 8
spirit, shall reape incorruption and eternall life, therefore
let vs liue in chastitie of bodie and puritie of hart, that
contemning vile pleasure and momentaneous delighte, we
may receyue in heauen vnmeasurable and vndecayable 12
ioyes.' The king being delighted with the wise discourse
of his spouse, and smelling thereby that she had purposed
to liue a perpetuall virgin, willinglie assented vnto her,
yielding her free power to serue Christ alone. Wherefore 16
building herself a monasterie at WINBURNE, in the honour
of the B: Virgin, there with other virgins did she serue
God in fastings and prayers, giuing no rest to her bodie,
and humble and meeke to all. And at last knowing her 20
death to be at hand she called her sisters aboute her,
giuing them wholsome admonitions and counsell: aduising
them to be myndefull of their calling, and to walke warilie,
redeeming the time for that the dayes are euill: She 24
exhorteth them to consider the deceits of the worlde,
which they had forsaken, and not in hart to retourne
backe againe into ÆGIPT, but with all custodie and watchfullnes to keepe their hartes moste studiouslie to please 28
Christ in all things, to whome they had consecrated
themselues, that so they might deserue to be loued againe
of him and crowned: And after that she had receiued her
holie VIATICUM or voiage foode the last of August, she 32
departed this life to enioye her beloued Lord and Sauiour
IESUS: /

The life of S! Withburge Virgin about the yeare: 650:

This holie virgin WITHBURGE was daughter to ANNA king of the East Angles, and sister to S! AUDRIE and
4 SEXBURGE Queenes aboue mentioned, whose puritie of soule (written monuments and records fayling) her bodie did testifie aboundantlie. For it being taken vp three hundred fiftie and fowre yeares after her decease, was founde intire
8 and incorrupt. Her monasterie was at DERHAM, which she herself built, and in it receiued her monasticall weede: where after she had spent her dayes in greate holines, she rested in Christ. Fiftie fiue yeares after, her corps was
12 found so sounde and free from all corruption, together with her garments thereon, as if they had beene then interred. When the Danishe furie wasted England and perturbed all estates, the virgins of her monasterie were
16 chased out thence, and it left desolate, and afterward it became a parishe, which to this day with his name remayneth in Northfolke. S! ETHELWOLDE bishop of Winchester in king EDGARS time, repayring the Abbie
20 of ELIE defaced by the Danes, adioyned the Abbey of DERHAM vnto it: and the yeare 974: by that holie Bishops procurement (as it seemeth) her bodie was translated by the Abbot BRITHNOTE from DERHAM to her sister
24 ETHELDREDS bodie at ELIE./

Her bodie incorrupt after 354 yeares.
Derham in Northfolk her monasterie.

The life of holie Inthware [1] *Virgin and martyr: aboute the yeare:* 700: /

This virgin INTHWARE was well borne and an Englishe
28 woman, as by her owne name is coniectured, and by her sisters names which were S! EADWARE, S! WILGITH, and S! SIDEWLLA, all as well vnited in singular holinesse, as conioyned by vnitie of bloud and birthe. This INTHWARE

[1] In Capgrave nov. leg. Angl. her name is Iuthware.

was giuen moste studiouslie to all vertues, albeit lyuing in
her fathers house, and in intertayning and seruing pilgrimes
moste carefull and obsequious. Her father being dead and
she much enuied by a wicked stepmother, by her fraude   4
and malicious deuice, her owne brother named BANA was
made beleeue, that this his sister INTHWARE was an harlott;
Her martyr- whereupon he in a rage slew her with his owne handes,
dome.
as she came from seruing god in the Church; But god   8
testified her holines and chastitie presentlie with a strange
miracle : For she hauing her head cutt of, did afterward
A miracle. with her owne handes, take vp her head and carried it to
the Church, whence she came : and withall in the same   12
place, where she was killed there sprong a lyuelie
fountayne : And not with these onelie, but with diuerse
moe miracles, did god iustifie and magnifie her dead, who
had beene by men so slandered, iniuried, and disgraced 16
aliue./

The life of S! Frideswide Virgin aboute the yeare: 740 :/

Holie FRIDESWIDE was daughter to one DIDANE, a pettie
Prince and SAFRIDE his wife, both religious persons and 20
dwelling at Oxford. This happie branch of that vertuous
stemme being shott vp beyond infancie, began to attempt
workes of maturitie, and rare pietie, refrayning sleepe,
vntill oppressed after long enforcing she must needes yield 24
Her prime nature her due : yet that was on the bare grounde, whereon
vertue.
allso she lay allwayes prostrate when she prayed : Her
bodie she allowed but such like short and simple foode,
stanching hir hunger with herbes and barlie bredd, and 28
her thirst with onelie water. By these priuate proofes of
her self, she prepared her self to a higher profession, that
She entered is monasticall profession, which she earnestlie seeking, and
religion and
12. others her vertuous parents gladlie assenting, obtayned her holie 32
by her
example. desire, and was inuested with religious weede, at whose

example other twelue noble virgins being prouoked and
inflamed did in like manner forgoe the worlde, and in
regular life of monasticall institution followed Christ.
4 There did she fast and pray with greate importunitie,
bowing her knees an hundred times a day in prayer, and
as often euerie nighte. The diuell enuying these her
vertuous studies, thought to supplant her, wherefore
8 taking a companie of his like liers, he taketh on him the *Satan appeared to her in the forme of Christ.*
shape of Christ, and of a number of bright Angells as it
were attending on him, and in this fayned forme of glorie
appeared vnto the virgin and sayd: 'My beloued spouse
12 hitherto I haue beheald and liked thy vertuous behauiour
and loue towards me, wherefore come now my deare and
receiue this immarcessible crowne which thou hast deserued,
embrace my feete which thou hast so longed for, and adore
16 me prostrate, for to this end haue I now appeared vnto
thee, that worshipping me in this thy mortall bodie, I may
translate thee to immortalitie.' The virgin of Christ being *Her answer.*
endued with her true beloueds spirit, vnderstood well who
20 this counterfett Christ and his retinew was, wherefore
embouldened in her Lord, she sayd to the fiend: 'What
meanest thou miserable wretch, to promise that which thy
self lackest nor canst any wayes obtaine, throughe thy
24 exceeding pride: I had beene partaker with thee in perdition, had not my Sauiour Christ his grace preuented me,
and deliuered me from that danger, and brought me into
hope of his happie presence and kingdome: he is the
28 beginning, he is the end of my wayes and hopes': With
these and such like humble answer the Enemie was putte
to flighte, yet albeit in his owne person he could not
preuaile, he hoped by some impe or member of his to ouer-
32 throw her. Hereuppon he incensed one ALGAR a litle *Satan inflamed a yong Prince with loue of her, but God defended her.*
Prince, and sette him on fire with loue of the virgin, which
donne this Prince addresseth messengers to her, to will
her to come to him, or if she refused, to bring her perforce:
36 who being ouer importunate, and vrging their Lordes desire

and will so egrelie, that they would needes force her to come to their sicke soueraine, God in defence of his spouse stroke them with blyndnes; whereat they acknowledging their faulte, and crauing the virgins fauor, she besought her Lord and sauiour, who presentlie restored them their sight. For all this the Prince nothing relenting his furie, God willed the virgin by his Angell to flie thence, and so saue her from the danger that was imminent. She did so, wherefore taking two sisters for her companions, away she hied her. After which presentlie came ALGAR in person to Oxford, threatening to rase the cittie if they deliuered her not to him; for he imagined them priuie to her escape. But when he came thus mynded to the gate, he was striken blynde, and thus was his hotte pursuit frustrated. After three yeares, the virgin retourned to Oxford againe, where meeting a poore man, horriblie payed with the leprosie and kissing him, he was forthwith cured. After that being admonished by gods Angell of the day of her death, she kindled within her all her spirituall lampes and with those ghostlie lightes expected the comming of her beloued. The day of her decease being come, S! CATHERIN and S! CECILIE, whome she had in especiall reuerence appeared vnto her, to whome she sayd with audible voice; 'I come my Ladies I come,' and with that she gaue vp her blessed ghoste: withall forthwith the house was all replenished with wonderfull light sent from heauen, and such a sweete odoriferous sauour ensued, and that so aboundantlie, that all the towne was filled withall.

Miracles.

Her Patroncases appeare.

Her glorious death.

The life of holie Walburge Virgin: who flourished about the yeare: 746:

After that BONIFACIUS that famous english Monck, had conuerted the Germane nation, and was placed in the See of MENZ, sondrie of his contrie followed him, amongst

whome were holie WILLEBROBD and WINNEBOLD brothers, *Her blessed brethren and she went into Germania.*
and their no lesse religious sister WALBURGE, a moste chaste
spouse of Christ: The first of which was made Bishop of
4 EISTETEN, the other brother giuing himself whollie to
Christs seruice in monasticall profession, liued moste
holilie all his dayes in a place called HYDENHERIN[1]: where [[1] r. Helden-heim, Capgr. Heydan-hem.]
after that he had gayned manie to lyue vertuouslie by his
8 saintlie conuersation, he went vnto his Lord, to receiue his
crowne. He being dead, his sister WALBURGE, the glorie
of her feminine sex, shewed her self a patterne of holinesse, *Her vertue.*
to all that knew her: For she was now Abbesse of the
12 monasterie of virgins at HYDENHERIN, and a notable
gouernesse, so whollie eleuated towards heauen by contemplation and prayer, that whatsoeuer she asked of God,
she obtayned it. It happened once that when she retourned
16 from the Church at euen, GUNWALD the *Custos*, would giue
her no lighte: She nothing moued at that iniurie when
she came into the common place of rest or Dorter, sod-
daynlie there shyned such claritie of light, that all her *Light from heauen sent to her.*
20 sisters allmoste amazed with admiration, came running to
her with greate exultation, certifying her of that exceeding lighte. She thereat bursting into teares, with her
handes and eyes lift vp to heauen sayd: 'I thanke thee
24 my Lord Iesus Christ moste hartilie, that hast vouchsafed to comfort me, thoughe vnworthie with this
lighte, and withall hast reuiued and quickened the
mindes of thy handmaydes my sisters.' When vpon her
28 brother WINNIBOLDS death she was somewhat immoderatlie greeued, to vnburden somewhat her mynde from
sorrow, goirg out of the monasterie, she came to the
house of a certaine riche man, who not knowing her but
32 deeming her some pilgrime or strange woman, feared
leste his dogges would haue runne on her, and torne her:
She nothing afeard of the dogs, tolde him that she was
WALBURGE, and entering into his house, requested him to *She telleth things absent.*
36 lodge her in that chamber, where his daughter lay sicke

allmoste vnto death. They hearing of their daughters
sodaine sicknes and crying oute for sorrowe, the virgin
WALBURGE went into the forenamed chamber, where she
prayed all that night for the health of the mayd, and on
the morning following, she presented her whole vnto her
parents. They for so greate a miracle rendering greate
thankes vnto God, offered also greate gifts to the holie
virgin, which she would not receiue, but desiring to please
Christ onelie, retourned to her monasterie, giuing her self
to so much the more straight life, by how much more
she felt her self fauoured of god. At length when she
was adorned with manyfolde vertues, she departed this life
like a conquerour, and her bodie was moste honourablie
buried in her monasterie. ORGARIUS[1] that was bishop of
EISTETEN next after WILLEBRORD, was admonished by an
assured vision, that he should transferre the bodie to the
monasterie of EYSTETEN, which he did: and the yeare
of our Lord: 893: ARNULPHE being Emperour, the
sepulcher wherein ORGARIUS had placed her being opened,
there happened a miracle not of ordinarie wonder, and
whereof there were moste euident testimonies, which was
as followeth. There was a certaine mayde named FRIDERIDE,
who was a dilligent and dutifull seruant to one EDERANNE
and his wife: This carefull seruant sodainlie fell sicke
and was tormented with intollerable paines, and when the
excesse of her griefe somewhat remitted, she became so
greedie of meate, that no store thereof could fill her famine:
yet could she not stand on her feete; so that now her
parents tooke perpetuall matter of sorrow by her: At length
when the rauenous hunger did more increase, so that she
was despayred of, they broughte her to the Church of S[t]
WALBURGE, where she praying three dayes together verie
earnestlie, to the greate ioy of her parents, recouered the
vse of her feete: Her maister and mistresse hearing
thereof came thither and offered her to the perpetuall
seruice of S[t]: WALBURGE: At that time one HUBILA was

Her death.

[1 Capgr. Otgar.]
Her bodie by vision was caused to be translated.

A strange miracle and storie.

Abbesse of the Nonnerie, who refusing to receiue her,
after a few dayes sent her home to her maister and
mistresse perfectlie sounde. But as soone as she was
4 come home, her olde disease latelie cured seized on her
againe, in such vehement manner that she was forced to be
sent backe to the monasterie, where presentlie she was
healed of her griefe, but her rauennous hunger remayned :
8 Wherefore she being much ashamed, opened vnto the sister,
that had charge of such matters of the house named
THEILTILD, her disease. She pittying her afflicted case,
obtayned of one MUNDUS a Priest, a peece of holie bread,
12 which she gaue her to eate : which as soone as she had
tasted, she perceiued her rauening so sensiblie to vanish
away, that for the space of allmoste halfe a yeare, she
could eate nothing but a litle cheese, nor drinke but a
16 litle milke : Afterward all desire of foode was so whollie
extinguished in her, that if she had taken any foode, she
must forthwith vomite it vp againe. All admired hereat,
and iustlie suspected some fraude lurking : in so much that
20 they forced her to feede after the manner of others. She
thereuppon that she might not seeme to contemne others or
preferr herself, tooke some of the smallest sorte of sider :
but presentlie she cast it vp at her eyes and nostrills with
24 such violence that she was bereft of her sight, and made
starke-blinde. This strange case being brought to the
Bishops eares, he as others had donne before, suspected
leste she were deluded by some cunning of the subtill
28 diuell, and that by some secret conueyance, she had meate
putt into her. Wherefore by the aduice of his friends, he
committed her to the custodie of a moste religious Priest,
willing him to watch her moste dilligentlie, whether she by
32 any guile had deceiued others : but after carefull triall, she
was found to vse no fraude, for whole three yeares together,
without any meate or drinke taken, she did her taske and
worke as the other sisters ; and as often as she receiued the Nota.
36 heauenlie bread of life, she was presentlie molested with

vomitting, if presentlie after she had not taken a litle sleepe. This strange worke thought I good to sett downe, that we may learne, how easilie god can worke things surpassing our capicitie. After this ERKENBALD bishop of EISTETEN moued with greate deuotion towards the holie virgin commanded her holie Reliques to be digged vp,

Her bodie incorrupt and moste odoriferous.

which were founde not onelie intire, but also bedewed with a small moisture, whence issued a moste fragrant sauour of incredible sweetnes, and a litle peece of her reliques being taken out, which was carried to the monasterie of

Miracles.

MONHEIME, by the way gaue health to a boy grieued with the falling sicknes: An other that was contracted from his natiuitie, in his sleepe was willed by St. WALBURGA, to go to her Church where presentlie he was cured, and all his members made so strong, that all his life after he was of greate mighte, and serued god in that Churche. There chanced of late a meruailous thing, which vnlesse it were testified by many witnesses, it would seeme to many scarce

A moste admirable storie.

credible. When many flocked to the Church of holie WALBURGE, one amongst the rest being in a Pilgrims attire prayed moste earnestlie, and with such attention of minde and perseuerance that all admired him. This man tolde a strange thing, and which maketh greatlie to the glorie of this virgin. For the yeare past when a cruell famine had taken away many a man, two that were in greate want, to auoyde that calamitie thought to leaue their contrie: and as they went on their way, a third person offerred himself

[¹r. whither]

into their companie: They asking him whether¹ he was going, he tolde them, 'to S⁺ WALBURGE, for deuotion sake': 'So do we,' said the other, 'to pay our vowes which we haue made to the holic virgin.' Whereupon that their iournie might be more comfortable, and also more safe, they accepted of the lone mans companie. When throughe trauaile and fasting they waxed hungrie, they sate downe all three to refresh their hungrie bodies; and when they had filled their bellies with meate and drinke, they gaue

themselues all to sleepe a while. The two perceiuing the
third to be fast asleepe, fall vpon him, and moste cruellie S! Walburge
murder him. They after the slaughter being verie anxious pilgrime slaine and
the dreadfull
4 in mynde what they should doe with the dead bodie, at last vengeance
donne
one of them, tooke him on his shoulders, and thought to therfore.
cast it into some by-place, where no man should come.
But see the wonder; when he would haue cast him from of
8 his backe, he felt the bodie to be so fast clasped to him by
the armes of the dead man, that by no force or mighte, he
could vnloose himself from it. What should the miserable
mansleyer doe now not able to conceale his villanous deede?
12 As he wandered vp and downe, one of his friends happened
to meete him : who beholding the ded bodie, and wondering
thereat, asked the other that carried it, whence he became
so loaden. He trusting him as his friend, tolde him the
16 whole troth, praying him withall to haue pittie of his
miserable case. His friend forthwith drew out his sword,
and attempteth to hacke the armes in peeces that clasped
the murderer aboute so fast, that so he might deliuer his
20 friend from that ignominie. Then might you see a new
and moste wonderfull miracle. For as soone as he touched A new
miracle.
the armes of the dead bodie to cutt them of, he himself was
ioyned moste fast to them both, so that he could not
24 separate nor vnlose himself from them. Wherefore
touched with repentance and lamenting for his sinnes
committed, he conuerted himself to god by humble
prayer, beseeching him at leaste for the merits and inter-
28 cession of S! WALBURGE virgin, to haue mercie on him; and
withall ernestlie beseeching holie WALBURGES patronage and
helpe, he was losed from that horrible coniunction, so that
he could goe where he listed. For all this he left not the
32 miserable murderer still holden, but followed him to the
banke of RHENE, where the wretch being werie of his
burden and shame, flong himself hedlong with the dead
bodie sticking to him into the Riuer. But the Rhene not
36 enduring the horrible murderer, presentlie cast him vp to

the shore. The other beholding this, was thereat terriblie frighted, yet reioycing at his owne deliuerie departed from him; with teares bewayling the wretches miserie, and comming with greate speede to the monasterie of S: WAL-BURGE, he tolde openlie what had happened. Also the vnhappie homicide did often attempt to come to the Church of the holie virgin, but he was not able to approche to it or the boundes thereof; that all men may thereby playnlie perceiue, with how horrible a crime he had intangled himself, that was repelled so farre of from her Churche.

<small>Note the credit of the storie.</small> Many saw this miserable wretch so loaden, with the filthie carcasse of the dead bodie: wherefore none may iustlie doubte of the veritie thereof. These miracles rehearsed were wroughte after the eleuation of the B: Virgin WALBURGES bodie, and are surelie greatlie to be meruailed at: yet in sundrie places els in the kingdome of France, which are famous for her reliques there honoured, mo miracles are wrought and more strange, by the powre of our Lord IESUS, who lyueth and reigneth withoute end. Amen. /

The life of S: Wenefride Virgin and Martyr: Whome I suppose to haue beene about this age of 800: and 700: albeit euident proofe of her time as yet I finde not. / Certaine it is she was before the Conquest and since the Britans were driuen into Wales, and when some Paganisme was amongst them, which seemeth not to haue beene at their first comming thither, when they onelie possessed it and were Christians: all which was after 600.

<small>Benno his vertua.</small> **Benno** a verie holie man was of the West parte of BRITTANIE, who leauing his contrie soile, chose voluntarilie to be poore and of monasticall profession; wherein he so profited, that he prouoked sondrie others to follow his vertuous example, and for them erected diuerse churches

and houses, wherein they might attend on their Lords
seruice our Sauiour Christ. After this the holie man was
admonished by god, to leaue his abode there with his
4 religious brethren : Wherefore departing thence he came to
a certayne potent personage, whose name was THENITH;
beseeching him to grante him a peece of grounde, whereon
he might build a Churche, and therein pray for him the
8 giuer of that benefit. The noble man yielded vnto his
desire, and beside his grant of grounde, he more commended
vnto his education and instruction, his onelie daughter
WENEFRIDE. Who after that she had long listened
12 attentiuelie to her religious maisters preachings and
teachings, she openeth her mynde vnto him, and tolde him *She voweth her virginitie vnto Christ.*
that she had resolued, to forgoe the riot and pleasure of
the worlde, and to dedicate her virginite vnto Christ:
16 wherefore she besought the reuerend man, to worke her
parents in such manner, as that they would agree
thereunto. The proposition being made to them for her,
their pietie was such, that they easilie assented, knowing
20 themselues more happie by offering vnto Christ, their
daughter a voluntarie virgin, than receiuing her a virgin by
nature for the worlde, so prouing their greate Christian
faith fertill in soule, as they had beene in bodie by bearing
24 her bodilie: nay more deuoute in religion, than ordinarie;
in yielding all vnto god; for that they had no more to
fructifie to this life. The holie virgin being thus fardered
by her good parents well lyking ; hauing now no externall
28 impediment to withholde her holie affection and studie,
with all sweetnes sucked vp and exhaled her maisters
declarations and praises of her celestiall Loues excellencie
and roialtie. After that she had in her fathers house,
32 thus serued her heauenlie spouse, in bodie being in the
worlde, but in spirit with her beloued aloft : one sunday her
parents going to Church, she remayned at home : when lo
king ALANUS his sonne whoso name was CRADOK
36 steppeth into the house, and impudentlie vrgeth her to let

him hauo his pleasure of her. She to auoyde this sodaine
danger, feyneth that she was rudelie arayed, and vnseemlie
attired for to haue companie with so greate a personage
as he was. Wherefore she prayoth him to expect, 4
vntill she had fitted and feated her self more decentlie.
The yong man thinking that some reason, permitted her
to goe to her chamber, thinking she would haue donne as
he imagined, and then retourned. But she as soone as she 8
was gone from him, secretlie by a posterne gate stale away,
and ran with all speede she could towards the Churche. /
The impious Prince hearing that she was so slipt away,
runneth presentlie after her, and ouertaketh the innocent 12
lambe, and he renewing his former filthie suite, but she
denying him, affirming that she was ioyned vnto Christ,
wherefore she could not, neither would euer couple herself

*She is be-
headed and
a fountaine
riseth in the
place.*
with man, the furious youth raging at her answer, with 16
his sword cuttes of her head: which falling to the earth,
deserued of god to haue a fountaine of water to spring in
the place, which to this day continueth, and the head still
tumbling downe the hill, came rowlling into the Churche, 20
where her maister and parents were: who being astonished
at that sighte BEUNO tooke vp the head, and with it he
goeth out to the homicide, moste sharplie reprouing him for
the fact, and calling on god for punishment of so heynous 24

*The murder-
ers cruell
punishment.*
a crime. Whereupon the yong man fell dedd to the
ground, and in the view of all that were present, the
bodie so sodainlie strokeu, melted as it were, and so
vanished cleane out of sighte, as thoughe it had so slonck 28
into hell with the soule thereof. But the holie head of
the martyr deceased, BEUNO kissed many times, and
brought it with the bodie to the church: which when
he had wrapped in his cloke, he went to Masse: which 32
being absolued he declares vnto the people, how she had
made a vow to our Lorde to dedicate her self vnto him,
remote from the worldes societie, but by this speedie and
vnexpected death, was hindered from putting it in effect: 36

wherefore he requesteth all there present to assist him
with their prayers to God for her. They willinglie yielded,
and when ioyntlie they had all besought gods mercie for
her, she reuiued and was whole; her head fast reunited to *She reuiued.*
her bodie, so that onelie remayned a litle scarre, like vnto
a white threed, compassing the necke aboute, denoting
onelie the cutte thus made but now healed, and testifying
gods mightie worke, not reseruing any paine or mayme to
the bodie. Vpon this white marke which in Welch is called *Whence*
WEN, they say she was called WENEFRIDE, being before *called Wenefride.*
named BREUNA, as the Britans record. The stones of that *Of the stones*
fountaine or well of St WENEFRIDE, which sprang where *and mosse of the well.*
her bloud was shedd, as well on the banke as in the water,
seeme all besprinkled with bloud: and the mosse growing or
cleauing to those stones is odoriferous and verie sweete, somewhat like frankincense. At these miracles the people there
neere aboute were so moued, that they thereupon receyued
the faith. But the virgin tooke at BEUNOS hands the holie
veile of professed virginitie, and gained many virgins mo *She receiued*
to follow her in that chaste and religious purpose. Whome *the veile of professed*
after that she had instructed in all regular discipline, and *virginitie.*
had shewed her self a patterne of all perfection (her maister
seruing our Lord some fiftie miles of from her) she was admonished by god, to goe seeke oute one SATURNUS: who
directed the virgin to a place called WITHERIACK, where
she founde ELERIUS a man of greate holynesse, who made
her gouernesse ouer an other Couent of virgins: Whome
after that she had instructed religiouslie in Christs loue
and seruice, she there ended her life, and was buried neere
St CHEBEE and SENANE flourishing after her corporall
decease with glorious miracles. For yong infants, in what *Miracles.*
sort soeuer they be infirmed or sicke, being throwne into
the head of this spring are wont to come forth whole and
perfectlie sounde.

The life of holie Modwen Virgin aboute the yeare : 870 : /

Modwene daughter to king NANGTHEE an Irish Prince, and CHOMAN his wife, forsooke the worlde, and all the gaye shewes and pranked profers thereof, and taking the sacred 4
veile of professed virginitie, became the mistresse of verie many like professed and holie virgins, and the foundresse of sundrie such monasteries. Her vertue did also her

Her brother and kins-woman follow her.
brother RONANE and her Cousine ATHEA emulate and 8 earnestlie imitate. First before others, building a monasterie on a certaine hill, where they lyued with her, feeding on raw herbes, and labouring with their handes for their necessarie sustenance, as she did also, full often digging 12 with a mattocke, and sowing seede in the earth. To her

Her renown.
did flocke noble matrons and like worthie virgins, yea and Queenes. Of all which BRIGIDE and ORBILA are of especiall name. Whereof ORBILA being to be appoynted Abbesse 16 or gouernesse ouer a monasterie of one hundred and fiftie virgins, by her mother MODWEN, who was to leaue that place and to goe other-where, excused her self from that charge saying, that if she went thence, she feared leste 20 youthfull blouds neere by, would for her bodilie beautie and fayre hayre offer her violence and take her thence perforce.

Orbila her disciples preseruing from danger of her beautie.
Thereat MODWEN comforting her tooke her owne girdle, and with it girded ORBILA, then making the signe of the Crosse 24 on it, and blowing on ORBILA, presentlie her head waxed gray, and her face wrinkled, yet venerable thoughe seuere like an olde woman. And to giue her to vnderstand, how that she was sette ouer that holie companie not to play the 28 Ladie but to serue others commoditie and ghostlie profitt,

Orbila called Seruila.
she changed her name from ORBILA to SERUILA, which signifieth 'a litle seruant.' After this she vnderstanding how certaine Priests were slayn on the way as they 32 trauailed, by theeues and robbers; taking some companions with her, she goeth to gather vp the^{ir} bodies.

The murdering theeues vnderstanding their purpose, determyned among themselues to take them, euerie one, one: and the captaine or cheefe of these fellowes, was called
4 GLUNELACH. The virgin perceyuing their intent prayed forthwith to our Lord for ayd; when lo all those theeues fell asleepe, wherein they continued from Thursday vntill Satersday, in which deepe sleepe the Captaine GLUNELACH
8 his soule was taken out of his bodie, and carried where he behelde the terrible torments of the damned and the wonderfull rewardes of the Iust. Then awaking he falleth prostrate at the virgins feete, asking pardon of his faulte,
12 and crauing help at her holie handes, withall beseecheth her to instruct him in the faith, and how to saue his soule: which she did: by whose example his sonne named ALFIN, did the like. so that they were both baptized, and after-
16 ward proceeding in vertue, became both bishops and finished their liues verie religiouslie. There was at that time a religious Bishop called CHEUIN, who for loue of more quiet and free attending on heauenlie contemplation, had for-
20 saken his Bishopricke, and had now lyued seuen yeares solitarie in the wildernes. This man did the diuell vehementlie incense against the holie virgin; for that some tymes she had promised GLUNELACH the forenamed theefe,
24 as worthie a reward and palace in heauen, as he had seene in his trance prepared for this Bishop CHEUIN: which the Enemie relating vnto Bishop CHEUIN, added withall. 'In vaine doost thou thus afflict thy self with fasting and other
28 like austerities, if so notorious a theefe and homicide, is to be made thy equall in heauen, as MODWENE hath promised him. Wherefore better shall it be for thee henceforth to leaue of this rigour, and with more ease to be content,
32 with that which is ordayned, and which may with lesse labour be compassed, seing so notable a malefactor shall be thy equall.' When CHEUIN had vnderstood thus much, he leaueth the desert, and arming himself and others, which
36 he had associated with him, he comes to the virgin in

A Captaine of theeues conuerted.

Theeues became Bishops.

The diuell incenseth a holie man against her.

greate choler, resolued to kill her and to destroy her
monasterie. As he approched thus with his retinew, the
She saw the diuel hanging on her enemie. holie spouse of Christ saw the diuell hanging on his left
foote, in forme of a litle blacke boy, also whyspering in 4
his left eare wicked counsell, and inspiring into his hart
naughtie desires. Whereat the virgin besought our Lord,
that he would make CHEUIN himself see these things;
which she obtayned. Wherefore when he had behelde the 8
diuells deuices and deccites, in himself being greatlie confounded he gaue ouer his enterprise, and retourned to his
She cured Alured the king of Englands sonne. wildernesse againe, well informed and amended. At this
time was ETHELWOLD or ETHELWOLFE king of the West- 12
saxons in England, whose sonne ALURED, was sicke of an
incurable disease. The father therefore hearing of the
excellent vertue of MODWENE sent ALURED his sonne vnto
her, beseeching her to pray to god for his recouerie: which 16
she did, and restored thereby the childe to his health. She
afterward was spoiled of all she had by a Tyrant of her
contrie, wherefore with three other sisters accompanying
her, to weete LUGE, BRIGIDA, and ATHEA, she fledd thence. 20
She came into England. And comming to the sea side to passe, and not fynding any
bote or shippe to transport them, as they prayed to god
for ayd, the earth where they lay prostrate in prayer, was
seuered from the other continent and floated into the Sea: 24
where the Angell of God directing it they arriued therewith in Britanie or England. Then came she to ALUREDS
The king receiueth her honorablie, and commendeth h's daughter Edith to her. father king ETHELWOLFE, who receiuing her verie honorablie
commended to her education and gouernement EDITHA his 28
daughter (others call her his sister) to be instructed in
monasticall discipline by her, and withall gaue her land,
where and what she would, to build her monasteries.
She built two monasteries. [1 r. Pollesworth.] Whereuppon she erected two monasticall houses, one at 32
PAULEWORTH,[1] where she placed ATHEA and EDITH, an other
at STRENSHALEN, where she her self serued god. One day
EDITH sent sister OSITHA with a booke to her: who in the
way passing ouer a bridge, by greate happ fell into the 36

Riuer; with whose force she being carried away, was
drowned, and being sought three dayes together, and not
to be founde, MODWENE was admonished by an Angell to
4 go oute, and seeke the virgin lost. She went forth
presentlie, and comming to seeke her, she founde EDITH
seeking, with whome labouring long to fynde the dead
bodie, and not possiblie able, they fell both to prayer;
8 which after they had finished with teares MODWENE sayd
with a loud voice, 'OSITHA, OSITHA, OSITHA, in the name of *She raised Ositha to life being drowned.*
the holie and vndiuided Trinitie come forth.' She had
scant thrice repeated these wordes, but that the mayd
12 came oute of the water with the booke, and said 'beholde
here I am,' thrice: and being perfectlie sounde and well
she retourned home with EDITH to their monasterie, but
MODWENE went backe to her Cell againe: And not long
16 after taking BRIGIDA for her companion, she passed backe *She passed into Ireland.*
into Ireland, where with the goods that the king of the
Westsaxons had bestowed on her, she repayred her monasterie at CELLISCLINE, which had beene rased to the grounde.
20 Eight of her virgins, that were of greate vertue once all- *Miraculous clothes.*
moste killed with colde for want of clothing, she praying
to her Lord for help, so many garments were sent from
him so fitt and iust for them, as if they had beene made
24 after a measure taken from their bodies. She was once
inuited on a time with her sisters to a friends house, where
she blessing his meate and drinke they thereuppon so increased and augmented that her hoste was bolde to inuite
28 the king to his house: where he abyding two dayes with
all his retinew, could not consume a litle drinke which he
had. Whereuppon they all glorified god in his holie virgin.
After this she went into Scotland to king CONAGALL her *Her acts in Scotland.*
32 kinsman reigning there: by whose helpe she erected there
many monasteries, at STRIUELIN one, at EDENBURROW an
other, in GALLWEY three, at LONFRONTIN one, where she
lyued in greate austeritie of life, yet withall had often com-
36 forts of Angells, who to her view appeared offering before

the face of God her prayers and her sisters. But one
night she was depriued of this vision, beholding her
sisters prayers ascending scant vnto the roofe of their
Church: she inquiring the cause thereof, one of the sisters
confessed, that comming into the monasterie from the worlde
the day before, she brought with her some sockes giuen
her by some bad man, and had kept and vsed them
secretlie against the rule of her Order: which being
cast into the riuer, her wonted visitation of gods Saints
was restored her. She went to Rome on pilgrimage thrice,
barefoote, and cladd with a hayre-smocke next her bodie,
hauing one virgin for companion in her iournie named
LAZARA, whence being retourned she built her an oratorie
in an Ile of TRENT called SCALECLIFFE, which Oratorie, she
dedicated to the honour of St ANDREW; whereupon that
Ile vnto this time was named ANDRESIA, where she lyued
seuen yeares an Anchorets life, remote from all companie.
A mayde by profession a gentill, ignorant of true religion,
hearing MODWENS greate fame and renowne of holines came
to see her, and by her instruction and holie persuasion,
beleeued in Christ, yet by sodaine death she departed
without Baptisme; which MODWENE vnderstanding presentlie
cried to god with feruent prayer for her, so that she obtayned her life againe, and then she was baptised, and
moreouer receyued the habit of monasticall profession,
wherein she lyued and died moste saintlike. God gaue her
greate grace of curing diseases, so that greate concourse of
people was made vnto her for help out of diuerse contries:
with which assemblies and multitudes she was so wearied
and grieued, for that so she was become as it were a cittisen
of a solitarie woman, that she left the place, and passed
againe into Ireland, leauing behinde her in that place of
ANDRESIE sister LAZARA and sister ATHEA. Departing she
gaue commandement, that wheresoeuer she should be taken
out of this worlde, her bodie yet should be broughte and
buried there in ANDRESIE. When she came into Ireland,

soone after she fell sicke, wherewith she died, being then
an hundred and thirtie yeares olde. On her death bed she
made thys Testament or last will. 'My spade, rake, and *Her last will and testament.*
4 other implements wherewith I haue wroughte, also my
wooden combe, I bequeath to the monasterie of CELLISCLINE,
but my bodie and my staffe let be carried into England.'
After this the blessed Apostles PETER and PAULE appeared
8 vnto her, and so she departed this life the thirteenth of
Iulie to euerlasting life. After her decease the Irish,
English and Scottes contending for her bodie, by diuine
miracle God deciding the matter, it was brought into.
12 England, and buried in ANDRESIE, as she had before
ordeyned.

*The life of holie Ositha Virgin and Martyr: about the
yeares: 880: /*

16 **Ositha** daughter to FRITHWALD a litle Prince, and WIL-
BURGE his Ladie of the stocke of king PENDA of MERCIA,
was disciple to the former St MODWENE, and was three
dayes drowned in the bottom of a Riuer, and by her
20 Abbesses prayers raised to life, and leaped out of the water:
whence with her Ladie EDITHA she retourned to the monasterie, where she lyued regularlie and veiled with a blacke
veile, albeit she was no Nonne, but there brought vp *Note how virgins were brought vp in monasteries.*
24 vertuouslie, fitt to doo well in what estate she should after
chuse, as it seemeth. MODWENE her spirituall mother deceasing, she retourned home to her parents, where when
she was fitte for mariage, SIGHERE a litle Prince of the
28 Eastsaxons desired hir to wife, whereto her parents con-
senting, persuaded her to accept of the good offer made.
To whome she answered. 'Virginitie pleaseth me far better,
and I would to god it would so please you, that I might
32 so continue.' They not liking her holie choise, promised
her allthoughe vnwilling to the sayd Prince, and with all
princelie preparation for the wedding deliuered her vnto

him, in matrimonie. She being thus in danger to be putt from her chaste purpose, with feruent prayer recommended her holie desires vnto her heauenlie husband, beseeching him to preserue her vndefiled from mans companie. And after that she had many dayes kept her self from her husbands bed by diuerse pretenses, at length the Prince being now mynded to enioy her more freelie, lo a speedie messenger commeth to him, telling how a goodlie harte or stagge, passed along before his gate. At which newes he presentlie in all haste, pursueth after in chace. That while the Queene signifieth her purpose to the Bishops and Religious persons thereaboutes of the Eastsaxons; whereuppon they came with speede, and giuing her the religious weede and virginall veile they consecrated her a Nonne. The king retourning home, and seeing her in religious attire, and perceyuing her to haue made her vow to Allmightie god, waxed sad and sorrowfull, yet would not in any wise molest her therefore. Afterward a monasterie being built her, and many virgins associating her in that holie profession, she gouerned them in greate vertue and godlines, vntill the Danish Pirates arriued at CHICHE, where the monasterie was. Who apprehending OSITHA, with the rest commanded her to denie her faith. But she nothing terrified with threates, refused vtterlie euer to do so. Wherefore by the Captaine of those theeues she was sentenced to lose her head; which was donne about the yeare of our Lord: 883: When her head was cutt of, she is sayd to haue taken it vp, and to haue carried it to the Church of S̊ PETER and PAULE, three miles of. Yet by her parents meanes, she was buried at AILSBURIE in a Church there (by which it may be coniectured, that they dwelt thereaboute) and after her death she was glorified by god, with many miracles. /

These two virgins following I deeme to haue beene about this time, if not before; for that mention is made of Ethnike Princes there dwelling, which seemeth not probablie to haue beene after this. The Contries hauing beene begunne to be conuerted an hundred or two yeares before this, if not more. |

The life of St Maxentia Virgin and Martyr.

Maxentia was daughter to the king of Scotts named MARCOLANE. By natures gift she was of rare beautie, and by gods grace, as comelie for the loue of all vertue and zeale of virginitie. A pagane Prince and a Barbarian by grew vehementlie in loue of her, and for satisfying his suite and desire, had obtayned of her father a promise of her in mariage. The chaste virgin hearing that, and fearing least she might be barred from keeping her self pure and vndefiled vnto Christ onelie: After that she had ernestlie commended her case vnto god by many prayers, taking an olde man named BARBANCIUS, and a mayd attendant on her called ROSOBEA for companions, she flieth thence and getteth her into France: where in a village of BEAUUAISE she lay secretlie with her two fellowes, seruing god in all dutie and deuotion. The promised husband and louer, vnderstanding that she was fledd pursued after with all speede and dilligence, directing euerie way messengers, to harken and espie her oute: who did their endeuour so effectuallie, that at length they founde her. The enamoured Prince came to her, and laboured all he coulde to prouoke her like carnall affection and assent vnto him, as he bare vnto her, and to retourne home with him to temporall ioy and glorie. But she had so fixed her loue and hart on the glorious king Christ Iesus, that all those labours were lost on her: all carnall worth seeming to her vile and so base as vnworthie whollie to be balanced or weighed with so supreme a Prince, and so stable and per-

She fled into France.

Her martyrdome.

fect glorie. The earthlie lord disdayning that his hoate flame should be dashed with so colde regarde, his loue tourned into such furie, that he slew with his own handes

A miracle.

both her and her companions, and so away he went. It is written that when he was gone, the virgin tooke vp her head in her owne armes out of the place where it was cutt of, and carried it to the place where it now lieth: where afterward there was a Church erected, and God glorified his louing spouse with miraculous wonders. Charles that was then king is sayd to haue much affected that holie Virgin, and thereupon honoured her sacred corps with sundrie roiall gifts. /

The life of S? Oswen or Osman Virgin. /

𝕿𝖍𝖎𝖘 holie woman was by nation an Irishe woman, of stocke descended from kinglie bloud, albeit ETHNICKS. She being but a girle receyued the faith of Christ, wherein she grew so feruent and stoute, that her parents soliciting her from her religion, she boldlie rebuked them and reproued their endeuour. She being after to be placed in marriage, and that to an Ethnike and enemie of faith,

She fled into France.

priuilie she leaueth her Contrie, and accompanied with an onelie maide that wayted on her, named ACLITENIS, she

Her austere life.

came into France: where in a wood neere the riuer of LOIRE she liued vnto god verie austerelie, being clad if not rather couered with bull rushes, and feeding her hungrie

A wonder.

bodie with onelie herbes. She lyuing there in that manner, one day a bore being chased by hunters came runne vnto her, as it were for succour, and the huntsman notwithstanding being egre to kill him, strake him with his hunting speare, thinking to thrust him throughe, but with all his force and endeuour he was not able once to pearce

She is suspected to be a witche.

the poore beastes skinne. Hereupon she was suspected to be a witche, and brought to the Bishop. Who fynding her to beleeue in Christ, and to desire to be baptized, he did

baptize her, and gaue her a contrieman, who should keepe
her garden for her releefe and liuelyhood. The enemie of
all good hoping to harme her by this her gardener, taking
4 on him a mans shape, came one day vnto the fellow, saluted
him verie courteouslie, and kissed him, promising him a The diuels deuice against her.
greate summe of golde, if he would goe and all to reuile his
mistresse and so prouoke her to anger and impatience. He
8 accepting of the offer, and vndertaking that enterprise,
homeward he comes to do his purpose. But as soone as he
was come home, he was striken blynde, that he could not
see her whome he had thought to iniurie. Whereby per-
12 ceyuing himself to haue beene deceyued and deluded, he
cried out and sayd, how one had circumuented him, and
withall crauing pardon of his mistresse, for that his former
intent purposed against her, she easilie pardoned him, and
16 pittying his calamitie also healed him. She perseuering
still in that holie conuersation was thence called vnto
Christ, whome she so loued and faithfullie serued. /

The life of holie Elflede Virgin about the yeare : 950 : /

20 **This** virgin was borne of ETHELWOLD her father and
BRITHWINE her mother: who hauing a free towne wherein
they dwelt named CLARE, the father deceasing bequeathed
that land to founde the ABBIE of ROMSEY, for his soules Romsey Abbie founded.
24 health, and redemption of his spirituall debtes: which he
dedicated to our B: Ladie the mother of god: Which will
his wife caused verie carefullie to be perfourmed, but thereuppon grew their deuoute daughter into greate pouertie
28 and distresse: which the good king EDGAR perceyuing, he
placed her in the sayd monasterie of ROMSEY, vnder the
holie gouernment of the vertuous Ladie and Abbesse
MERWENNE: who loued her as her owne daughter, and Merwenna.
32 taught her, as her owne bowells: so that vnder this regular
institution, she so profitted in gods fauour, that he honoured

her one day with a miracle. For going in tyme of mattins, to reade a lesson or some such thing, with the light in her hand, the candle by happe going oute, such brightnes issued from the fingers of her right hand, that all aboute were able to reade by it. At which strange euent she became in greate veneration with the other sisters, so that after the decease of the Ladie Abbesses MERWEN and EL-WINE, she was chosen gouernesse of the house. Who can recounte what plentie of teares she shodd[1] for her owne sinnes and the necessities of gods church? Who can recorde the aboundance of her almes deeds? Whereas from her first Nouiceship, what she could spare from her owne bellie by fasting, that would she bestow priuilie on the poore, and pilgrimes. Moreouer when by her exceeding bountie and large releefe of the needie, her houses welth, and cofers were greatlie emptied and exhaust, in so much that the Prouost or officer of the reuenewes did checke her sharplie for exceeding lauishnes, with many teares she made her mone to her supreme Lorde, crauing his helpe, whereat the emptie chests were againe filled as before, by Gods gracious recompence and approbation of her beneficence. Her wisedome was no lesse than her charitie, whereby she resisted, and putt to silence a calumniating Countie[1] thereby, who with false fictions and fayned faults framed against her, laboured to harme her, but indeed shamed himself. After that she had by long well dooing fraighted and replenished her self with vertuous treasure and celestiall riches, withall she sayled safelie out of this worlde, and happilie arriued at the heauenly porte, about the yeare of our Redemption 950. /

The life of S: Edith, Virgin and Abbesse: 980: /

King EDGAR in his youthlie heate enamoured with the beautie of a yong maiden that was veiled in a religious house, named WILFRID, with some violence tooke his

pleasure of her, but did sharpe penance therefore many
yeares after, by S̃ DUNSTANS constrainte. By that fact he
begat on WILFRID this virgine EDITH, whome her mother *Her birth.*
4 leading a monasticall life in the nonrie of WILTON, brought
vp with her in the seruice of Christ moste religiouslie.
For after that she had beene deliuered of that childe, she
lyued so vertuouslie there, that she obtayned the honour
8 and estimation of holines. Her daughter EDITHE, de- *Her vertues.*
meyned her self so regularlie there, that amongst the
sisters, she was an other paynfull and obsequious
MARTHA, in spirituall solitude with Christ, she was an
12 other MARIE. She serued the sicke and leaprous persons
with greate charitie, so farre, that looke how much more
deformed and ouglie any one was, by disease, so much the
more pittifull was she by compassion, and the more dilligent
16 in attending him. Her brother king Edward the martyr,
being slayne by his stepmother, some of the nobilitie
laboured to sette the crowne on EDITHS hed, this our
Nonne, but she could by no persuasion or force, be remoued *Note.*
20 from her holie purpose. S̃ DUNSTANE once dedicating a
Church, which she had built in the honour of S̃: DENISE,
as he was at Masse, he had reuealed vnto him, that she
should shortlie be taken out of this worlde. Wherewith *A vision of her death.*
24 he presentlie burst into teares, and wept bitterlie: Being
asked why he so wailed, fetching a deepe sighe he sayd.
'This starrie gemme shall ere long be taken from vs into
the Saints contrie, for this wicked worlde, is not worthie
28 to enioye the presence of so cleere a lighte.' Wherefore
when she was twentie and three yeares of age, in the yeare
of Christ 984, the sixteenth of September, she was called *Her death.*
hence vnto Christ, Holie Dunstane assisting her vnto her
32 last gaspe, and after burying her, in the forenamed Church
of S̃: DENISE, where also she departed, Angells singing at
her decease, and conducting her soule with such harmonie *Angels sing.*
vnto heauen, as one Angell signified to one of the virgins
36 of the monasterie. On the thirteth day after her obite,

she appeared verie glorious vnto her mother WILFRIDE or VLTRUDE, and tolde her that she was verie acceptable vnto her king in euerlasting glorie. She sayd more: 'Satan accused me before my Lord, but by the patronage and fauour of the holie Apostles, I crushed his head, and in Christs crosse I ouerthrew him, trod vpon him, and triumphed ouer him.' After some yeares also she appeared vnto S⟨t⟩: DUNSTAN (as also S⟨t⟩: DENISE did vnto him confirming her request) willing him to take vp her bodie. And for proofe of the vndoubtednes of the vision, she added farther saying. 'All my bodie shalt thou finde vncorrupted (except those partes, which I haue somewhat abused by childish leuitie as my eyes, handes, and feete) for I neuer was subiect either to lust or gluttonie, and the thumbe of my right hand, whereby daylie I signed my self with the holie Crosse, thou shalt also finde vncorrupt: that by this thou maiest perceiue gods benignitie and bountie in the parts kept intire and vnperished, and his fatherlie chastisement, in the partes consumed.' When one had vsurped on a peece of land which belonged to S⟨t⟩ EDITH, and preuented by sudden death had not repented him thereof, after that he had lien dead a while he reuiued, and spake 'Helpe me all my friends, aide me all faithfull people, for beholde the indignation of S⟨t⟩ EDITH is intollerable, excluding me the vnhappie inuader of her possession out of all places in heauen and earthe; no-where permitteth she me to abide, neither in my bodie nor oute of it': And when the land was restored, he forthwith gaue vp his ghoste againe. /

There was an other holie EDITH Aunt to the foresayd virgin and sister to king EDGAR who lyued in the monasterie of POLLELWORTH in Warwicke-shire, and whose vertue the later her Neece studdied with all dilligent indeuour to imitate. / Of a third see the life of Sainte MODWENE. /

The life of holie Wulfhilde Virgin and Ablesse.

Alfrede King of the Westsaxons in England, passing thoroughe a woode as he was hunting, he heard the voice of an infant crying on the toppe of a tree. Thereuppon causing some to clymbe the tree and to looke what was there, they founde an Eagles neaste, and in it a goodlie man- childe, wrapped in a purple cloake, with golden bracelets aboute his armes, and on his bodie some token, as if he were of Princelie bloud. He tooke the infant thence, caused it to be baptized, and of the neast whence he had him, he named him Nesting. He more brought him vp verie noblie, and after made him an Earle. He afterward tooke a wife and begatt a sonne named WITHBURDING, who likewise growing to ripenesse and marriage, left a sonne named WULFHELME, who was father to our WULFHILDE virgin. Her father hauing had sondrie children by his wife, of religious zeale agreed with his wife to lyue chaste euer after for the loue of god; which when they had performed eighteene yeares together, they were thrice admonished by diuine vision, to keepe company againe, for that now in their more chaste age they should bring forth a spouse of Christ: who being borne, they should reassume, their former chaste custome, and continue it withoute interruption. They obeyed gods appointment, and this infant being borne, she was called WULFHILD. After that she was capable of religious education, and godlie institution, she was committed to the religious virgins of Winchester to be brought vp. Where seruing god, some time after, King EDGAR in his britle youth grew into greate desire of her, yet durst not take her out of the Cloister from the Churche, albeit she seemeth not to haue beene professed as yet. Wherefore by flatterie sometimes, otherwhiles by threates, he calleth her, and willeth her to come out thence vnto him. But she

(margin notes: A strange thing. The familie of Nestinga. Her stocke. Her strange birth. King Edgar wooeth her.)

being nothing moued with any thing he could doe, he dealt
with the virgins Aunte a Ladie named WENFLEDE, who
dwelt at WEREWELL, to do her endeuour to entice her to
come thither, where he might be bolde to catche her and 4
stay her. The Aunte in hope to aduance her Neece to be
Queene was as readie to worke in this busines, as the king
to require her. Whereuppon she feyneth herself verie
sicke, and in danger of death; which donne she certifieth 8
the holie virgin of her case, requiring her to come with all
speede to see her before she should leaue the worlde, for
that she also purposed, to make her heire of all that god
had lent her. The simple lamb fearing no fraude, came 12
confidentlie to the olde foxe her Aunte, where arriuing she
found the king EDGAR present, farre beyond her expectation
and desire. Who reioycing to see her whome he so loued,
wooed her afresh to consent to be his wife, promising her 16
riches in all aboundance, honour of the highest degree, as
that he would make her Queene and Ladie of all England,
beside other delightes what a Prince could procure for his
best beloued. And besides this, leste she should escape 20
out of his handes, being now in holde, he appointed watchmen about the house, to see that in no wise she might
depart withoute his leaue. Aboue promises in presence,
he feasted her roiallie, and at the banket he placed her by 24
his owne side: but her hart being full of better loues, litle
lyked those profers, and seeing herself so circumuented and
enuironed, could make no meate go downe for sorrowe.
Her hart was absent, and wished her bodie not there 28
present, which for all the watche she with gods helpe
thought to attempt. Wherefore by a secret hole vnder

She gott out of the king's hands to Wilton Abbie.

grounde she gott away and came to her monasterie at
WILTON. The king vnderstanding of her flight followed 32
after, and comming to the Abbie requested to speake with
her, but she would none, refusing any communication,
hauing beene so latelie deceiued by fayned speache. The
king not so contented, sett some to watche when she 36

should passe throughe the Cloister, and so by cunning
caught her withoute the Churche, and as he triumphed to
her of his preye, she slipt suddenlie from out of his hands,
4 and ran away. The king following after caught her by
the sleeue, as she entered in at the Church dore; but the
sleeue lightlie came of, and remayned in the kings hand.
But she escaped into the church where prostrating herself
8 before the Altar, with hartie lamentations and teares, she
besoughte her Lord to keepe her chastitie vndefiled: which
the king beholding, he blushed at his owne impudencie,
perceyuing by the sleeue as it were cutt of from her
12 garment by gods helpe, how Christ his spouse was
deliuered oute of his handes. Wherefore now amended, *The king overcome*
he came to her, and bad her not be afeard, assuring her *and his liberalitie to-*
that from thence forthe, he would no more molest her, but *wards her.*
16 farder promised that he would farther and defend her in
her holie purpose. Which he performed. For he gaue
her the monasterie of BERKING, which being then much
decayed (by the Danes as it seemeth) he repayred, and
20 with princelie munificence restored it to his auncient glorie
and worthines. / Againe the monasterie of HORTON, which
the virgin had founded of her owne patrimonie, and was
equallie distant from WILTON, SHAFTESBURIE, WARRAM and
24 HAMPTON, he did so enriche and endowe, that both for
multitude of virgins, and greatnes of reuenewes and possessions, he made it equall vnto the Abbie of BERKING. She *A miracle.*
being afterward consecrated a spouse of Christ or pro-
28 fessed virgin, there appeared a moste white doue which
came from heauen and rested on her head: After that she
had for many yeares gouerned those two aforesayd monasteries, throughe the enuious ambition of the Priests of
32 BERKING, they were broughte into that monasterie by
Queene ALFTRUDE mother to king ETHELRED, and the holy
virgin with her Sisters cast oute. But going out at one *Her troubles*
gate of the Abbie with her company, and the Sisters *and prophecie.*
36 lamenting at that their expulsion, she comforted them,

saying. 'Be of good cheere and trust in our Lord, for this day twentie yeare hence, at this verie gate shall I with you retourne hither, and be restored': which came so to passe. For then appeared blessed ETHELBURGE, the first foundresse of BERKING, vnto the Queene ALFTRUDE being sicke, attired in a vile weede ragged and rent, complayning of her iniurie donne by ALFTRUDE, withall threatening her, that vnlesse she restored WULFHILDE oute of hand to her monasterie, she should presentlie perishe. Therewith the Queene being corrected, recalled home the holie virgin with all her sisters, and she withall recouered hir health. After this she lyued seauen yeares, gouerning both monasteries in greatest glorie, and in her life-time, and after her death shined with miracles. She foretolde the day of her decease, and then leauing this life she was buried at BERKING. Where thirtie yeares after, her bodie, with all the clothes thereof, were founde intire and vncorrupted. She died at London, for that there she then remayned with her sisters for the greate sturres, that the Danes made euerie-where. As the bodie was carried to BERKING, a fellow against whome the virgin liuing, was offended for his lewde life, putt his hands to the beare with others to carrie with them: but presentlie the corpse waxed so heauie, that no multitude could once stirre it. Whereat all exclayme against him, calling him a wicked man. He departing the bodie was lighte againe, and moste easie to carrie: Then began the fellow to bethinke him of his estate, and sorrowing and confessing his faultes, retourned to the others that carried her, and then no alteration was felt, but that he was permitted to beare with the rest euen to the Monasterie. /

Alftrude y Queenes vision.

Her death: and bodie long after incorrupt.

A lewd fellow impenitent was not permitted to carrie her dead bodie.

The life of S! *Margaret Queene of Scotland: liuing in the yeare of our Lord:* 1100 : /

Edward being the yongest sonne of EDMUND IRONSIDE
4 king of England, together with his elder brother EDMUND, was by king CANUTE the Dane banished. Being there abrode he married the Emperours daughter called AGATHA, *Her stock.* on whome he begat with others, this MARGARIT. Who from
8 her tender age, began to loue god aboue all things, to exercise sobrietie and honestie : In so much that WILLIAM Conquerour getting England, and her mother AGATHA thereuppon flying for feare with her children into Scot-
12 land, where by king MALCOLME the third, they were courteouslie entertayned ; he was so enamoured with the beautie and vertue of MARGARIT, that he would needes haue her to wife. Whereto her mother, assenting ; being
16 coupled vnto her in marriage, he was also vnited so to her *She made* in Religious loue and christian zeale, that he became more *her husband of rare* holie than all his Predecessours had beene. And by their *vertue.* exceeding vertue others were so prouoked to godlines, that
20 the Queenes mother AGATHA, and her sister CHRISTINE forsooke the worlde, and vndertooke monasticall profession ; and the king himself by her example, was whollie addicted to the repayring and increasing of religion throughe
24 his Realme ; restoring two Bishoprickes of foure decayed, *Their acts :* and founding two other new, also building the Church of DOBRAM all new. The vertuous Ladie was compelled to *In the* manage worldlie matters, yet her hart was far from louing *Realme.*
28 them. By her wise counsaile and commandement all was donne that was conuenient, by her aduice were the lawes of the kingdome ordered, by her industrie gods glorie and honour cheefelie aduanced. None more firme in faith than
32 she, none more composed and stayed in countenance. She was so patient in suffering, so mature in counselling, so iust in iudging, so sweete in communication as none more.

In the place where she was maried, she built a noble Church to the moste holie Trinitie, endowing it with diuerse ornaments and riches. Her children she brought vp with all diligence, instructing them no lesse in vertuous behauiour and pietie, than in other good and princelie qualities, oftentimes in her owne presence and person teaching them the faith of Christ, and true pietie. And this did she daylie request at gods hands with teares, that they might in this life serue their creatour, and afterward reigne happilie with him in heauen. By gods help concurring with her, she inflamed her husband to all vertuous workes, making him moste prompt to all good actions: for he perceyuing Christ to dwell in her, moste gladlie did he obey and yield vnto her in all things. Her hart was so wounded with the feare of god, that she did often request her Confessour to tell and reprooue her secretlie, if he marked any thing that was amisse in her actions. Whereas she had espied many things practised amongst the nation of Scots, contrarie to the sacred customes of the vniuersall Church, she caused sundrie Counsells to be gathered, thereby to reduce the people from their errours, vnto the truthe, in which endeuour the king her husband did especiallie assist her. She herself premised a speeche to the estates of the kingdome, wherein she noted vnto them the abuses then current: as of the euill obseruation of Lent, not beginning it on Ashwednsday, as the Church vseth, but on the munday of the weeke following. Againe how at the holie feaste of Ester, they vsed not to receiue the holie Sacrament, against the expresse commandement of holie Churche. Thirdlie that they sayd Masse in some places, against the vse of the Churche. Fourthlie that they wrought seruile workes on the holie dayes. More that some married their stepmothers, others their brothers wife after his deathe./ All which she with sound reason and authorities, both of scriptures and Fathers, did before them refute and conuince of falshoode or faulte. She talking of the state of her

What toward her Children.

Her greate feare of God.

What for religion.

The abuses then in Scotland.

Her deuotion.

soule, and heauenlie sweetnes, with her Confessour, would
vtter moste gracious speeches, and withall would resolue
into teares. She would neuer talke of secular affaires in
4 the Churche of god, nor doe any terrene or worldlie act
there. When she went abrode multitudes of Widows and
Orphans, and other distressed people, would flocke aboute
her as their mother, from whome none departed withoute Her greate charitie.
8 some comforte. Neither did she conteyne her munificence in
the poore of her owne people, but to strangers of all
contries in necessitie was she pittifull and liberall. She did
send secret spies throughe other prouinces and remote
12 places, to see if any were hardlie vsed and to redeeme
them. Innumerable English captiues did she sett free,
paying their ransome, and sending them home. She did
often visit in her owne person Heremits and other religious,
16 that liued recluse, commending her self to their prayers,
and granting them whatsoeuer they demanded. After that
she had taken her rest the former part of the night, she
arose, went to the Church, where she said the matins of
20 the Trinitie, of the Crosse, and of our Ladie. After that Markx.
she sayd the office for the dead, and the whole psalter.
She was also present at the Canonicall houres or Church-
office songue by the Clergie. That being donne she retourned
24 to her chamber, where she washed the feete of sixe poore
persons, and then gaue them monie for their releefe. That
dispatched she permitted her bodie to take a litle nodd or
sleepe. The morning being come she arose, and then had
28 she nyne poore infants that were orphans, and voide of
friends, whome she fedd on her knees, with tender and
suckling meates agreeable for their infancie, putting meate
into their mouthes, with her owne handes. Besides all
32 this, she had this custome to haue three hundred poore
people, brought in within the Courte of their Palace, then
the gates being shutte, the king on the one side, and she
on the other did serue Christ in them. That absolued she
36 went to the Church where with long deuotion, teares, and

sighes, she sacrificed herself vnto god, and before the
highe masse, she would heare fiue or sixe priuate masses.
Before dinner she had fower and twentie other poore
Her fasting. folkes, whome she serued moste humblie. When she did eate, 4
she rather did taste than feede. Fortie dayes before Easter
and Christmas, she did afflict herself with incredible abstinence. By reason of which extreame fasting she vnto her
dying day endured moste sharpe payne and torment of 8
stomacke. She had a new Testament verie curiouslie
bounde, and adorned with golde and precious stones,
wherein she vsed much to reade and studie; which by
negligence of him that kept it, fortuned to fall into the 12
water, where it remayned a whole day and a nighte, yet
tooke no manner of harme: and her booke wherein she
prayed, the king tooke greate pleasure to handle it and
kisse it. Towards her end she called her Confessour 16
Her com- TURGOTTE, to whome it is almoste incredible, with what
punction. compunction and weeping she made her generall confession
of all her life, gushing oute whole streames of teares allmoste at euerie worde. And when all was donne, she 20
taking her leaue and bidding her Confessour farewell: she
sayd, 'God be with you: I shall not long remayne in this
life; but you shall liue a litle while after me'; Half a
yeare before her end, she kept her bed allmoste continuallie, 24
sicknes growing on her more and more: when one day
Her pro- she was more heauie and sadd than wonte. For beholding
phecie. in spirit the death of her husband and sonne Edward,
that were slaine then in the warre, she sayd: 'This day so 28
greate misfortune is befallen on Scotland, as perhaps in
long time before hath not happened the like to that
Her rare Realme.' Soone after, her sonne EDGAR comming and
patience. relating the whole storie, she burst into these wordes. 'I 32
thanke and laude thee God omnipotent, that wouldest now
at my departure exercise me and purge me, as I hope, with
so greate sorrowes and anguishes of harte.' She had the
blacke Crosse of Scotland in greate reuerence, and now 36

especiallie often kissing it, and signing her eyes and face
with it, she died praying, and whereas she was pale-faced
before her death, being dead a comelie white and red *Her comelines after her death.*
4 adorned her countenance. She left behinde her vertuous
children, true inheritours of their mothers vertue: MAUDE *Hervertnons Children.*
that was married to the king of England, HENRIE the
first. She was so charitable towards the poore and pitti-
8 full persons, that she was termed 'MAUDE the good.' EDGAR
and DAUID, that were both moste religious Princes one
after the other, who had both miraculous fauours of All- [¹ Hector BoeceChro:!.
mightie god, as in BOETHIUS,¹ in their liues sett forth in Scot. lib. xll.]
12 our English chronicles may appeare./

*The life of holie Mectilde Virgin: who liued about the
years 1200: or somewhat before: Out of a verie good
Author¹ that liued a litle after, to weete, 1238./*

[¹ In Brit. sancta this author is Thomas Cantipratensis " in the 2. book

16 '**Mechtild** who is proued to haue deceased in our time of the miracles of his
(saith the Author) was daughter to a king of Scotts, and as own time, Cap. 10."]
we haue heard by credible relation had foure brothers: one *Foure holie Brothers.*
a duke, who forgoing his wife for Christs loue became a poore
20 man, and as it were a banished man or pilgrime from his natiue
contrie, to assure him self the better of the celestiall contrie
that is endlesse happie with god aboue. An other was an
Earle, yet for heauenlie honour contemned secular dignitie,
24 and became an Heremite. The third was an Archbishop, who
forsaking his Episcopall regiment, entered the order of the
Cistertian moncks, seeking by such humilitie, to be more
exalted in the kingdome of our humble Lord, who therein
28 moste approued heere, was aloft therefore moste exalted.
The fourth and yongest named ALEXANDER, being but
sixteene yeares olde and vrged by his father to manage
the kingdome, his sister MECHTILDE, being then twentie
32 yeares of age, aduised him in this wise. 'Deere brother
ALEXANDER, what meane you, your elder brothers haue all

forsaken the worlde and their contrie glorie, the earth and
all therein, to purchase heauen, and immortall kingdomes:
Wilt thou then take this temporall dominion onelie, and
for it leese the supreme glorie that knoweth no end?' 4
Herevpon ALEXANDER melting into teares sayd withall;
'Alas good sister, what will you aduise me to doe; what
you thinke best that am I redie to putte in practise.' She

She left her contrie with her brother Alexander.
reioycing at this resolute answer, forthwith changing her 8
attire and her brothers, ouer the seas she goeth with him.
Where she taught him to milke kine, to tourne milke into
curde, and to make cheese in the best manner. Then came

He entred religion.
they into France, to the monasterie of CISTERCIANS called 12
FONE; where she placed her brother for a milker of kyne,
and there he proued himself a moste cunning maker of
Cheese. He being a conuert and brother of that Abbie,
his sister aduised him in this manner. 'Good brother greate 16
meede and reward shall we purchase at Gods hand, for
leauing our Contrie and friends, but especiallie shall we
augment this glorious crowne of ours, if for the time of
our pilgrimage in this life, we shall be content to bereaue 20
our selues of the sight of each other, vntill we shall meete
happilie in our euerlasting contrie.' Her brother at these
words wept bitterlie, deeming this to be a more difficult

They part for Gods sake.
and irksome pointe than all hitherto. Notwithstanding 24
he commandeth and ouerruleth his owne affection, and
separateth himself for euer and whollie from his beloued
sister. She then went nine miles of to a village called
ALAPION, there-by getting her a litle vile cottage like vnto 28

Her pouertie.
a place to keepe geese in. There dwelt she lyuing of the
onelie labour and worke of her handes. She could by no
force be made to receiue any gifts or almes of others, nor
thereto could be induced by any intreatie. Neither would 32
she with other poore people lease corne in the fieldes at
haruest, but if she did gather any, it was after all others,
onelie that which remayned verie rare, which was permitted

Her austeritie.
to the swine. She would hardlie admitte any thing vnder 36

her when she slept, to keepe her from the grounde, and
her head would she lay euen with her bodie on the plaine
withoute pillow or any like supporting staye. She would
4 not eate or drinke, but kneeling on her bare knees, which
were verie hard by much vse, and so did she pray and that
verie long./ In her deuotions and prayer she would often
be so abstracted and taken from her senses, that she did
8 neither heare thunder nor see lightening then being.
ALEXANDER her brother remayned vnknowne vnto his *Alexander
death, when his Prior of his obedience willing him to known vntil
declare what he was, he confessed himself brother to death.*
12 blessed MECTILDE of ALAPION, and sonne to the king of
Scotts. His glorie and worth god testified after his
death in this manner. A moncke of his monasterie, that
had a sore vlcer in his brest, and now growne to a fistula,
16 came to Alexanders toombe before deceased and there
prayed. He thus praying brother Alexander appeared *He appear-*
vnto him more bright than the sunne, carrying two *death most*
crownes, one on his head, the other in his handes. Thereat *glorious.*
20 the moncke admiring tooke hart, and demanded what that
double crowne meant. He answered, 'The crowne in my
handes, is for the temporall crowne which I forsooke for
Christs loue, the other on my head, is that which I haue
24 receyued common with other Saintes, and that you may be
more assured of the veritie of this vision, according to
your faith shall you be now cured of your infirmitie, which
dooth vexe you.' Holie MECTILDE his sister, was descried *Mectild is*
28 what and whence she was by certaine souldiours (who had *her griefe.*
seene her in Scotland) nine yeares before she died. Whereuppon she presentlie had fledd thence, bicause she desired
to be vnknowne in this life, to be better knowne in the
32 next, but the people where she dwelt, would in no wise
permitte her to depart. She was glorified by God with
miracles manifoldelie bothe lyuing and dead.' /

FINIS.

A TABLE OF THE SAINTES NAMES BEFORE SETT DOWNE; IN ORDER OF THE ALPHABET. /

	PAGE		PAGE
S^t: Brigid	40 *(52)	S^t: Keyna	39 (50)
S^t: Cuthburge	77 (107)	S^t: Kinesburge	71 (38)
S^t: Dympna	43 (55)	S^t: Kineswide	71 (98)
S^t: Eanswide	51 (67)	S^t: Margaret	109 (160)
S^t: Edburge	49(64 & 66)	S^t: Maxentia	99 (143)
S^t: Ebba	65 (88)	S^t: Mectild	113 (167)
S^t: Edithe	102 (150)	S^t: Milburge	60 (81)
S^t: Erkengode	55 (73)	S^t: Mildred	63 (84)
S^t: Ermenild	58 (78)	S^t: Modwen	92 (131)
S^t: Ethelburge	52:54:55:74 (68:71:73:102)	S^t: Ositha	97 (140)
		S^t: Oswenne	160 (145)
S^t: Etheldred	67 (91)	S^t: Sexburge	54 (71)
S^t: Elfled	101 (147)	S^t: Walburge	82 (116)
S^t: Frideswide	80 (112)	S^t: Wenefrede	88 (126)
S^t: Helene	30 (38)	S^t: Werburge	59 (79)
S^t: Hilda with her Sister Hereswide	56 (74)	S^t: Withburge	79 (110)
		S^t: Vrsula and the 1100 (0) Virgins	36 (46)
S^t: Hildelitha	76 (105)		
S^t: Inthware	79 (111)	S^t: Wulfhilde	105 (153)

* The numbers in brackets are those of the MS.

HEERE FOLLOW

CERTAIN LIUES OF OTHER SAINTS WRITTEN BY FAMOUS DOCTORS OF THE CHURCH, AS NAMELIE

PAGE

The life of Sᵗ: MONICA written by Sᵗ: AUGUSTINE her sonne . . (177)

The life of Sᵗ: AGNES written by Sᵗ: AMBROSE . . . . (223)

The life of Sᵗ: GORGONIA by Sᵗ: GREGORIE NAZIANZENE her brother . . . . (244)

The life of Sᵗ: NONNA by Sᵗ: GREGORIE NAZIANZENE her sonne (274)

The martyrdome of JULITTA by Sᵗ: BASILL . . . . (293)

The admirable vertue of a Christian maid captiue in IBERIA . (300)

The life of Sᵗ: MACRINA by Sᵗ: GREGORIE of NYSSA her brother. (306)

An admirable miracle of Sᵗ: MACRINAS grandfathers . . . . (351)

The Life of S: *Monica mother to S:* *Augustine the Doctor taken out of his bookes, Of Confession : /*

Whereas *this holie woman could not haue a better witnesse of her vertues and blessings, than her holie sonne, nor the reader can iustlie wish, a more vndoubted relater, than so sincere a Sainte, and greate doctour of truthe : whereas also his relations, are either his owne knowledge or her vnfayned report of her self, and all are by him to God himself spoken, heereby both his narration shall be more veneruble, and his owne Confession before God of her shall be more delectable to reade, than to alter his person, in speaking with hindrance of holie affections, which his forme of speach, and spirit talking with God himself doth works. Therefore I thought best, to giue his onelie wordes, albeit digested and disposed, somewhat otherwise than he hath putt them, to weete according to the naturall euent and course of them, as they were donne, yet onelie out of him, so helping our vnderstanding by the one, as not hindering our deuotion for want of the other, and so studious to conserue his spirit speaking, that yet we will not omitte the naturall order and proper progresse of the matter for memorie. /*

Confess.
lib: 9.
[Cap. 8.]

'**Receiue** my Confessious and thankes giuings my God, for innumerable things, which I passe ouer in silence, yet will I not omitt any thing which my soule dooth bring forth of her thy seruant, who begott and bare me both in flesh to this temporall lighte, and in hart to eternall light : I will recounte not so much her graces as thy gifts in her, for she neither made herself, nor gaue education to her self. Thou diddest create her, neither did her father or mother know, what a one should be borne or bredd of them. And the rod of thy Christ, the gouernement of thy onelie sonne,

Childerne
are Gods
more than
of their
parents.

did teache and instruct her in a faithfull house, a good
member of thy Churche. Neither did she so much commend the diligence of her mother in bringing her vp, as
4 the care and industrie of a certaine olde woman thy
seruant, who had sometime carried her father in her
armes, as vsuallie bigge wenches are wonte to beare
children aboute the house. For which cause, as also for
8 her olde age, but speciallie for her excellent good conditions and manners in a christian house, she was honoured *Her Gouer-*
of the maisters thereof. Wherefore she had the charge of *nesse.*
her maisters daughters to teache and gouerne them; which
12 she performed diligentlie, for she was (when neede required)
throughe holie seueritie vehement in correcting them, and
sober and prudent to instruct and teache them. For besides
those howres, when they fedd at their parents table, which
16 also was verie moderate, she permitted them not to drinke,
no not water, allthoughe they had beene verie thirstie,
thereby bewaring to breede an ill custome, and adding
withall wholsome exhortation, saying: 'You now drinke *Temperance*
20 water, bicause you haue not wine in *your* power, but when *in childe-*
you shall haue husbands, and be mistresses of pantrie and *hood.*
buttrie, water will be then vile vnto you, but the custome
of drinking will preuaile, and continue': With this reason
24 of persuasion and authoritie of commanding, did she bridle
the greedinesse of yong yeares, and framed the thirstines
of the maydes to an honest fashion, so that at length they
desired not that which was not decent. Notwithstanding
28 there crept on her, as she thy seruant tolde me her sonne,
there stole vpon her, loue of wine: For where-as she was
assigned vsuallie by her parents, to draw the wine, being
reputed by them a sober and abstinent mayden, at first she *A secret ill*
32 began to sippe onelie of the pott wherewith she filled the *custome.*
flagon, sense not abyding much after her good custome of
abstinence aforesayd, and she dooing so not of dronken
desire, but of youthes superfluous excesse, which boileth
36 with wanton motions, and is wont to be repressed with the

weight and grauitie of elders. She then daylie adding litle to litle, not considering that he that despiseth small things, dooth by degrees fall, slipped into such a custome, that soone she could suppe vp allmoste a full cuppe of wine, and that with delight. / Where was then the sage mistresse? Where the vehement prohibition? Was there any prouidence or remedie against a secret sore, vnlesse thy medicine Lorde did watch ouer vs? In the father, mother, and gouernesse their absence, thou Lord wast present, who art creator and caller, who also by men rulers doost worke much good for the health of soules. What didst thou then my Lord and god? How didst thou cure her, how didst thou heale her? Didst not thou produce a hard and sharpe reproche out of an other soule, as it were a Surgeons iron out of thy secret prouisions and at one blow didst cutt of that rottennes? For an other mayd which vsed to accompany her, when she went for wine, falling out one day with this her yong mistresse, as it often befalleth, being both alone vpbrayded her with this vice, calling her with bitter insultation, 'winebibber.' She being striken with this sting, beheld her owne foulenesse, and withall presentlie condemneth her owne faulte, and casteth it cleane from her: So that as flattering friends do often peruert, so enemies chyding dooth often correct; and yet thou rewardest in them, not that which thou workest by them, but what themsellues would; for she being angrie desired to afflict her yong mistresse, not to heale her, and therefore in secret; either for that so it happened time and place to finde them, or leste perhaps she herself might haue beene indangered, for so late bewraying the fault, if it had beene heard by their elders. /

But thou Lord ruler of heauen and earth turning to thy vses, the depth of the brooke, and ordering fittlie the turbulent waues of this worlde, didst likewise by the furie of one soule heale an other; that none marking this may

God onelie can cure secret vices, as he onelie seeth them.

God vseth but rewardeth not things proceeding from vs, yet not intended or willed.

attribute it to his owne power, if by his speach to one, an
other than whome he intended be corrected therewith. She [Cap. 9.]
being therefore bredd vp chastelie and soberlie, and rather
4 by thee made obedient to her parents, than made subiect
by them to thee, being full ripe for mariage, and matched
with a husband, she serued him as her Lord, and endeuoured *Her vertue in mariage and zeale to saue her husbands soule.*
with all diligence to gayne him vnto thee, preaching thee
8 to him by manners, wherewith thou hadst made her
beautifull, amiable, and admirable to her husband. And
in such manner did she beare the iniuries of mariage- *How patient and wise in bearing the tribulat'ons of matrimonie*
bed, that for any such matter she neuer had brable
12 or strife with her husband: For she did expect thy
mercie vpon him, that beleeuing in thee he might be
chastified and made chaste. And as he was for kyndenesse
and beneuolence inferiour to few, so for anger he was
16 verie hotte : but she knew not to resist her angrie husband,
neither with worke nor word, and when he was calme and
quiet, spying oportunitie, she rendered him a reason of her
fact, when he chanced to be inconsideratelie offended.
20 Farther when many matrones, whereof some[1] were verie [[1] lat. quarum viri.]
meeke and quiet, bare on them the markes of stripes, and
ware a blacke or blew badge in their face, in priuate and
friendlie talke they would complayn of their husbands life
24 and demeanure, she as it were merilie would correct their
speache, telling them, that since that time, they had heard *Her counsell to wiues that had curst husbands.*
recited the tables or Indentures of mariage, they should
repute themselues by those instruments, to haue beene
28 made handmaydes : wherefore they should be myndefull of
their condition, and not to waxe proude toward their
Lordes. And when they meruailed, that neuer any heard,
nor by any signe it could appeare that PATRICIUS had
32 beaten his wife, or that they had disagreed any one day for
any domesticall contention, knowing that she had a verie
fierce husband, and demanding of her familiarlie the cause
thereof, she tolde them the manner of her behauiour, as is
36 sayd ; And they that obserued her fashion did congratulate

her good experience; they that did not, were vexed with forceible subiection. She so ouercame her mother in law with dutifullnes, which had bene incensed against her by tale-carrying maydes of the house, and perseuered so patient and meeke, that her mother in lawe of her owne accord, reuealed to her sonne those that brought her the tales, whereupon she had beene offended with his wife MONICA, and required him to reuenge himself on them. Therefore he obeying his mother, and to shew his care of the discipline of his familie, and to establish concorde in his house, after he had corrected them, yet at the arbiterment of the bewrayer his mother; she promised them all the like reward at her handes, that should afterward bring her any ill speeche of her daughter in law, thinking to purchase themselues fauour at her handes by such tales: so that thenceforward none daring to doe the like, they liued in memorable sweetnes of good will together. This greate gift also didst thou my god and my mercie bestow on this thy handmayde, in whose wombe thou createdst me, that whomesoeuer she knew to be at variance and discording, so much did she studie to make peace where she coulde, that hearing of both partes verie bitter speaches of each other, such as swelling and vndigested discord is wont to belke oute, when to his friend cruell hatred doth breathe out sowre language of his absent enemy, she notwithstanding would neuer reueale the ones speeches to the other, vnlesse it were such as might farder the meanes of their reconcilement to eache other. This qualitie might seeme small to me, vnlesse with griefe I had tried innumerable multitudes, I know not with what horrible pestilence of sinnes spreading it self verie wide, so to be infected, that they doe not content themselues to reueale the speeches of angrie enemies to the others like angrie, but they will add more of their owne: whereas contrariwise to a humane, friendlie, and mercifull mynde, it should not suffice not to increase enmities of men by ill report, vnlesse by good speeches, he studie cleane to ex-

She ouercometh vniust anger with goodnes.

Her desire to make peace and wisedome therein.

marke the horriblenes of talecarying or susurration.

tinguish them, as she did by thy internall teaching in the
schoole of her brest. Moreouer her husband did she gayne — She gayned her husband
vnto thee, in the end of his temporall life, neither did she — to God.
4 bewaile that in him now a faithfull man, which she had
tolerated before in him not beleeuing. She was also the
seruant of thy seruants, for what seruant of thine knew — Her humilitie and holie
her, that did not praise, honour, and loue thee in her, — conuersation.
8 feeling thy presence in her hart, the fruites of her holie
conuersation being witnesses thereof. She was the wife of
one husband, she had yielded mutuall dutie to her parents :
she had gouerned her house religiouslie, she had testimonie
12 in good workes, she had bred vp her children, whome so
often she bare againe with greate paine, as she beheld them — Her greate spirituall
to stray from thee. For thou didst send thy hand from — griefe at her childrens ill
aboue my Lord god, and didst heale my soule out of the — doing. [lib. 3
16 deepe darknes of the errour of the MANICHEES, when my — cap. 11.]
mother did weepe for me to thee, more than mothers bewaile
their corporall corses and dead children : for she by thy
faith and spirit receyued from thee, beheld my death, and
20 thou didst heare her, not despising her teares, which flowed — Her abundant tearcs
so plentifullie, that they watered the earth in euerie place, — for her sonne
where she prayed to thee, and thou didst heare her for me. — Austine.
For whence was that dreame wherewith thou didst comfort — A vision
24 her, so that she beleeued that she did lyue with me, and — S!. Augustine doubteth
that I had one table with her in the same house, which she — not to call it of God.
had now refused to haue with me, flying and detesting the — She would not dwell
blasphemies of my errour. For she saw herself standing on — nor eate with her
28 a lynnen rule and a beautifull yong man comming with — blasphemous sonne.
merrie countenance to her, who smyling to him self, while
she was weeping and sadd, asked of her the cause of her
sorrowe, and so daylie weeping : which he did not so much
32 to learne himself, as to instruct her. She answering that
she so sorrowed for the perdition of my soule her sonne ; he
to make her secure, bad her beholde and see, 'where she was,
there I also was' ; which when she had beheld, she seeth
36 me standing by her on the same rule. How could this be

vnlesse thy cares were attentiue to her hart ! O thou God allmightie that so doost care for euerie one, as if thou hadst care of him onelie, and so all, as euerie one. And whence came this also, that when she had related to me what she had seene, and I endeuoured to draw it to that sense, that she should not despayre, but that she should be in time as I was then, she presentlie without staying answereth; 'No not so, for it was not sayd to me, where he is, there thou, but where thou art there he.' I confesse vnto thee my Lord, what I remember, and which often I haue tolde others, that I was more moued at this answer of thine, giuen by my vigilant mother, seeing her nothing troubled at the apparant and mere falshood of my interpretation, and how redily she espied that which indeede was to be considered, and which my self before she had spoken it did not marke; and so hereat (I say) was I more touched than at the dreame it self; wherein to the godlie woman was foretolde ioy so long after to ensue, to the comfort of her present sorrowe: For there followed allmoste nyne whole yeares, after all which time I still wallowed in the mire of my profunditie and in the darknes of falshood: albeit I often endeuoured to arise in the meane tyme, yet fell backe againe with greate bruising; when that chaste religious and sober widdow, such as thou louest, althoughe in hope she was more reuyued, yet in weeping and wayling nothing relented, neuer ceasing when she prayed to weepe to thee for me; and her prayers entred before thee, yet thou permittest me to wallow and to be ouerwhelmed in the mist. And moreouer thou gauest her an other answer, which I remember; allthoughe I passe ouer many things, hastening to those, which vrge me more to confesse, and I forget many. /

Thou gauest I say, an other answer by thy priest, a certayne bishop brought vp in thy Church, and excercised in thy bookes; whome when she on a time requested, that he would vouchsafe to talke with me, and refell my

errours, to vnteache me my euill, and to teache me good
(which she still vsed, when she found any fitt thereto) he
would not, and indeede verie wiselie as I perceyued after-
4 wards: For he answered her, that as yet I was not docill,
or fitt to be taught; bicause that I was puffed vp with the
noueltie of my heresie: She replied and tolde him, that I
had vexed many vnskillfull persons, with certaine questions:
8 He answered, 'let him alone as he is, and onelie beseeche our
Lord for him, for he by reading shall by himself finde his
errour, and how greate impietie he maynteyneth.' He added
more that himself being a Childe was by his seduced mother
12 deliuered to the MANICHES to be taught, with whome not
onelie he had readd allmoste all their bookes, but also had
coppied them forth; not withstanding by himself, none disputing against him, or conuincing him of errour, to haue
16 discerned the fowlenes of that sect, and to haue forsaken
it: Which when he had spoken, and she yet would not
leaue him, but intreating him and weeping bitterlie, be-
sought him to see me, and to dispute with me, he somewhat [¹ lat. ita vivas.]
20 offended with her importunitie; 'goe your wayes, sayth he, An heretik would deride
and lyue so,¹ for it can not be that a childe of so many S! Aug. and Monica for
teares should perishe': Which wordes (as in priuate talke making ac-
she often tolde me after) she receyued, as thoughe, he had that former dreme or this
24 spoken from heauen. speach.

Thou wroughtest also with me Lord, that some should Lib: 5: [Cap. 6]
persuade me to goe to ROME, and rather to teache there Confes:
that which I taught at CARTHAGE; and the cause why I was
28 persuaded hereto, I will not let passe to confesse vnto thee,
for that herein thy deepe counsailes, and moste present
mercie towards vs, is to be considered and commended. I
went not to ROME in hope of greater gayne, or greater
32 preferment, which my friends that persuaded me thereto,
had proposed, albeit these things did also mooue my mynde,
but the cheefest cause was for that I vnderstood, that
Students there were more quiet and orderlie, not rushing
36 malepertlie and violentlie into the schoole of the maister

(which they heard not) withoute his leaue, better than at CARTHAGE, where the licence of schollers was foule and intemperate, they pressing in impudentlie, and allmoste with furious forhead, perturbing the order prescribed by the maister to his Auditors: Many iniurious trickes committ they with meruailous blockishnes, and worthy of punishment, vnlesse custome did patronise and seeme to allow thereof; therein shewing themselues moste miserable, in that they doe euill, and yet deeme it lawfull, which indeede shall neuer be approued or allowed of thy eternall law. And they thinke themselues not punishable therefore, when they are punished with the verie blyndenes of such vsage, and so endure incomparablie worse, than they doe whome they so vex. I therefore did then indure perforce in others such ill manners, being now a teacher, which I would not acknowledge and amend in my self, when I was a scholler: which to auoide, I remoued thither, where I was assured no such vnrulinesse to be practised. But thou my hope and my portion in the land of the lyuing, for the sauing of my soule, didst at CARTHAGE putt spurres to me to hale me thence, and didst shew me allurements at ROME to draw me thither. And all this didst thou by men, who loued this dead life, heere committing madd prankes, and there promising vaine things, whose peruersnes, as also myne, thou didst vse with secret wisedome, to the correction of my pathes; for both those that disturbed my studies, were blynde with ouglie woodnes, and those that inuited me otherwhere did taste nothing but earth, and I who detested heere true miserie, did also desire there false felicitie. But why I departed hence and went thither, thou my god, well vnderstoodest, and yet didst not tell me, neither my mother, who lamented maynlie my departure, and who followed me vnto the sea side: but I beguiled her, forceiblie staying me, to the end either she might change my minde or at leste go with me: And I feyned my self so friendly to her, that I would not forsake her till the wynde serued,[1]

Whose moste miserable.

Blindnes in euill the che fe punishment.

Gods secret wisedome in working.

[1 lat.: et finxi me amicum nolle deserere donec vento furto nauigaret.]

when I lied to her, althoughe so rare a mother, and away
went I from her, and passed safe, bicause thou mercifullie
didst spare me, keeping me from the waters of the sea,
4 althoughe I was full of execrable filthines, vnto the waters   Baptisme the waters
of thy grace, wherein I being washed and cleansed, the   of grace do cleanse
flouds of my mothers teares might be dried vp, wherewith   sinne.
she watered the earth vnder her daylie for me; who refusing
8 to retourne home without me, I could hardlie persuade to
stay one night at the memorie of blessed CYPRIAN, which   The memorie of S!
was neere our shippe: That night did I slippe from her,   Cyprian
sayling on my iournie, and she remayned behinde praying   where Monica
12 and weeping. And what did she request of thee my God,   prayd.
with so many teares, but that thou wouldest not suffer me
to saile thence? But thou deepelie prouyding, and hearing
the hinge or principall weight of her desire, didst not
16 respect what she then asked, that thou mightst bring to
passe that which she allwayes wished. The windes blew
and filled our sailes, and carried the shore out of our sighte:
That morning was she mad, filling thine eares, with griefe,
20 complaynt and lamentation, which thou contemnedst, haling
me by my desires to fullfill them, and beating that carnall
desire of hers with the iust whip of sorrowe. For she
loued my presence as mothers vse, and much more than
24 many doe, litle knowing what ioye thou wast in working
her by my absence, and bicause she knew not, therefore
she wept and cried, and in those perturbations she prooued
her self of the reliques of EUE, when she sought with
28 sorrow which she had borne with griefe./ And yet after
that she had accused my treacherie and crueltie, tourning
her againe to beseeche thee for me, she retourned to her
home, and I went on to ROME. And beholde there am I   [Cap. 9.]
32 apprehended by the whip of corporall sicknes, and so
hastened towards hell, bearing all my sinnes with me,
which I had committed against thee, my self, or others,
which were many and greeuous, ouer and aboue the band of
36 originall sinne, whereby we all dye in Adam; for thou

haddest not yet pardoned any of them in Christ, neither had he (according to my errour) dissolued in his flesh the enmitie, which I had incurred by my sinnes. For how shouldest thou lose and vndoe it by fantasticall suffering 4 on the Crosse onelie, which I did beleeue of thy sonne; so that how false then did seeme vnto me the death of the flesh, so trulie was my soule indeede dead; And looke how true and certaine, the death of Christs flesh was, so false 8

Impenitent sinners by sicknes hasten towards he.l. was the life of my soule not beleeuing it. Thus my feuers increasing, I went forward towards death and perdition; for whither els should I then haue gone, if I had dyed, but into the fire and torments due to my desertes, by the 12 veritie of thy iust order. And this did she litle imagine; yet for me did she pray absent; but thou weart allwayes present, hearing her where she was, and shewing mercie to me where I was; so that I recouered the health of my 16 bodie, albeit I remayned mad in sacrilegious soule. For then did not I desire thy baptisme, allthoughe in such danger, and better was I being an infant, when I (in a

[Confes. 1. 11] sorte) did craue it in my mothers pietie, as I haue confessed; 20 but now had I growne in shamefullnes, and did deride the counsaile of thy medicine, of madnes; albeit thou didst licence me to escape double death: With which wounde if my mothers hart had beene stroken, she had neuer re- 24 couered it. For I can not sufficientlie expresse her mynde

She bore her sonne Augustin in spirit with greater griefe than first in bodie. towards me, who bare me now in spirit with greater care and griefe, than she had donne my bodie in fleshe. Wherefore I see not how she could haue endured it, if my death 28 in that state had pierced the bowells of her loue; and where had beene then, her so many prayers without intermission, but with thee! Couldest thou god of mercies despise the contrite and humble hart of that chaste and 32

Wayting on Saints. Hearing of Masse daylie. sober widdow, multiplying almes-deedes, seruing and wayting on thy Saintes, and omitting no day the oblation and sacrifice at the Altar; visiting thy church daylie twice, morning and euening without any intermission, not to talke 36

there of vaine toyes or olde wyues deuises, but to heare
thee in thy speaches, and to be heard of thee in her
prayers. Couldest thou neglect such a ones teares, or
4 repell such a one from thy helpe, whom by thy grace thou
hadst made so good? and who asked of thee not golde and
siluer, nor any mutable and transitorie thing, but the
saluation of her childes soule? No Lord, rather wast thou
8 then present, and didst worke for her, yet in that manner
and order as thou hadst predestinated to be donne. God
forbid thou shouldst deceyue her in those visions and
answers of thine, which I haue rehearsed, and others which
12 I haue omitted, which she still conserued in faithfull brest,
and euer praying did suggest vnto thee, as thy handwrittes; for bicause thy mercies are eternall and endlesse,
thou vouchsafest to such to become debter by thy
16 promises, to whome thou remittest all their sinnes.
Thou didst recouer me from that sicknes, and didst saue
the childe of thy handmayd then in bodie, that he might
lyue and be capable afterward of thy greater and more
20 certayne saluation of soule. O my hope from my youth, [Lib.6,sap.1]
where wast thou, and where didst thou decline from me?
hadst not thou made me, and seuered me from fowre
footed beastes and birdes of the ayer: thou madest me
24 wiser, than they, and capable of true wisedome, yet I walked
in darknes and slipperie wayes. I sought thee withoute Lib: 6: c: 1.
me, and could not fynde thee God of my hart. I had now
descended into the bottome of the sea of errour, and did
28 distrust and despayer of euer fyndinge the truthe, when my S. Augus-
mother strong in pietie came vnto me, following after me tine de-
by land and sea, still secure of thee and thy promise, in spayreth to
whatsoeuer perills she passed: For in dangers on the sea, truthe.
32 she comforted the shipmen themselues, who vsuallie are
wont to cheere fresh water passengers, being perturbed
therewith, promising them safe arriuall, for that thou See her fnith
hadst promised her this by vision. Comming then she of those
36 fyndeth me allmoste despayring to fynde out thy truthe;

FEMALE SAINTS. K

Margin notes:
See S. Aug.
calleth the
aforesayd
dreames,
visions and
diuine.

which when I had intimated to her, declaring that I was now neither MANICHEE nor CATHOLIKE, she did not leape for ioy thereat, as if she had heard an euent vnlooked for; but allreadie secure in parte of release of my miserie, so dooth she now bewaile me dead, as neere to be raised vp to thee : wherefore on the beere of her cogitation, she carieth me out before thee, that thou mightest say to the sonne of the widow, *Yong man, I say vnto thee, Arise;* and so he mighte reuiue and beginne to speake, and thou then giue him to his mother. Her hart therefore did not exult with any turbulent ioye, hearing so much to be wrought of that she wept for, that I now was freed of my falshoode, althoughe I had not obtayned the truthe: nay rather bicause she was without doubte that thou wouldest performe and perfect which was wanting, whereas thou hadst promised the wholle: moste quietlie and in hart confidentlie, she answered me, that she hoped in Christ, that before she departed this life, she should see me a faythfull Catholike. And this did she to me. But to thee Lord, fountaine of mercies, did she offer more thicke prayers, and plentifull teares, that thou wouldest accelerate thy helpe, and illuminate my darknes, that I mighte (!) more studiouslie runne to the Church, and there be suspended at the mouth of AMBROSE, to sucke the mounting waters into life euerlasting: For she loued that man as the Angell of God, knowing that by him I was brought to that staggering, wherein I was, hoping verilie thereby, and thereto concurring this new fitt and sharpe perill, as it were a criticall accesse of my sicke humour or ague, that I would passe throughe from sicknes to health. She one day visiting the memories or reliques of the Saintes, and bringing with her thither meate and wine, as she had vsed in AFRIKE, the dorekeeper not permitting her to enter therewith, when she vnderstood that the Bishop AMBROSE had so prohibited, so religiouslie, and obedientlie did she yield and submitte herself, that I meruailed thereat, to see her more easilie

Marginal notes:
S: Ambrose chcefflie brought Augustine from his Manicheisme heresie.

[Cap. 2.]
She visited holie Saints reliques or bodies.
This vse of bringing meates to Saints sepulchers was begun to releeue the

to accept of his prohibition, than to defend her custome; yea rather to forgoe it, than to dispute or contradict AMBROSES commandement. For she was not possessed with
4 the loue of wine, neither did such delight spurre her to the hatred of truthe, as it dooth many men and women, who as much lothe the song of sobrietie, as bibbing folke, doe loathe watered wine. But she when she had brought her
8 litle basket fraight with her solemne meates to be tasted by her self, and to be bestowed on others, on her self she bestowed onelie a litle supping or drinke, soberlie tempered, whence she could hardlie be incensed. And albeit there
12 were sondrie memories of the dead, which seemed worthie to be honoured in that manner, to weete sondrie places with sundrie messes, yet she caried one aboute all, both watered well and key colde (!) : Which she tasted and destributed to
16 those that did accompanie her, for she sought for pietie, not for pleasure therein. Wherefore learning that it was the will of thy worthie preacher and prelate of pietie, AMBROSE, that none should any more vse that fashion,
20 were they neuer so sober therein, fearing that by it any occasion of swilling and ryoting might be giuen, and withall for that this vsage seemed to resemble the funerall festiuities of the Gentills, she therefore, moste willinglie
24 abstayned, and insteede of a basket full of earthfull fruits, she learnt to bring a brest fraight with religious vowes and desires, to the memories of the martyrs, and to bestow on the poore, what she was able; And if the communication
28 of our Lords bodie was there celebrated, to participate therein, for imitation of which passion the martyrs were immolated. And[1] it seemeth to me my Lord and god, as thou best seest, that she had not so easilie forgone her
32 custome, if she had beene forbidden by an other, whome she had not loued as she did AMBROSE, whome for my saluation she honoured highlie, and whome he on the other side did much reuerence for her moste religious conuersation: for
36 that she was so feruent in spirite, therewith multiplying

poore there in the honour of the Saint : as Christians vsed in the honour of Christs mysteries...1Cor: 12; which in time people conuerting to their owne recreation, now began to be prohibited : albeit vertuous persons (as this woman) did perhaps this, that their abstinent refection might be sanctified by the Saints there

Celebrating and worshiping at the Christs bodie there communicated.

8 : bodies. [1 r. but]

K 2

goode workes, and frequenting the Churche; in so much
that often times seing me, he would burst oute into her
commendation, congratulating with me, that I had such a
mother; althoughe he knew not, what a sonne she then had   4
of me, who doubted of all those things, and despayred that
I shculd euer finde out the way of life. /

  She also once asked thy seruant and bishop AMBROSE his
counsell and sentence touching the fasting on saterday: he   8
answered that not preiudicing the customes of other churches,
she should keepe his, and should fast the Saterday while
she lyued at MILANE, and at ROME to obserue the custome
there. Afterwards I hauing receiued, the grace of thy   12
Baptisme thou that makest men of one mynde to dwell in
one house together, didst consociate and ioyne vnto me
besides others EUODIUS a yong man, being borne in the
same towne with me, who hauing beene a souldiour, was   16
conuerted to thee, and baptised too before me, and more
now forgoing his temporall warfareing girdeth and armeth
himself to thine. We were together and dwelt together,
and with holie consent did seeke what place might fitt vs   20
best, and seruing thee together retourned into AFRICA. In
the way coming to OSTIA at the mouthe of TIBER, there
dooth my mother dye; But first Lord, to vs all thy seruants,
through thy gift that speake vnto thee, and who before her   24
death were vnited in one consociation to thee, so did she
serue, as if we had beene all her fathers, such care had she
of vs, as if she had beene all our mothers.

  I disputing one day of order and gods prouidence, with   28
LICENTIUS, TRIGETUS, ZENOBIUS and others, she commeth in;
who vnderstanding the question, demandeth how far we had
proceeded; Whose comming in and demande when I had
after our manner commanded to be written, as other   32
speaches and discourses were: 'What meane you (sayth she)
did you euer reade in your bookes, that women were
brought into these kinde of disputacions?' I answered, 'yea:
with our auncestors, women had disputed and playd the   36

Side notes:
Fast on Saterday.
Epist: 112 (86).
Lib: 9: Confes. [cap. 8]
Baptisme giueth grace.
[Cap. 9, and]
Her humble seruice of Augustine and his holie fellowes.
Lib: 1: de ordine[cp. 11]

philosophers, and that¹ philosophie pleaseth me much; for [¹ r. thy]
that you may vnderstand, this greeke word PHILOSOPHIA in
latine signifieth the loue of wisedome. Whereupon the
4 diuine scriptures which you greatlie embrace, doe not
vniuersallie or absolutely command philosophers to be
auoyded and derided, but the philosophers of this worlde:
And that there is an other worlde farre distant from our
8 sight, and which the vnderstanding of a few sounde heads
doe discerne, Christ himself dooth sufficientlie signifye,
saying: *My kingdome is not of this worlde:* he dooth not
say, my kingdome is not of the worlde, but not of this
12 visible worlde. And whosoeuer thinketh all philosophie to So say heretiks
be eschewed, will nothing els, but not to loue wisedome. vpon ca: 2:
I should therefore contemne you in this my writing, if you ad Colos.
were not a louer of wisedome: but I might not despise you,
16 albeit you did but meanelie loue it, much lesse if you loued
it, as much as I doe: But whereas you loue it more than
me, whome I know how greatlie you loue, nay seeing that
you haue so profited therein, that not the feare of any
20 misfortune, nor the horrour of death, which to men moste
learned is wont to be difficult, can terrifie you, w*hi*ch all
confesse to be the toppe of philosophie, can I with reason,
not admitte you, amongst the students and professors of
24 philosophie ?' Hereat she mildelie and religiouslie answering that I neuer had tolde such a lie, and we perceyuing our
selues to haue spoken and written much, to the iust
quantitie of a booke, our wryting tables also fayling, and
28 somewhat also to ease my stomacke, it was thought good to
deferre the question. /

Not long before we were at MILANE, this Church, began Lib: 9: c: 7:
to celebrate this kinde of consolation and exhortation; to vsque ad: 13:
32 weete of singing together with voices and harts: For a
yeare before or litle more, when IUSTINA, mother to VALEN-
TINIAN the Emperour, yet a childe, did persecute thy seruant
AMBROSE for the loue of the Arrian heresie, wherewith
36 she was seduced, thy religious people did watche in the Vigils of olds.

Church being readie to dye, with their bishop thy seruant. There was likewise my mother, thy handmayd, bearing a cheefe part in this care and watchings, and lyuing by prayer. I yet colde from thy spirite, was notwithstanding troubled, the Cittie being so amazed and perplexed: Then was it appointed, that like as the Churches of the East vsed, so their hymnes and psalmes should be song, that the people mighte not throughe tediousnes of griefe faynte and be dismayed. From which time that vse hath beene continued to this day, many churches, yea almoste all thy flockes throughe the worlde imitating the same. Then diddest thou lord, shew by a vision to thy bishop, in what place the bodies of thy martyrs PROTASIUS and GERUASIUS lay; which so many yeares thou hadst shutte vp and conserued incorrupt, in the treasure of thy secret: whence thou mightest when oportunitie required, bring them forth to represse the womanish furie of the Empresse: For when they were reuealed, and being taken vp were translated with due honour to AMBROSES churche; not onelie possessed persons were deliuered, the diuells confessing, but also a blynde man, and a cittisen, that had beene so many yeares knowen to the whole Cittie, hearing the tumultuous exultation of the people, and enquiring the cause; that knowen, he leapeth vp, and willeth his leader to bring him to the bodies; whither when he was broughte, he requested and obtayned to be admitted so neere, as that he might with his handkerchife touch the beare of thy Saintes, whose death is precious in thy sighte; which when he had donne, and had putt it to his eyes, they presentlie are opened. Thereat runneth aboute the fame thereof; thereat issue out thy feruent and glittering praises; thereat the mynde of the Aduersarie woman, was stayed from her persecuting furie, althoughe not plyant to be cured therewith. Thankes be to thee my god; whence and whither hast thou ledd my memorie O Lorde, that I should confesse these things, and forgett greater matters; and for

all this, when the sweete odour of thy spirituall oyntments *Spirituall benefits:*
did so smell, yet did not I runne after thee, and therefore *Spirituall oyntments.*
did I more aboundantlie weepe, amidst the Canticles of
4 those thy hymnes: first gaping and gasping for breath to
thee, and at last breathing out after thee, as much as my
poore litle breath could afforde from my house of haye. /

But I being by thy grace come home to thy Churche,
8 and therein proceeding towards thee our eternall home in
heauen, we retourning to our natiue soile, to fix our tents
before thee and for thee, my mother in the way is taken
away from vs to thee: And being at OSTIA, her day *Of her death.*
12 approching when she was to departe, this life vnknowen to *[Cap. 10.]*
vs, but foreseene by thee; It happened by thy procurement but by secret wayes of thine, that I and shee stood
one day leaning, at a certayne windowe which looked into
16 a garden of the house where we lodged; being there alone
and remote from companie, after the labour of a long
iourney, we now repayred and restored our strength against
our passage ouer the sea: We talked heere moste sweetlie,
20 and forgetting things past, and extending our selues
towards the things to come, we soughte betweene vs,
before the present truth which thou art Lord, what a life
that eternall life of Saints is to be, which neither eye hath
24 beheld, or eare heard, nor hart conceiued, and we gaped
with the mouth of our hart at the supernall waters of the
fountaine of life, which is with thee, that being sprinkled
therewith, as we were capable thereof, we might in some
28 sorte conceiue it. And when our speeche proceeded
forward to that end, so that the delighte of carnall senses,
were it neuer so greate or corporallie cleare, in respect of
the ioye of that life, was not onelie vnworthie of com-
32 parison therewith, but of naming also; and ascending
higher with more ardent affection, to that which is allwayes one and immuteable, we mounte by degrees aboue
all corporall things, yea aboue the heauen whence the
36 sunne and moone, and starres send forth their light vpon

the face of the earth. And soaring higher by thinking
and talking of thee, and admiring thy workes, we come
to consider the excellent nature of our myndes, which yet
leauing beneathe vs, we passed farther, hoping to attayne   4
to the region of indeficient aboundance, where thou feedest
ISRAEL with the foode of truthe for euer, and where wisedome is life, by which wisedome all these things were
made, and all that hath beene or shallbe, it self not being   8
made, but still remayning as it was, and so euer shall be, or
rather wanting 'was' or 'shallbe,' hath onelie 'is'; bicause
it is eternall: for 'was,' and 'shallbe' are not eternall. And
while we thus common and gape hereat, we did touch it 12
a litle, with the whole force of our hart, and sighed and
left the first fruites of our spirite there tyed, and retourned
to the noyse of our mouthe, talking againe with wordes
which haue beginning and end: and what is like to thy 16
worde, O Lord, allway lasting without oldenes, and
renewing all things. We sayed therefore, if the tumult
or trouble of flesh must be silent (before any), let likewise
the fansies or representations of earth, water, and ayer be 20
silent; yea the Poles, and the soule it self let it be hushe:
But ascending beyond it self not thinking of it self, let
dreames moreouer, and imaginarie reuelations, euerie
tongue and signe, and whatsoeuer is made (by any inno- 24
uation or mutation) be silent: for if you listen what they
say, you shall heare them speake thus, all these things;
'We made not our selues, but he made vs, who abideth one,
eternallie:' This being spoken, if more they dare not, but 28
are silent, for that they haue erected their eare to heare
him speake onelie that made them; and if he speake alone,
not by them his creatures, but by himself, to the end we
may heare his worde, not by a carnall tongue, nor by the 32
voice of an Angell, neither by the sounde of a cloude,
neither by the obscure signification of a similitude, but
by himself whome we loue in these, let vs then heare him
without these, as we now extend our selues: and with 36

swift cogitation not staying there, doe touch the eternall wisedome lasting aboue all things: O that this might continue, and that other visions and sightes of inferiour kynde mighte be withdrawen: so that this one mighte carrie vs, and swallow vs vp, and hide vs beholders, within the interiour and inward ioyes, that our life for euer might be like to this moment of vnderstanding, after which wo sighed. Is not this, that: *Enter into the ioyes of thy Lords.* And when shall this be? Perhaps when all we shall arise: but yet all shall not then be changed, (to weete into impassibilitie and glorie). We talked thus, if not in this manner and with these verie wordes: Thou Lord knowest, that when we talked such things, this worlde with all his delightes became vile in our sighte and sense. Then sayd she; 'Sonne for my parte, I am delighted with nothing in this life, What shall I lyue longer, why doe I remaine heere? I know not; the hope of this worlde being cleane spent within me. One onelie thing was there here-tofore, for which I desired to stay a while, which was that I might see thee a Catholike Christian, before I died: which now God hath granted me with aduantage, hauing brought to passe that I see thee (all earthlie felicitie despised by thee) to be his seruant: What then make I longer in this worlde?' What I answered her to this at that time, I doe not now perfectlie remember: Within few dayes after, she fell sicke of an ague: And while she lay thus sicke, one day she fell into a swounde or traunce: She being thus from her sense of these present things, we come runne aboute her; and retourning quicklie to her self againe, she looketh at me and my brother, and speaketh in manner of demanding thus, 'Where was I?' And seeing vs striken with griefe; 'You shall (sayth she) lay your mother heere.' I held my peace and repressed my teares: My brother sayd some thing to her, wherewith he seemed to wishe and hope, as more happie, that she mighte dye in her owne contrie and not abrode; which when she heard, looking

Her speach:

See the name of Catholike peculiar to the faithfull onelie: other names to others: as Christian; Manichee: etc.

[Cap. 11.]

See Saints litle care of their bodie, buriall, and, Contrie.

at him with a sterne countenance, for that in mynde he tasted such things, she forthwith tourneth her eye to me and sayeth, 'See what he sayeth': And then to vs bothe, 'Lay this bodie (sayeth she) wheresoeuer you list: let no care thereof troble you, onelie this I request of you, That at the Altar of our Lord, wheresoeuer you be, you doe remember me:' Which when she had sayd the best she coulde, she was silent and the disease increasing, she was more exercised. And I considering thy gifts my god inuisible, which thou puttest into the harts of thy faithfull, and whence proceede admirable fruites, reioyced thereat, and gaue thankes vnto thee, remembering what before I knew of her, to weete, with what care she allwayes desired, to be buried by her husband, for which cause she had prouided and prepared her sepulcher there: For hauing lyued with him verie peaceablie and quietlie, her will and desire was (such is the mynde of man lesse capable of diuine things) to haue this addition to her felicitie, and to be remembered of men, that it might be granted her after her pilgrimage ouer the sea, both bodies of her self and her deere husband to be interred together. But when this inanitie or vanitie first began to leaue her harte, throughe the greatnes of thy bountie, I knew not: yet now reioyced I and admired that she was thus disposed; althoughe in that speache of hers with me at the window, when she sayd, 'what doe I heere in this worlde,' she seemed not to desire that her olde wishe, to dye in her contrie. I heard also afterward, how that she being at OSTIA, with certayne of my friends, I being absent, of her motherlie confidence one day discoursed of the contempt of this life, and of the commoditie of death. Whereat they admiring the vertue of the woman which thou hadst giuen her, and asking her if she were not afeard, to leaue her bodie so farre from her Contrie? 'Nothing (sayeth she) is farre from god, neither may I iustlie feare, but that he will knowe what is myne at the later day to raise it to life.' /

The ninthe day then of her sicknes, and the fiftie and sixth yeare of her age, and the thirtie three of myne, did that vertuous and religious soule leaue her bodie. I closed her eyes, and aboundant sorrow ouerwhelmed my hart strings: so that it burst oute into teares; yet there also did myne eyes, throughe the forceible commandment of my mynde drinke and drie vp their owne teares, with which conflict I was much payned. When she gaue vp her ghoste, my boye ADEODATUS, cried playne oute, but being reproued by all vs, he held his peace;…Neither did we thinke it decent, to celebrate that funerall with weeping complaynts; for that with such vses, the miserie of them that dye is to be bewayled, or their death as vtter destruction to be lamented. But she neither dyed miserablie, neither dyed at all; which we beleeue for the greate documents and exemplar forme of her manners, for her faith vnfeyned and other certayne reasons. And what was that which wrought me so greate griefe within me, but this new wounde made by this sodaine breache of our sweete and deere conuersation with eache other. I tooke some comfort of her testimonie, that being pleased with my attendance on her, and dutifullnes in her sicknes, she called me good and kinde childe, and she testified with greate affection of loue, that she neuer heard fall from my mouthe, any roughe and contumelious speache. But what was that my god, my maker, what dutie or honour donne her by me, was comparable to her seruice and care taken for me? Being berefte of so greate a comfort, my soule was wounded, and my life, which was in a manner composed of hers and myne owne, was by this separation torne in twoo. We hauing stilled the childe ADEODATUS, EUODIUS opened the psalter, and began to sing the Psalme *Misericordiam et iudicium cantabo tibi Domine* etc.: to which all we in the house answered; which being heard, many brethren and religious women came together to vs, and while those did dresse the corse to whome it appertayned, I going into a conuenient roome by, with those that remayned with me, did dispute and discourse of such things as I thought fitt for the time: and with that foode of truthe did I mitigate my griefe onelie knowne to thee, when others did attentiuelie listen to me, and litle thought what I felt; yea imagined me to haue no feeling of griefe: but I in thy hearing, where no man was, did reprooue my ouersoft hart, and did bridle the headines of my sorrowe, which yielded a litle, but breaking out afreshe, althoughe not into teares or change of countenance, I knew well what I repressed within my hart: And bicause it greeued me much that humane affections were so potent within me, which notwithstanding by course, order and debt of our condition must needes happen, with one griefe did I grieue at the other, and so with double affliction was it wasted. / When the bodie was caried forth, we goe with it, and retourne thence without teares, neither in those prayers which we powred forth vnto thee, when the SACRIFICE of our price was offered for her, The bodie standing by the sepulcher, before it was buried, as the fashion is there, in all this did I not weepe, but all the day was I within full of sorrowe, and with troubled mynde did I beseeche thee, as I was able, that thou wouldest heale my griefe, which thou diddest not, for that cause, I thinke better to commend to my memorie by this document, the band of generall custome, albeit somewhat repugning to our mynde, which is fedd now not with deceyuing wordes. I also thought it conuenient for me to goe wash my self in the bathes, for that the Greekes terme is βαλανεῖον, for that it repelleth anxietie of mynde: And I confesse vnto thy mercie, O Father of Orphans, that I washed my self; yet remayned I all one, as before, for I could not sweate out from my hart that bitternes of sorrow. Afterward I slept, and awaking thence, I felt my griefe much aswaged, and being in my bed alone, I remembered the true teaching verses of thy seruant AMBROSE, saying, *Thou God art maker of all, and ruler of the pole, Cladding the day with*

See how to strugle with naturall affections.

Masse the sacrifice of our redemption offered for the dead.

St Ambrose his verses.

*comelie lighte, with gratefull sleepe likewise the night, That
wearie bones may be refreshed, And wasted mindes redressed,
And griefe demisd that it oppressed.* Then began thy
4 handmayd afreshe to retourne to my minde, her godlie and
religious conuersation towards thee, and her mylde and
sweete behauiour towards me, which now I was bereft of;
wherefore I now listed to weepe before thee for her, and
8 touching all that of her aboute my self also, and for my
self, and I permitted my teares now to runne their pleasure,
which before I had contayned, strowing them vnder my
hart, which rested in them, for that thy eares were there
12 and not mans, who proudlie might interprete my weeping.
And now Lord I confesse to thee in my writings, reade
them that list, and interprete they as they please, and if
it were a sinne for me to weepe for my mother a litle peece
16 of an houre, being dead in my sighte, who had wept for me
many yeares, that I might liue in thy sighte, let him not
laughe at me, if he be greate in charitie let him weepe too
for my sinnes, to the father of all brethren of thy Christ.
20 But I being now cured of that wounde, whereby carnall [Cap. 13.]
affection might be reproued, doe poure oute vnto thee our
God a far different kinde of teares for her thy seruant, Prayer for the dead.
flowing from a contrite spirite, throughe consideration of See originall
24 the perills of euerie soule which dieth in Adam. Albeit sinne killeth.
she was reuiued againe in Christ, and in her life so lyued,
that thy name is lauded in her faith and manners, yet dare Baptisme
I not say that since thou didst regenerate her by baptisme, reuiueth to Christ.
28 no one worde escaped her against thy commandement; and See Saints
it was sayd by the truth thy Sonne *If any say to his brother,* feares of small sinnes, and
foole; he shall be guiltie of hell fire; and woe also to the laudable of the paine therefore in
life of men, if thou discusse and trie them withoute mercie: Purgatorie.
32 but bycause thou doest not exact faults we haue greate
confidence, that she hath founde a place of indulgence with
thee: And whosoeuer dooth number vnto thee, his true True merits
merits what dooth he but recounte thy gifts? O that men against heretiks
36 would know them selues, and that those that doe glorie albeit Gods gifts.

woulde glorie in our Lorde. I therefore, O my praise, my
life, and god of my hart, setting by a while her good acts,
for which with ioyfull hart I thanke thee, now doe I
beseeche thee for the sinnes of my mother, heare me by
the medicine of our woundes which hung on the Crosse,
who sitteth at thy righte hand and dooth intreate for vs: I
know she shewed mercie to others, and from her hart
forgaue others that had offended her, their offences, remitte
her likewise her offences and debts, if she hath incurred
any these many yeares, since the water of health, forgiue
her lorde, forgiue her, I beseech thee; enter not into
iudgement with her, let mercie ouerweighe iudgement, for
thy speaches are true, and thou hast promised mercie to
those that are mercifull; and she to be such was thy gift,
who wilt haue pittie on those whome thou pittiest, and wilt
performe mercie on whome thou hast pittie. And I beleeue
thou hast donne this allreadie, which I beseeche thee; yet
my voluntarie oblation approue good lorde; for she (her
houre of death approching) had no minde or cogitation to
couer her bodie sumptuouslie, or to be dressed with spices,
neither wished a braue toombe, or buriall in her contrie;
she commanded vs none of these, but this onelie that she
might be remembered at thy Altar at which she serued
thee (no day omitted) knowing that there the hoste or
victime was dispensed or imparted, wherewith the hand-
writing of spirituall debt, contrarie to vs was cancelled,
and wherewith our aduersarie that counteth and obiecteth
our sinnes, was lead in triumphe, seeking somewhat to
obiect against him, and fynding nothing by him [1] we ouercame. Who shall poure againe backe to him, that innocent
bloud? who shall restore him the price, wherewith he
bought vs out of the handes of that common enemie? At
the Sacrament of which price of ours, thy handmayd bound
her soule with the band of faithe. Let none separate her
from thy protection, let neither the lion, nor the dragon by
force or snares interpose themselues against her: for she

[1] Lat. in illo in quo vincimus.

will not answer that she hath no debts, leste she be conuinced
and gotten by the craftie accuser; but she will answer her
debts to haue beene forgiuen by him, to whome none can
restore equall, for that he payed for vs without any
obligation: Let her be then in peace with her husband,
before whome she was neuer maried to man, and after
whose death she neuer tooke husband: whome she serued,
bringing thee forth fruite in patience, to the end she
might gaine him vnto thee. Inspire my Lord and god,
inspire thy seruants my brethren, thy children my maisters, <small>He beseecheth others to</small>
whome with tongue and hart and learning I serue, that <small>pray (at the
Altar) for</small>
whosoeuer shall reade these things, they will remember at <small>her and his
father.</small>
thy altar thy seruant MONICA, with her husband PATRICIUS,
by whose fleshe thou broughtest me into this life, how I
know not. Let them remember with pittifull and deuoute
affection, in this transitorie life my parents and my brethren,
vnder thee our Father, and in our Catholike mother the
Churche, and my Cittisens in eternall HIERUSALEM, after
which the pilgrimage of thy people doth long and sighe,
euen from the beginning to the end, from their entrance in,
vnto the going oute; that what she requested of me in her
end, may be more bountifullie performed, by the prayers of
many better than by my confessions, and prayers onelie.' /

*The life of S! Agnes Virgin and Martyr written by S!
Ambrose the latine doctour Bishop of Milane, to
Religious Virgins, in his 3: tom: Serm: 90:*[1] /

'**The** Seruant of Christ AMBROSE to the holie Virgins. /

Let vs celebrate the festiuitie of this moste sacred virgin,
let psalmes sounde on one side, and lessons be heard on the
other. Let the multitude of people reioyce in one parte, and
let Christs poore be releeued in an other. Let vs all then
be glad in our Lord, and to the edification of virgins, Let
vs call to mynde, how and what blessed AGNES suffered:
Being now thirteene yeares olde, she destroyed death and <small>Her age: 13:</small>

[1] See Migne P.C., tom. 17, p. 735 ff.

found life, bicause she onely loued the Author of life: Her infancie was reputed equall to many yeares, being yong in bodie, she was moste olde in mynde: for time vnskillfull, but in truthe graue and wise; fayre of face, but more for 4
faith. /

When she on a time retourned home from schoole, the Gouerners sonne of ROME was enamoured of her, whereupon he harkeneth after hir parents, and fynding them he 8 beginneth to make greate offers, to giue large promises, if they will consent to his suite. Besides to obtayne AGNES good will, he presenteth her with precious iewells and ornaments, which she reiecteth as dirte. Whereat the yong 12 man began to be more earnest, and thinking that she looked for richer things, he bringeth her far more costlie attire, and layeth before her all the glorie of all sorts of rare and precious stones: beside he soliciteth his purpose by himself 16 and friends, by kinsfolkes and acquaintance, promising substance and houses, possessions and families, and to be short all kinde of worldlie commodities, if she would accept of him for her husband. Whereunto AGNES is sayed to 20 haue retourned this answer: 'Away from me thou fewell of sinne, thou nutriment of iniquitie, thou foode of death. Auant from me, there is an other louer that hath preuented thee, who hath made me fayrer offers than thou canst, who 24 hath giuen me richer iewells, than thou hast; who hath betrothed me to him with the ring of faith; who surpasseth thee in stocke and nobilitie. He hath adorned my right arme with an inestimable bracelett, and my necke 28 with precious stones aboue price: he hath putt on myne eares margarites vnualuable, and on euerie side hath besett me, with glittering and glorious gemmes: he hath placed in my face a signe that I can not admitte any wooer to me 32 beside him: He hath attired me with a gowne of cloth of golde, and hath bedecked me rounde aboute with chaynes vnmeasurable for worth: and with all and aboue all, he hath shewed me such incomparable treasures, as can not be 36

[margin: She is wooed vnto mightilie.]

[margin: Her answer setting forth the excellent graces of a spiritnall spouse and Christ him selfa.]

tolde, which he hath promised me moste faithfullie, if I will remayne sure to him. I can not therefore to the contumelie and disgrace of my first louer, beholde any new, and leaue
4 him to whome in charitie I am fastened: whose gentilitie is more excellent, whose power more mightie, whose countenance more louelie, whose loue more sweete, and exceeding all fauour: who hath allreadie prepared me a
8 mariage bed, and who with organes and other musicall instruments and voices dooth delight me: From his mouth haue I tasted honie and milke, his embracings haue I allredie enioyed, my bodie is coupled to his, and his bloud
12 hath beautified my cheekes; whose mother is a virgin, whose father neuer knew woman, who hath Angells to waite on him, whose beautie the sunne and moone doo admire, whose smell dooth raise vp the dead, whose touch
16 dooth confirme the weake, whose riches neuer decaye, and treasure neuer decrease. To him doe I onelie giue my faith, to him doe I yield my self with all deuotion, for louing him I doe remayne chaste, and touching him I am not *Other priuiledges of*
20 defiled, and enioying him I continue still a virgin: neither *spirituall mariage.*
do children want after this marriage, where the ofspring is produced without payne, and daylie fertilitie aboundeth.'/

 The mad yong man hearing this, is seised on with blynde
24 loue, and throughe anguish of mynde, he fetcheth his winde verie short, wherevpon he is caried to his bed, and by deepe sighes his loue is made manifest to the physicions. His father hath intelligence thereof, and for his sonnes sake
28 he maketh the same offers and promises, to purchase the maydes good will and consent of friends, which before his sonne had donne. The blessed AGNES denieth saying, that she can not for any thing breake her faith giuen too her *The Prefect assalteth*
32 first louer. Thereto the yong mans father replieth; that he *her but she excelleth in*
was Prefect of the Cittie, and therefore none was more *constant faith.*
worthie than himself: withall he demandeth verie earnestlie, what he was, and who of whose power AGNES made such
36 vanting. Then stepped forth one Parasite, who tolde him

that Agnes was a Christian from her infancie, and that she
was so bewitched withall that she affirmed Christ to be her
husband. / The Prefect hearing this waxeth verie glad and
sending men for her, commandeth them to bring her to the
benche and tribunall seate; where first he dealeth with her
in secret, making her fayre promises, if she will consent vnto
their suite: which not proceeding he layeth on her with
threates. But the virgin of Christ, was neither seduced by
flatteries, nor shaken with terrours, but keeping one
countenance and one mynde, dooth alike deride him
flattering and threatening. SEMPHRONIUS the prefect,
beholding such constancie in the yong mayde, he soliciteth
earnestlie her parents; who bicause they were of nobilitie
he could not enforce, wherefore he pretendeth against them,
that they were Christians also. /

Well the day following, he willeth AGNES to be brought
before him, to whome againe and againe he repeateth, how
his sonne did loue her. All which speaches when he
perceiued to be in vaine, he then giueth commandement to
bring her to his Tribunall seate, who being there presented,
he beginneth thus to her. 'The superstition of the Christians,
whose magicall artes do make them[1] verie bragge, thou
must needes cast from thee, or els thou canst not forgoe
thy madnes of mynde, and be capable of sounde counsell
and aduice. Wherefore thou shalt be sent to the venerable
goddesse VESTA, if thou like so to perseuer in thy purpose of
virginitie, and on her sacred sacrifices shalt thou attend.'
To this holie Agnes replied: 'If I haue refused thy sonne,
being a liuing man, thoughe taken with vniust loue,
being (I say) a man endewed with reason, able to heare and
see, feele and walke, and capable of this flourishing lighte
and of the good thereof: If for the loue of Christ by no
meanes I can abide to beholde him, how may I endure to
worship dumbe and deafe idolles voide of reason or sense,
and to the iniurie of the supreme god, bowe my necke to
vaine stones.' The Prefect hearing this answered, 'I am

[1 r. the]

desirous to pittie thine infancie, wherefore yet I deferre to
punish thee blaspheaming the gods, seeing thy yeares not
yet arriued at sense and vnderstanding: doe not therefore
despise thyself, to incurre thus the wrath of god.¹' S[t] [¹ r. the gods.]
Agnes replieth saying, 'doe not so despise in me my corporall
infancie, as to thinke that I desire mercie or fauour at your
handes, for faith goeth not by yeares, but by true sense,
and God omnipotent dooth more approoue the mynde of
men than their yeares. But for thy gods, whose
indignation thou wouldest not I should incurre, permitt
them hardlie to be angrie at me, let them speake, let them
command me, let them giue charge to be worshipped and
adored: I perceiue you intend that which you shall not
bring to passe, wherefore doe as you shall thinke good.'
Then sayd Semphronius, 'choose one of these two: Either
sacrifice to the goddesse Vesta, with her virgins, or els
thou shalt be thrust into the stewes, and there shalt be
enforced to be an harlot, and thy Christians who haue thus
inchanted thee, shall be farre from helping thee, howsoeuer
thou wilt seeme to endure this calamitie prepared, with vn-
daunted spirite. Wherefore as I haue sayd doe honour to
Vesta, and so honour thy stocke and kinne, or to thy house
and families ignominie, thou shalt be a publicke queane.' /
To this sayd holie Agnes with bolde spirite: 'If thou diddest
know, who is my god, thou wouldest not let such speaches
passe from thy mouth. I therefore that know the power of
my Lord Iesus Christ, securelie doe contemne thy threates,
trusting that I shall neither sacrifice to thy Idoles, nor be
defiled by others filthie follie: For I haue the Angell of my Angell keeper.
Lord the keeper of my bodie: for the onelie begotten sonne
of God, whome you know not, is to me an impregnable
wall, and a defender that neuer sleepeth, a protectour that
neuer faynteth or faileth. As for thy Gods, they are either
made of iron, wherewith pots were more fittlie to be made
for mens vses, or of stone, and then more conuenient to
paue the streetes withall: for diuinitie dwelleth not in

stones but in heauen, not in brasse or in any mettall, but is resident in the supreme kingdome. But thou and thy like, vnlesse you leaue speedilie worshipping them, you shall all with them be ioyned in punishment: for like as they were 4 cast by the helpe of fire, so their adorers shall be cast into eternall fire; not there to be melted or founded, but to be tormented and confounded for euer.' Herevpon the madd Iudge commandeth that she be stripped, and so naked to be 8 leadd to the common stewes: The crier going before and proclay[m]ing, 'This is sacrilegious AGNES the virgin, that blasphemeth the gods, for which fact she is deliuered vp to the stewes.' 12

Her condemnation.

She is stripped as he willeth, which donne her hayre being also dissolued and lett loose, God forthwith giueth her hayre such vnwonted thicknes, that she seemeth more comelie attired therewith to the feete, than if she had 16 beene clothed. Being so brought to the place of turpitude, and entered therein, she fyndeth the Angell of God so readie to ayde her, that presentlie she was enuironed round aboute with a meruailous lighte: In so much that none 20 could abide to looke at her for brightnes thereof: for the whole cabbine glittered as the sunne in his greatest brightnes, and the more curiouslie one would fixe his eyes on her, the more was his sight blunted or dymned with the light. 24 And when she prostrated herself in prayer before our Lord, there appeared before her a verie cleare white garment long to her foote, which she taking putt on her naked bodie, and sayd withall; 'I thanke thee my Lord Iesus 28 Christ, that vouchsafest me among thy handmayds, and hast commanded this vestment to be giuen me.' This gowne was so fitte for her, and so conspicuous for brightnes, that none could doubte it to be made by Angells 32 handes. This while both this stewes become a place of prayer, whereinto euerie one that entered did there adore and doe reuerence, giuing honour to that meruailous lighte, and so came forth more cleane than they went in. After 36

Miraculous shadowing of her nakednes, and protection.

A garment sent from God made by Angels handes. /

this commeth the Prefects sonne (that had beene author of
all this mischeefe) with his youthfull companions, thinking
now to insulte on the poore mayde and to take his lasciuious
pleasure on her, to her despite and shame. First his companions with rage and filthie crueltie entering in to her,
they retourne oute with greate reuerence and admiration,
which he reputing and exprobating to be impotencie of
spirite, iudged them vaine, whiteliuered and wretched
fellowes: and deriding them rusheth rashlie into the place,
where the virgin did pray, and beholding so greate a lighte
aboute her, did not for all that doe honour to god; but
pressing presumptuouslie to passe throughe the light to her,
before he could touch her with his hand, he fell flatte on his
face, and being choked by the diuell dyed in the place. / His
companions seeing him stay so long, imagined him to be
busie in his filthie workes, wherefore one that was moste
familiar with him, entering in to congratulate his scorne-
full insultation, and abusing of her, spying him to be dead,
crieth out with a loude voice and sayd. 'O yee pittifull
Romanes helpe; this harlot with witchcraft hath slayne
the gouerners sonne;' forthwith flocketh together the
people into the Theater, and the furious meynie make
sondrie exclamations: Some that she was a witche; Others
that she was innocent; Others that she was guiltie of sacri-
ledge. The Prefect himself hearing his sonne was slayne,
runneth with greate tumult to the Theater: and entering
into the place where his childe lay dead, with a loude crie
sayd; 'O moste cruell woman of all women, was there none
but my sonne, on whome thou couldest make shew of thine
art?' Which wordes he repeating often, and others moe,
and earnestlie asking of her the cause of his death, holie
AGNES sayth vnto him: 'He whose will he would haue
wroughte (that is the diuell) he hath receiued power from
God vpon him: For why are all the rest safe that entered
hither besides him: but bicause they all gaue honour to
God, who sent his Angell, who hath clothed me with this

The diuell hath speciall power giuen him on lasciuious persons, as on Saras 7: husbands.

garment of mercie, and hath kept my bodie, which from my cradle hath beene consecrated and offered to Christ? They therefore seeing the Angells claritie, and adoring departed all vntouched: but this impudent fellow, as soone as he was entered began to rage and be cruell; and when he thrusteth out his hand to touch me, the Angell of my Lord giueth him to this reprobate death as you see.' Then sayeth the Prefect to her, 'Herein shalt thou make manifest, that thou hast not donne this by magicall art, if thou beseeche the Angell to restore me my sonne aliue againe': To whome sayeth holie AGNES; 'Albeit thy faith deserueth not to obtayne this of our Lorde, yet bicause now is tyme wherein my Lord Iesus power may be manifested, depart you out all that I may offer my wonted prayer vnto him.' They being all oute she prostrateth herself flatt on her face, began to beseeche our Lord, that he would raise to life the yong man. And she so praying, the Angell of God appeared, and lifted her vp weeping, and comforting her mynde restoreth the yong man to life: Who going forth began with highe crie to proclayme and say: 'There is but one god in heauen, earth, and sea, who is the god of the Christians: for all the Temples are vaine, and the gods that are worshipped there, like vaine; not able to help themselues or others:' At these speeches, the Southsayers and cheefe priests of the Temples were troubled, so that they stirre a greater tumult than euer the people had donne before; And withall they crie; 'away with this witche, kille this sorceresse, who dooth change mens myndes and alienate affections.'

The Prefect seeing these meruailous workes was amased and astonied with admiration: yet fearing proscription and banishment, if he should seeme to take parte against the gentill Bishops, and defend AGNES, he leauing an other Substitute or vicar to iudge in his absence, departeth verie heauie, seeing himself not able to deliuer her, that had raised his dead childe to life. His vicar then ASPASIUS

Virginitie consecrated to Christ from infancie.

She raiseth vp the prefects sonne slaine.

The yong man reuiued exclaimeth at the Idols and confesseth Agnes god.

Infidels impute all miracles vnto witcherie.

commandeth a greate fire to be made in the sighte of all
the people, and Agnes to be cast into it: Which being   *Agnes is cast into the fire which hurteth onelie the furious people aboute.*
donne, presentlie the flame, diuideth it self into two parts,
4 burning the seditious people on each side; but not once
toucheth Agnes in the middest thereof. The furious people
not acknowledging Gods power therein, but imputing it to
witchcraft crie oute against her. Then blessed Agnes cast-
8 ing abrode her hands, in the middst of the flame prayeth
to god with these wordes: 'O omnipotent, onelie to be   *St Agnes praier in the fire.*
adored, worshipped and feared, father of our Lord Iesus
Christ, I blesse thee for that by thy onelie begotten sonne,
12 I haue escaped the handes of wicked men, and the filthines
of the diuell I haue passed ouer all withoute polluting my
self: And now moreouer the fire about me (being by thy
spirite sprinkled with the heauenlie dew) dieth, is diuided,
16 and the flame is powred on those that kindled it against
me. I blesse thee, O Father, worthie of all praise, who
permittest me cheerefullie to passe throughe the flames vnto
thee. Beholde now I see that which I did beleeue, now I
20 possesse that which I hoped for, now doe I embrace that
which I haue so long desired: I confesse thee with my
lipps and hart, and with all my bowells I long for thee.
Loe now I come to thee my liuing and true God, who with
24 our Lord Iesus Christ, thine onelie sonne, together with the
holie Ghoste, liuest and reignest world without end. Amen.'
When she had finished her prayer, the fire was so whollie
quenched that no warmthe remayned. Then ASPASIUS the
28 vicegerent of ROME, not enduring the peoples sedition and
tumulte, willeth one to runne her through the throate with   *She is runne throughe the throte with a sworde.*
a sworde. And with this end she being rinsed in her owne
red rose bloud, Christ consecrated her his spouse and his
32 Martyr. But her parents taking no kinde of griefe hereat,   *No griefe to be taken at friends martyrdome.*
tooke away her bodie with greate ioye, and buried it in a
litle ferme of theirs, neere the Cittie, in the way which is
called NUMENTANA, whither all the multitude of Christians
36 did flocke: Whereat the Pagans being offended, they lye in

wayte for them. The Christians perceyuing them to be armed, and to rushe on them, they flie away, who all escape, albeit some with stones were hurte. One notwithstanding named EMERENTIANA, a holie virgin, who had beene nursed of one milke with her, albeit she was but a Cathecumene, stayed boldelie, and reproued them saying. 'O you waste, you wretched, you corruptible and cruell fellowes, you haue slayne her that did worship the Omnipotent god, and with stones haue farther endeuoured to kill other innocent persons.' At which speeches and the like, the furious infidells flie vpon her with stones, vntill they had stoned her dead, where praying at Sr AGNES sepulcher, she yieldeth vp the Ghoste. No doubt but she was baptised in her bloud, that did so constantlie suffer death in the confession of our Lord, and for the defence of righteousnes. At the same houre was there a moste vehement earthquake, and allbeit the heauens were moste cleare, yet there was such thundering and lightening, that the moste part of the mad multitude, died in the place, so that no Christian that came to the S^{rs} sepulcher, was molested thenceforth. /

St Agnes parents with the priests came in the night and tooke away the bodie of holie EMERENTIANA, and buried it in the confines of the field, where St AGNES lay. And while they continued many nightes, watching at the Sepulcher of their holie daughter, in the deepe time of silence of the nighte, they beholde an hoaste of virgins, who being all attired in gownes of cloth of golde, passed by them with meruailous light. Amongst whome they see their blessed childe Agnes, in the same attire glittering, and at her right hand a lambe more white than snowe. When her parents and those with them saw those things, they were astonished in mynde, but holie AGNES requesteth her fellowes to stay a litle: And standing still she sayeth to her parents: 'Looke you doe not lament me as dead, but reioyce with me and congratulate, for that I doe possesse this lightsome seate

with these virgins, and am vnited with him in heauen,
whome liuing I loued with all my harte': and this being
sayd, she goeth on againe. This vision was daylie diuulged
in publicke, by those that had seene it; whereupon it came
to passe, that after some yeares, this action came to the
eares of CONSTANTIA, daughter to CONSTANTINE, related by *By this it is euident that she suffered immediatlie before Constantine.*
the parties who had seene it. This CONSTANTIA queene,
was a moste prudent virgin yet so besett with woundes (of
leprosie as it appeareth) that from the crowne of her head
to the soale of her foote, no part was sounde. She con- *Consider what greate good visions seene and vnderstoode doe worke.*
ceyuing hope of recouering her health, vpon counsell taken
commeth to the Sepulcher of the martyr in the nighte;
and albeit yet a Pagane, yet somewhat beleeuing, and of
good mynde or meaning made her faithfull prayers there.
The which while she was doing, she of a sodaine is ouer- *Constantia her vision and cure.*
taken with a sweete sleepe, where in a vision she beholdeth
holie AGNES speaking in this wise; 'doe constantlie
CONSTANTIA, and beleeue my Lord Jesus Christ to be the
sonne of God, and thy Sauiour, by whome thou shalt now
obtayne perfect cure of all thy woundes in thy bodie.' /
At this voice CONSTANTIA awaketh so whole, that no signe
of hurte did remayne. Retourning then to the palace so
sounde, she bringeth greate gladnes to her father and
brothers Emperours. All the Cittie is crowned with ioye
and triumphe, souldiors and others, all that heard this effect
exulted: Gentilitie was confounded, and our Lords faith
did reioyce. This donne she beseecheth her father and
brothers Emperours, that there may a Church be built to *A Church built to S.*
S. AGNES, and a sepulcher to herself there-by. This *Agnes.*
opinion runneth aboute to all, and whosoeuer beleeuing
came thither to her Sepulcher, they were cured of their *Cures at S. Agnes se-*
diseases whatsoeuer: which no man doubteth but that *pulcher.*
Christ worketh to this day. CONSTANCE the Emperours
daughter continued after in virginitie, by whome many
other virgins of the meane sort and of the Noble, yea and
of the moste excellent and renowned, tooke the holie veile. *Veiling of virgins.*

And for that faith sustayneth no damage of death, euen to
this day, many Romane virgins, doe imitate and waite on
holie Agnes, as if she were in bodie lyuing, and by her
example, doe courageouslie proceede and perseuer intire,
beleeuing vndoubtedlie, that if they perseuer to the end, they
shall obtayne the price and reward of perpetuall victorie.

These things I Ambrose seruant of Christ fynding
written in sacred bookes, I could not permitt to be hidden
with fruitlesse silence; Wherefore to the honour of so greate
a Martyr, as I vnderstood her gests were, so haue I
described them, and to your edification (O virgins) haue
I thought conuenient, to dedicate and direct the storie of
her passion; beseeching the charitie of the holie Ghoste,
that our labour may fructifie in the sight of our Lord, by
your imitation of her. Amen.'/

*The life of S.t Gorgonia a maried wife and sister to
S.t Gregorie Nazianzene a greeke Doctor, flourishing
in the yeare 370: written by him: taken out of his
eleuenth and fourteenth Oration*[1] *somewhat abridged./*

[Orat. 11 (8).] '𝕴𝔱 𝖇𝖊𝖎𝖓𝖌 to commend my sister, doe relate domesticall
things (who somewhat therefore touch my self) which
things are not false, bicause they are domesticall, but true,
and therefore commendable. They are true and more,
bothe iust and openlie knowne. Wherefore my speache
shall not passe throughe fauour or affection, but I will
praise her in seemelie manner, which any iust man will

Note the credit and sinceritie of this life.

approue; not fearing to exceede truthe, but rather that
I omitte nothing of her true and due praise, and so
diminish her glorie. For it is a difficult matter, to equall
my sisters vertues with my speache. Truthe then shall be
my rule and bounde, which onelie beholding, we will
commend onelie such things as are praiseworthie; neither
may I in pietie denie my bloud and kinne that due com-

---

[1] See Migne, *Series Graeca*, tom. 35, p. 790 ff. (Or. VIII.), and p. 986 ff. (Or. XVIII.); the former is the 'Or. fun. in laudem Gorgoniae sororis,' the latter 'in patrem.'

mendation, which is due to all good persons, nor of vertuous
dutie may I doe lesse to her worthines, than many bad
persons doe performe to their beloued, on corrupt affection
and carnall kyndenes./ But now let vs come to her praises,
without all affection of mynde, or affectation of speache :—
For such a one was she whome we intend to praise, withoute
paynting and forren colouring, her brauerie was to want   Her brauerie.
brauerie and trimming,—yet will we giue her her due;
whereby also we shall instruct and incite many to
imitate her vertues; which is our purpose and intent in
euerie worke and speach to better them that are com-   Note his in-
mitted to our charge. Some would praise her for her   tention in all
                                                                                            his speaches.
contrie and stocke, obseruing the lawes and rules of such
as commend the dead, wherein store of fayre wordes would
occurre, to him that would commend her for such externall
things; as for her beautie and venerable fayernes, for
precious stones, golde, and for her artificiall comelynes of
her handes, which doe controule deformitie by them : yet
beautie is nothing the lesse, albeit destitute of such
externall ornaments. I will commend her stocke by onelie
recording her and my parents, for pietie will not abide that
such worthie parents and teachers should be forgotten;
they being the new ABRAHAM and SARA of our age; I
meane GREGORIE and his wife NONNA, our father and   Her parents
mother, he becomming iust by faith in Christ, which before   and their
                                                                                            vertues;
mariage he knew not; and she being coupled to him in   Gregorie
                                                                                            and Nonna.
matrimonie, after a moste faithfull and religious man : he
like Abraham, being on a sodaine made a father of many
people, (soone after his conuersion and baptisme, being made   Orat: in
bishop and miraculouslie, that being foresignified also at   funere patris:
                                                                                            14 (18) Orat.
his baptisme,) and she likewise with him spirituallie
bringing forth; He forsooke his kindred and house, forgoing their errours and erroneous conuersation for the
happie land promised him therefore by God like Abraham;
but she aboue SARA (if it be lawfull to speake so) was
author and worker of her husbands foresayd holie de-

parture. (For he at mariage being depraued by the heresie of the HYPSISTARIJ, which interpreted signifieth 'moste highe,' who held some superstition of the Gentills, as reuerencing fire and candles, thoughe detesting Idolatrie: and with the Iewes kept the Saboth day, and abstayned from certayne meates, yet refused Circumcision: After that he was coupled to her, she neuer ceased fasting and praying, weeping and wayling prostrate before god, persuading and labouring him by all meanes, vntill she had vnited him in one faith and affection towards god.) He was now whollie deuoted vnto God, and now did she esteeme and call him her lorde, and therefore gott a new title of righteousnes. They also had their Isaac, whome they restored to the giuer; (yea she promised him to god before he was borne (*he meaneth of himself*) and being brought into this worlde, she presentlie consecrated to God; nothing terrified or doubting of the desired euent by gods good benefit, albeit the effect might haue seemed casuall throughe my vncertaine proofe.)/

Of these two then, this is the order, that the woman by prayer and shewing the way brought that good sheppheard to the faith, and thereby also gaue others example of well feeding and bringing forth: the man likewise, with his hart and good faith, forsooke the worship of Idoles, and more after expelled the diuells themselues from others; and the woman so hated that wicked worship, that she would not eate nor drinke with Idolaters, (nay would not endure to passe by or beholde their wicked Churches; neither would suffer her eares and tongue, that vsed to listen and pronounce diuine things, to be defiled with hearing or speaking any of the Ethnicall narrations, or Theatricall songs.)/ Who did not know these two equall for honour of one will and minde, no lesse vnited to God by vertue, than to each other in flesh; for numbers of yeares and gray hayres, prudence and worthie life, matches; for emulation and desire to excell in vertue contending with

each other, yet surpassing all others; who by bandes of flesh were somewhat holden heere, but in spirit had left this life, before their bodie and soule were separated; who
4 had the worlde and yet had it not: for that they contemned it, albeit they ruled in it; who decayed in wealth and riches, yet by cunning negociation and trafike abounded in riches: for that they despised the goods of this life, to gett
8 those of the next; who reputed the endes of this life short, but the next long: and who liued but a small time, except that they spent in vertue and godlines, but a long time was it, wherein they were before dead to this life. Thus
12 (to add this one thing of them more) were they fitlie dis- tinguished in sex, and so commodiouslie diuided for the good of others, that he might be an honor to men, and she of women, and bothe paternes of vertue. From these
16 receiued GORGONIA her life, and worthie renowne: from these had she the seede of vertue, from them had she that she liued religiouslie, and died full of all ioyfull hope comfortablie./ These are notable things verilie and not
20 easilie founde in many that glorie of their gentrie, and swell with pride of their auncestors; but we must talke of her more wiselie and more sublimelie: GORGONIAS contrie was heauenlie HIERUSALEM, that cittie which was[1] not
24 beheld with mortall eye, but is conceiued with mynde and vnderstanding, where we all are Cittisens, and whither we hasten with all celeritie, whereof Christ is a cittisen, and fellow Cittisens are all the worthie companie and Church of
28 the first begotten registred in heauen, reioycing in behold- ing that glorie, and dauncing without end, aboute that greate builder of that Cittie. Her nobilitie is the con- seruing of Gods image in herself, and the trimming and
32 conforming it to her exemplar, which wisedome and vertue make, with a pure desire of informing herself daylie more and more in godlie matters, and in the knowledge of her beginning, nature, and end why we were created, all which
36 make true and kindelie professors of supernall things.

See their admirable vertues.

Note for braggers of gentrie.

[1 r. is]

Her spirituall nobilitie and of Saints.

True Christian gentrie./

Wherefore I know her soule to be moste noble, and extoll
her therefore, not iudging of gentrie and basenes by the
rule of the common sort, that is by their stocke, but by
manners, not weighing the tribes and parentage of those
that I commend, as their persons and proper qualities. To
Her chastitie in mariage. come then to her vertues, for chastitie she was so worthie,
that whereas our life is diuided into two sortes, maried and
vnmaried persons, whereof as the one is more excellent and
diuine, so is it of more payne and perill: the other as it is
more base and abiect, so withall is it of lesse danger: she
auoyding the incommodities of bothe states, chose the
benefits of bothe, the excellencie of the one and the securitie
of the other: chaste withoute pride, and mixing the commodities of chaste life with matrimonie: by which worke
she prooued by deede, that neither of these states, were of
their owne nature such as did necessarilie tye vs to God or
the worlde, or whollie separate vs from them, that one of
them onelie were vtterlie to be shunned or chosen, but that
it was the mynde which did well gouerne mariage and
virginitie, and like the wise artificer vsing each matter to
Her spirituall minde in matrimonie. good, could worke each of them to vertue. For not bicause
she was coupled to flesh, was she therefore separate from
spirite, neither bicause she had a man to her head, therefore
did she forgett, or was ignorant of her cheefe head, but
obeying the worlde and nature, in parte to satisfie the law
of flesh, or rather to obey him that gaue that law, afterward
she consecrated herself whollie to god. She chose to
Her husband and Children. husband one (named VITALIANUS) who was not an importunate or imperious Lorde, but a true husband, and a fellow
Her vertuous education of her children and familie. seruant to all goodnes. And not content with this onelie,
she made the fruite of her bodie, that is her sonnes and
Nephewes (her sonnes being PETER and PHOCAS, her
daughters EUGENIA, NONNA, ALYPIANA, her nephew by
ALIPIANA maried by NICOBULUS, was NICOBULUS the yonger
with others) these I say she made spirituall fruite, purifying vnto god, not onelie all her children but her owne

familie too, like her owne soule, so making mariage laudable, by lyuing in wedlocke laudablie and acceptablie in gods sighte, and making the fruite springing thence like accept-
4 able vnto god : And while she liued, she made herself a patterne of all vertue to her children, and being called hence, she bequeathed to her familie, her spirit and will for a dumbe exhortation. The diuine SALOMON in his instructiue
8 wisedome, that is his PROUERBES, commendeth a woman that abideth at home, and loueth her husband, and against a light huswife often gadding out of her dores, impotent and infamous, and with wanton wordes and gestures alluring
12 excellent soules, he opposeth her who liueth honestlie at home, and fullfilleth all her womans duties and offices with constant and manlie mynde : keeping her handes euer busie at the spindle and distaffe, working her good man double
16 suites, making prouision of corne and like fruites in due tyme, and preparing fruite for her familie in conuenient manner : who intertayneth her friends with bountifull table, and dooth performe all things els, which he requireth, and
20 commendeth, in an honest and industrious Matrone. If I would fetch matter from those pointes, to commend my sister, I should imitate him who would sett forth a fayre image by the shadow thereof, or expresse a lion by his clawes,
24 and so should I with them, take the small for greate, and omitte the cheefe and excellent matters, to choose the baser. /

Who was euer more worthie to goe abrode and conuerse
28 with others, yet none more seeldome was seene abrode, nor any lesse to be seene of mens eyes ? Who knew better the iust meane of being sad or cheerfull, that she might not be vnciuill or sowre by sadnes, or dissolute and wanton by
32 mirth, but in the one might shew prudence, in the other courtesie, and so in bothe might be a paterne of moderation, by greatnes of spirit mixt with humanitie. /

Harken you women who are ouermuch prone to sett
36 your selues to the shew, who are too rashe and too easilie

How mariage made laudable.

Prou: 31:

Her rare vertues.

despise the veile and couer of your shamefastnes : None did
refraine and keepe her eyes like her ; none did more despise
laughing ; who thought it ouermuch almoste to smile : Who
did sett greater guards on her eares, not to listen euill
matters, and who had them more open to all godlie talke ?
yea who with more iudgement gouerned her tongue to speake
gods iustifications, and to sett order and moderation in her
wordes ? And to add this more to her praise, albeit she
esteemed it litle, as other modest and well manered women
doe likewise, yet is it vsuall throughe the faulte of such
women, as are to immoderate in trimming and decking
themselues, nor by any speache or teaching will be corrected,
whereby her commendation herein is the greater; she
trimmed herself with no goldesmiths art, wrought for
brauerie; no yellow haire or flaxen lockes, or friselled
tuffes, borrowed to deceiue and foullie shadowing an honest
head, came on her; there was not to be seene on her riche
garments, so lose as that they would flie aboute and open,
nor so thinne as that you might see throughe ; no glittering
of precious stones, altering the ayre and bodies aboute with
their braue colour, no art or counterfetting of paynters, no
vile beautie bought with small price, which earthlie work-
man frameth, and with false colours hideth gods worke ;
more disgracing it thereby than gracing and adorning it, so
proposing gods frame to wanton and shameles eyes, vnder
an harlots shape, and withdrawing the naturall image kept
for god and the next worlde, by fayned and forged
fayrenes. But she albeit she knew many and diuerse
dresses for women, yet accounted she of none like her
inward ornament of manners. That ruddines onelie liked
her, which shamefastnes and bashfullnes produced : that
whitenes onelie pleased her, which was caused by abstinence ; for as for paynted face, or colouring of eyes, and
such like brickle brauerie, she left them to women that play
or follow the stages, keepe common and open companie, who
thinke it a shame to blushe. /

*Rare fayr-
nes and
ruddines*

Her prudence and pietie who can with fitt wordes expresse; of which vertue, you will hardlie fynde many examples, if you tourne your eye from her corporall and spirituall parents, whose steps she onelie beholding (howbeit she was nothing inferiour to them therein) yet did she willinglie yield them the cheefe praise, for that she acknowledged them the fountaine of her light and other good whatsouer she had. /

What was more ingenious and sharp of witt than she, whome not onelie her kinne and familiars, but all her neighbors commonlie would consulte and craue aduice, and whose counsaile they followed, as an vndoubted rule and inuiolable law. There was nothing more considerate than her speaches, nothing more wise than her silence : And for that I haue happened to talke of silence, I will add one thing peculiar to her and which beseemeth women exceedinglie, and in these dayes hath much benefitted. / None knew matters belonging to god better than she, not onelie throughe her owne quicknes of witt, but also from gods scriptures and diuine oracles, yet none would talke lesse thereof than she, conteyning herself within womens boundes. Now touching that belongeth to a woman, that maketh profession of religion and godlines, and wherein onelie to keepe no measure is best, none adorned the Churches with gifts more than she, and not onelie other Churches, but this also with vs, which I doubt she being deceased, will hardlie henceforth be so decked. Yea more, who amongst men did so make himself a liue Temple of God as she did? Who did reuerence the Priests like her; especiallie him who was her maister of vertue, whose excellent seede are her self and a paire of sonnes consecrated vnto God? Who had her house more open to entertayne holy and vertuous persons, and more furnished it with diuine riches than she? and which is more, who with like modestie, holie steps and gate, gratefull vnto god, went to inuite them and receiue them? Who in afflictions had her

Her wisedome.

Her deuotion and rich liberalitie on Gods churches.

Holie hospitalitie.

mynde lesse afflicted ? who had more griefe and compassion at others griefes and calamities ? Who had a more liberall hand to the poore than she ? Verilie I doubte not to applie those words of Iob to commend her : *His gate was open to euerie one that came : no pilgrime was tourned away and made lie abrode, he was the eye of the blinde, the foote of the lame, and mother of orphans.* / so was she.

Of her humanitie and benignitie to widdowes, it sufficeth to record this fruite thereof, that none was there termed widdow. Her house was a common Inne or hospitall to her poore kinsfolke, and her goods were no lesse common to all poore people, than each mans owne. She dispersed and gaue freelie to the poore, and vpon Gods certaine promise, she layed vp much in the heauenlie barne, and by often deseruing well of many, she receiued Christ himself liberallie. And that which was moste to be magnified, she studied not so much to seeme excellent and best, as to be in verie deede, or rather in the secret sight of God, who vieweth all secrets, did she exercise charitie and mercie euidentlie. She tooke all from the Prince of this worlde, and transported all into those supernall barnes, to be euer safe : she left nothing for the earth but her bodie, but changed all for the hope of next life : These onelie riches, did she leaue to her children when she died, forsoothe the imitation of their mothers vertue, and the studie of her praise. Neither did she seeke to flourish so with liberalitie, or did so studie benignitie and beneficence that she might yet enioy carnall delightes, and vnbridled bellie pleasures ; which doe teare the soule, like as a mad and cruell dogge doth a bodie ; as the custome is of diuerse, who if they shew bountie to the poore, they thinke then they may liue more daintilie and delicatelie, and so they doe not heale vice with vertue, but doe change vice for vertue : neither did she breake her bodie with abstinence, that she left base and hard bed for others to medicine them withall : neither did she assume that help for her soule, that withall she might vse no moderation in her sleepe ; but

imposing that law on her self, as being not too much
wrapped and inthralled to her bodie, she did not in her *Watching all night in praier.*
watching straighte bow downe, and for werynes fall to the
4 grounde, when others stood vpright all night praying, which
notwithstanding is so laborious a worke, and so hard to
ouercome our selues therein, that onelie principall spirituall
men can performe as much, wherein she did not onelie
8 ouergoe women, but also moste strong and stoute men for
greatnes and valour of mynde. Likewise in prudent atten- *Attentiue prayer and reading with kneeling allmoste continual and teares.*
tion to psalmodie or vocall prayer, in reading or expounding
diuine scripture, in readie memorie, in paynfull kneeling,
12 and that so continuall, as that she seemed allmoste still to
sticke to the grounde, in teares from a contrite and humble
hart, which doe wash away the vncleannes thereof, in
prayers and eleuated spirit, carying her vpreared without *Her eleuated spirit.*
16 distraction, in all these or each of them, no man or woman
dare compare with her. And of her may this no lesse true *Note.*
than magnificall commendation be made, that vertues she
in part imitated and partlie performed in so exquisite
20 manner, that others did take example from her; againe
that some vertues she found out of her self, and some she
did surpasse. And albeit we grant that some others should
be equall to her in some one, yet in this she ouerwent all *A rare perfection.*
24 others lyuing that she one conteyned and possessed all
vertues. She kept so exactlie all the rules of vertues, as
hardlie any other obserued the rules of one in mediocritie,
and againe so excelled she in euerie kinde, as that it was
28 fullie sufficient like all. O homelie bodie and garment, *All her holie exercises and actions in order.*
onelie glittering for vertue; O soule keeping the bodie
almoste without meate, and as it were withoute substance,
or to speake more fittlie, O bodie imposing on it self necessitie
32 to dye before death, that the soule might thereby be free,
and deliuered of the impediment of senses. O nights
passed withoute sleepe, singing of psalmes, and continuall
standing at prayer, from the end of one day, to the
36 beginning of the next! O DAVID that in song art not long

or tedious to deuoute soules! O tender and weake members, layd prostrate on the earth, and exercising themselues hardlie beyond nature! O fluds of teares shedd throughe sorrow of hart, to cause a ioyfull haruest in heauen! O night-cries pearcing the cloudes and pressing to Gods owne presence! O feruour of spirit throughe egernes of prayer not feared by dogs of the nighte, nor by showres, thunders, haile or darknes! O womans nature that for the common conflict and victorie of saluation hast surpassed men, and thereby hast proued that men and women are onelie in bodie distinguished, not in mynde. O meruailous puritie euen from baptisme, O soule spouse of Christ, placed in a pure bed of her bodie! O aple, O Eue, mother of our stocke and sinne, and thou deceyuing serpent, with death it self, you are all ouercome by this womans continencie and sparenes of meate. O humiliation, exinanition, forme of seruant, and sufferings of Christ, honoured, and adorned, by her mortification. O how shall I either number vp all her praises, or not iniurie the readers by omitting many things of her?

Women and men not distinguished in minde.

How God glorified her in this life.

It is now time that we shew you the rewards of her vertue euen in this life: for the reward which the iust paymaister hath made her possessour of, now in heauen, no humane eye or eare can attaine vnto, nor cogitation comprehend: and oftentimes this serueth much to the edification of such as are doubtfull and weake in faith, by small and sensible things to helpe them to beleeue greater and inuisible things. But I will relate things partlie knowne to all, and partlie secret to the common sort vntill now, which she concealed, leaste she might seeme to much to please her-self, for the graces granted her by God, if they had beene knowne. / You know how furious the shee mules of our contrie are, that draw in chariots or beare litters, and you remember with what raging madnes, they ran away with her horse litter, so that all her bodie and members thereof, were bruised and broken moste grieuouslie, in such horrible

Saints greate works do often much edifie others weake in faith.

manner, as persons not well grounded in faith, might take greate occasion of offence and staggering, to see godlie persons fall into so greate affliction : But see how swiftlie
4 God corrected such infidelitie. After that all her bones and parts open and inward, were so broken to peeces, she would not vse any other physicion than him who had so striken her, God himself. And this bothe bicause she was ashamed
8 to be seene or handled by men, for she retayned modestie and bashfullnes euen in her paynes; and also bicause thus she hoped, her innocencie should best be defended, and all sinister opinion of her should be purged and cleared, by him
12 who had permitted her to fall into this calamitie : of whome therefore she seeking help did easilie obtaine it : by whose sodaine curing it came to passe that some were as much astonished at this healing of her, as at her calamitie ; this
16 miraculous recouerie being as vnlooked for as her striking. Wherefore it seemed a tragedie, that by affliction she should grow famous, she by griefe being touched as a man, but aboue humane sorte and vse being restored to
20 health : whereby moreouer aftercommers, tooke a lesson to learne faith in afflictions, she giuing there a paterne of so rare faith : and that they might take example of patience in greate perills, and beholde Gods singular goodnes and
24 mercie towards such persons : All this did this greate storie yield vs. For trulie was that comforte pronounced of iust men verified in her, *The iust person falling shall not be* [Ps. 36, 24.] *crushed to naught:* and a more meruailous thing was by the
28 Prophet added of him, *and thoughe he be broken, he shall be* [Ps. 145, 8.] *soone raised vp againe, and that with glorie:* which was also performed on her; for albeit she seemed extraordinarilie striken, so did she retourne to her former health aboue all
32 expectation so speedilie, as the cure almoste tooke away all feeling of the blow, and the medicine more aduanced her than the stripe. O laudable and admirable calamitie! O paine better than ease! O how trulie was that verified in
36 her, *He shall strike and heale, and after three dayes he shall* [Ose 6, 2.]

A miraculous cure.
Rare modestie.

By affliction she grew famous and others edified.

raise vp him, againe: which howbeit it be ment cheefelie of Christ, yet may it fitlie be applied to this affliction. The fame of this miracle came to all mens eares euen those that were far of, and together with other admirable workes 4
An other miracle. of God, in all mens tongues and eares did this storie sounde: But that which was hidden from the worlde, for pietie and humble wisedome, which abhorreth pride and ostentations, as I sayd, wilt thou O excellent Pastour and guider of this 8 holie sheepe (*he speaketh to his father, before whome it seemeth he made this oration*) that I reueale it; which was committed to our twoes knowledge onelie, or wilt thou we keepe our promise made to her still, thoughe dead? to me it seemeth 12 conuenient, that as then she lyuing, time was to conceale it, so now it is time to manifest it, both for gods glorie, and also for comfort of such as are in affliction; thus it was./
Gorgonias strange sicknes. She fell verie sicke of a cruell and vnwonted disease, or 16 rather a prodigious maladie, to weete a sodaine inflammation of all her bodie, all her bloud as it were boyling within her, and after a congealing of the same, whence such a numnesse and palenesse, dissolution of mynde and all members ensued, 20 and that so continuallie sometime, as it seemed not an humane or naturall euill: For no priuate iudgement of one physicion or common consultation of moe, no skill nor industrie coulde heale her griefe, no nor her parents teares, 24 which often were tried to be of greate power, nor publike
See how she was beloued of all: prayers and supplications, which all the people made for her, as if it had beene for their owne health, could preuaile: For all were so affected towards her, that they reputed her 28 health to be their owne, and contrariwise her calamitie and sicknes, they esteemed all theirs. What dooth this greate soule and worthie of the greatest things in this case, and what medicine dooth she applie to her griefe? for here is a 32 secret pointe worthie of obseruation. All humane helpe being despayred of, she flieth to the physicion of all mortall men, she obserueth the darke and dead time of nighte, and her infirmitie then somewhat remitting her vehemencie, to 36

the Altar she goeth, and there prostrateth herself, beseech- *At Christs altar and B: Sacrament she is cured.*
ing him that was there honored with greate crie (by all his
names and meruailous workes which euer he had donne, for
4 she knew the stories of bothe Testaments, olde and new)
and in fine, of holie and notable impudencie, she imitated
the woman, that for her incureable bloudie flux, pressed to
touch the hemme of Christs garment, and lo what she
8 did: with earnest crie and aboundant teares she putteth her
head to the Altar, like the woman (*Marie Magdalen*) who
long agoe watered Christs feete, and threatened that she
would neuer depart thence before she were healed; and
12 watering her whole bodie, and the Sacrament of Christs *Marke the vse of reseruing the B: Sacrament.*
precious bodie and bloud with teares, (O wonderfull worke)
presentlie she feeleth her self freed of her disease: and so
lightened in bodie and mynde she departeth, obtayning this
16 reward of her hope, that she got what she wished, and with
strength of soule purchaseth strength of her bodie. These
are greate and admirable things, yet true; which I wish
both whole and sicke to beleeue, that so you may either
20 conserue your health had, or recouer it lost. And none may
thinke I tell this storie of vaine ostentation, for that while
she lyued, I euer concealed it with silence till now; which still
I had left vnmanifested if I had not feared some perill to my *What peril is it then not to credit it, as Protestants easilie will.*
24 self, if I should not haue notified so greate a miracle to
faithfull people now lyuing and to come hereafter. /
And this was her life, and many things we pretermitte
that our speech may not seeme to exceede the meane; yet
28 her vertuous and worthie death may seeme to be iniuried,
if we should not record how notablie she behaued herself
therein, whereas the knowledge thereof I know is much
desired. She had greate desire to be dissolued hence, (for
32 she had greate libertie of spirit with god, who called her,) *Her greate longing to be with God.*
and to be with Christ she preferred before all earthlie
commodities, neither dooth any one loue this bodie so exceedinglie, as she to shake of the bandes of this mortalitie,
36 to be free from the dreggs wherein we lyue, and so to be

purelie vnited, with the cheefe good, and to enioy him
whollie, of whome she was beloued, and with whose small
beames we are now illumined, to know and feele that we
are separated from him. Neither was she frustrated of her 4
desire, and which was more, throughe her foresight and
She knew the time when she should depart before. many watchings she vnderstood before-hand the time, when
she should attayne that her longed loue: in a sweete
dreame and vision, the day being signified to her from god, 8
that so prepared and withoute perturbation she might dye:
She had receiued the purgation, clensing and new dedication
of baptisme before, or rather her whole life was nothing
els, but a heauenlie purgation and renouation; she had 12
beene regenerated by the holie ghoste, but she made it safe
by her former good life; so that in her alone, baptisme
(that I may speake somewhat boldelie) had rather the
worke of confirmation in former grace, than the benefit of 16
Her zeale of her husbands soule-health; and why: first and pure grace. And for as much as this one thing
she wished to be added to the rest, that her husband, might
be clensed with the purifying waters, (and if you would
that I should describe her husband in a word, I can not 20
deuise it better, than by terming him her husband) and
this wished she, that so in her whole bodie (consisting of
man and wife) she might be dedicated to God, and so dye
not halfe baptised but all: which desire of hers by prayers 24
she obtayned of god, who worketh the will of those that
feare him, and bringeth their petitions to wished end.
Hauing then all her desires so accomplished, and knowing
her last day to be at hand, she prepareth her self to de- 28
parture, and to obserue all that is vsuall to be donne on
death bed: for after that she had giuen such good admoni-
Her last speeches to friends. tions to her husband, children and friends, as beseemed a
woman so louing to husband, children and friends, and had 32
discoursed much and excellentlie of the life to come, and so
had made that day a festiuall and solemne day, she left this
[¹ left out: quos ne ipsa quidem exoptabat.] life, not full of dayes or many yeares,...¹ for that she knew
her dayes to haue beene euill to her, dustie and deceitfull, 36

but full of dayes spent according to gods will, and that so full of such, as I know not her matche amongst those that liued to verie olde age, and passed ouer a greate number of yeares. She was so dissolued, or to speake fitter, so was she assumpted, flew away, or changed habitation, or went before her bodie. But I had allmoste forgotten one thing of her, which her spirituall father, both obserued and notified vnto me (*he meaneth his father olde Gregorie*) which he would not endure to be omitted, as a notable miracle, much to her glorie, and our exhortation to vertue, and to wish like end: And verilie I am amazed and teares ouertake me recording this miracle. She was now dead, and had giuen vp the last gaspes, and greate companies of kinsfolkes, friends, and externes compassed her all-aboute, performing such duties of pietie, as are wont to be donne to the dead, with her decrepite mother, who beside her griefe also enuied her departure, and others for loue mourned, some recording her blessed memorie, others longing to heare somewhat and others wishing to speake yet durst not, notwithstanding all were silent: She this while for as much as by sight could be gathered, did neither breathe, nor moue, nor gaue forth any sound, so that all deemed that silence death of bodie. Then the good sheppheard (*her father*) who diligentlie obserued all her wordes and deedes, marking her lips a litle to moue, putt his eare neere to, (for his vertue and compassion made him bolde and hardie) and listening he heard that it was a verse of a psalme, which she muttered, and such a verse as was moste agreeable to such as were departing, and in her a testimonie of her freedome of spirite wherewith she left this life, and blessed be that person, who yieldeth vp his last gaspe with those words of hers, which were these; *In peace and him that is alwayes one will I sleepe and rest.* Thus didst thou moste excellent woman sing, and the wordes and truthe thereof together concurred, and thy Epitaphe and departure were conioyned, for that thou hadst thy mynde so excellentlie freed from affections;

Marginal notes: Who is trulie full of dayes; Note a strange and worthie action. Pietie onelie to be exercised about persons dying. Her last diuine wordes Psal. 4 (v. 10).

wherefore thou also obtaynedst an extraordinarie death, aboue the common decease of gods friends, lyuing and dying with godlie wordes. Verilie I doubte not but that thou now enioyest far more excellent things, than eye can beholde; 4

She had cleere vision of God. to weete, the voice of those that keepe euerlasting festiuitie, the quiers of Angells, the heauenlie order, the sight of glorie, and especiallie the pure light of the supreme Trinitie, which withdrew it self from our mynde shutte within the 8 prison of this bodie, and dispersed in our senses, but now offereth it self whollie to be embraced, and to be contemplated of our whole mynde, and euerie way lighteneth our soules, with the whole brightnes of his diuinitie. And 12 if thou make any reckoning of these honors, which we yield thee, and if this reward also be granted holie soules by God, that they haue any feeling of these things, accept

He prayeth to her. this oration or speeche of myne in steede of many, or aboue 16 many funerall gifts, which before thee, we offered to CÆSARIUS (our brother) and now to thee we present, seeing we haue beene reserued to yield these funerall speeches to our brother and sister.' / 20

Baronij martyrolog: The Greeke and Latine Churche, haue of olde kept and still keepeth her holie memorie the ninthe of December. /

The life of S:̣ Nonna mother to S:̣ Gregorie Nazianzene (the Greeke Doctor) S. Gorgonia and Cæsarius: written 24 *by S:̣ Gregorie her sonne in sondrie places,*[1] *whence this is collected.*/

Orat: funeb: Cæsar: [cap. 4 ff.] **Nonna** from her greate grandfathers, and by them long before was consecrated vnto god, of whome she receiued 28 vertue as a naturall Inheritance, which she did not possesse to her self alone, but deriued it to her children also: making her self and them holie flowre of holie corne; which more she so increased and augmented, that the 32 absolute vertue of her husband in all kinde of pietie (I

---

[1] Or. fun. in laudem Cæsarii, Migne 35, p. 755, and Or. fun. in patrem, *ib.* p. 985.

dare speake so of her, thoughe it may seeme strange) can
be ascribed to none but her, as some thinke and report;
and that she (an admirable thing to speake) in reward of
4 her vertue and godlines obtayned more aboundant and
perfect holines. She was maried to GREGORIE of NAZIANZUM   Orat. funeb.
                                                           patris [Cap.
in CAPPADOCIA, not descended of good and godlie Christians 5 ff.]
as she was, nor himself then a good Christian, but of a   Her hus-
                                                           bands stock
8 preposterous and monstrous superstition framed of two   and first
                                                           qualitie.
contraries, to weete of the fond errour of Gentills, and of
the legall vanitie of the Iewes, flying both partes in some
thing, and embracing them yet in others: of the Gentiles
12 (albeit detesting their idoles and sacrifices) yet retayning of
theirs the worship of the fire and candles: of the Iewes,
hating Circumcision, yet with them keeping their Sabaoth,
and abstayning from some certayne meates. The professors
16 of this base and abiect sect, arrogate notwithstanding to
themselues the name of HYPSISTARIES, that is, 'moste highe,'
and they worship onelie the omnipotent. Albeit in opinion
he was an alien, yet for all honestie and humane vertue, he   Morall
                                                              honestie in-
20 then inclined towards vs; for temperance excellent, and   clineth to
                                                              Christian-
therefore moste beloued, for iustice more singular, who   itie.
albeit he liued in greate offices in the common wealth, yet
he neuer increased his substance one farthing, allthoughe
24 he saw others scrape all they could with BRIAREUS the
giants handes, and by the like offices to swell with riches
quicklie: For which and other honest actions, as also
throughe his godlie wyues endeuours (vnlesse I be deceiued)
28 soone after he mett with her, he attayned Christs faith for
a reward. For his wife NONNA burning with loue of Christ,   Her zeale to
                                                             saue her
through her excellent faith, could not indure that her husband husband.
should be of a diuerse religion from her self; and albeit other- [patr. Cap.
                                                                 11.]
32 wise she was a moste patient woman, and of rare courage of
spirit, yet this could she not abide with quiet harte, that
she halfe onelie should be conioyned to God, her other part,
that is her husband being separate from him, greeuing to
36 be ioyned in bodie and not in mynde. Wherefore day and

night lay she prostrate in prayer to god, for the saluation of her head, with many fastings and teares, beseeching Gods mercie for him: And withall she herself dealt with him moste busilie and instantlie, labouring diuerse wayes to gayne him, by admonitions and dutifullnes, by falling out with him, and by that which is the cheefest, good behauiour, and feruent affection to godlynes, wherewith principallie is the mynde bowed and freelie drawen, and mollified to loue and embrace vertue. Neither could it be, but the stone should be pierced and made hollow such daylie droppes falling on it, and that her holie studie and labour should be effected, as by the sequele shall playnlie appeare. This did she aske, and this did she vndoubtedlie hope to obtayne, for that she was more feruent in faith, than in youthlie age: and none had such confidence in these present and visible things, as she had of things hoped: And no meruaile, when before she had experience of gods liberalitie, and the reall fruite of her holie hope. For by her prayers she had before obtayned me of god, and before I was borne she promised me vnto him, nothing doubting of the future euent; and after I was borne she presentlie consecrated me to wayte on him: a worthie attempt was it of her, and a greate benefit of god, that she had not beene made whollie frustrate of her hope and vowe, and that her oblation had not beene refused (*he meaneth thoroughe his owne faulte*)./

To her husbands recouerie and ghostlie health, helped not onelie his good wiues wise manner of curing, which by litle and litle he admitted, but also a vision shewed him in his sleepe, as God vseth often to benefitt and blesse a soule worthie of saluation; which vision was this: He thoughte (that which he neuer had donne before, althoughe his wife was verie frequent and often in prayer) that he song that part of DAUIDS psalmes; *I haue reioyced at those things which were sayd vnto me; we will goe into the house of our Lord.* This was a new song and vnaccustomed, and with this new song, a new desire also entered into his hart:

Which when his wife vnderstood, hauing her wish, tooke
the occasion offered, and expounding the vision, in the best
and ioyfullest part, and declaring the greatnes of that
4 benefitt, with gladnes of mynde added that health was at
hand, and withall wrought that nothing might chance,
which might hinder his calling, or interrupt and quash her
intended desire. Wherefore at that time, many Bishops *The 1: Nicene Councell.*
8 hastening to NICEA there to suppresse and exterminate the *Note the time of Nonna in which she flourished: to weete the yeare: 325:*
mad doctrine of ARIUS lately risen, by which the diuinitie
was diuided (he affirming the Sonne of god to be of inferiour
substance to his Father) GREGORIE her husband committed
12 himself to God, and those preachers of truthe, opening to
them his desire of truthe, and beseeching them to helpe
him to obtayne the common health and saluation; amongst
whome was our famous LEONTIUS, bishop of our mother
16 Cittie. At his Conuersion, God gaue notable testimonie *Two miracles at olde Gregories conuersion.*
by two miracles, which I may not passe with silence, with-
out iniurie to Gods grace by which they were wroughte:
and of the first there are many witnesses. At his first
20 initiation or Cathechising, a spirituall errour was committed
by the maisters of exact discipline or priests, whereby notwithstanding Gods supernall grace did foresignifie, what
was after to come; The forme of priestehood or Bishops
24 degree being mingled with his Christian and prime institution (O instruction and Cathechisme not thoughte of) for
he receyued the Elements of faithe kneeling (which he
should haue donne standing, bishops being onelie then *[add. by the transl.]*
28 created kneeling) whereuppon many bothe of quicke iudgement, and of ordinarie vnderstanding were confirmed not
on lighte and obscure signes to thinke and foretell of him,
that which followed, to weete that he should be Bishop.
32 Not long after an other miracle was added to the former. *The second.*
He comming to that regeneration, whereby we are borne *Baptisme changeth vs and maketh vs new persons; which the miracle following proueth.*
againe by water and the holie ghoste, where we professe
our selues, to be created, consecrated and named Christians,
36 and where we are changed from earthlie persons to spirituall,

he I say comming hereto with burning deuotion, aboundant
and cleare hope, and purged before-hand all he could in
bodie and mynde, far more diligentlie than the Iewes were,
being to receiue the tables of the Law by MOISES; being
baptized and comming out of the water, light and glorie
shined all-aboute him worthie of his mentall affection,
wherewith he came to the gift of faith; which diuerse
others beheld: yet bicause euerie one thought themselues
onelie had seene it, they for a while made no wordes thereof
to any, but after conferring thereof amongst themselues,
they acquainted each other what they had seene: but to the
Bishop LEONTIUS who was the BAPTIST and renewer, the
lighte was so cleare and euident, that not conteyning he did
openlie protest, that he whome he did annoynte, should
succeede him in the Bishopricke./

By this we see, how according to the scripture a worthie
woman and a good mariage is a speciall benefitt from god;
wherewith accord well those wordes of the profane Poet
(HESIODUS) *No possession better than a good wife; nothing
more pernicious than a wicked wife.*/

*By Gregorie she had three children all Saints: Gregorie the
Doctor or greate diuine after; obtayned by prayer as is
sayd before; after Cæsarius a moste excellent learned physicion, honorable with the Emperours, yet more with God:
the third Gorgonia no lesse holie wife than her holies mother./*

'These two were verie louing to their children and also to
Christ; which is not vsuall among men: nay they loued
Christ more than their children; whereas they tooke this
onelie fruite of their children, to haue them knowen and
named of Christ; defyning moreouer, that it was no happines to begette children, vnles they by vertue be conioyned
with god. Bothe were kynde and curteous, full of mercie
and pittie, taking much from the spoile of mothes theeues
and the prince of this worlde, (by charitable bestowing of
them); and withall transporting themselues from this pilgrimage and muteable abode, to the certayne and stable

seate and habitation in heauen; heaping vp to their children, an aboundant and rich patrimonie, the glorie of the life to come. And she was not onelie giuen to her husband by
4 God to be a helper, but which is more to her praise and admiration, to be captaine and leader to all goodnes, by life and speeche and excellent example. And albeit in other things according to the lawes of matrimonie, she thought it
8 best to obey her husband, yet she feared not for faith and godlines to professe her self maister: which act of hers howbeit it is greatelie to be commended, yet more admirable is his praise in that he so willinglie yielded. For she is such
12 a one, as where other women glorie and vaunt of their naturall or artificiall beautie, she contrariwise made reckoning of that beautie onelie which consisteth in the adorning of her soule, and in preseruing and purging of Gods image
16 there with all diligence: and that onelie did she vouchsafe of the name of beautie, for other paynting and trimming by art, she repelled it from her, and left it to women, that delight to be at playes and shewes, to see and to be seene.
20 Also she reputed true nobilitie to be in vertue and godlines, and in knowing whence we came and whither we tend. She accounted these the safe and inuiolable riches, to powre these earthlie things oute vpon God and the poore, and such
24 poore kinsfolke especiallie, as by misfortune had decayed, and fallen into penurie: For to bestow on them onelie necessaries, she thought it rather a renewing of their miseries, than an ease and lightening of their burden: but
28 liberallie and with large benignitie to comfort them, and embrace them, that sayd she was honorable and full of solace. Now where other women, some attend to augment and amplifie their houses and housholde commodities, others
32 giue themselues to pietie and holines onelie, for that it is hard to doe bothe, she for both praises surpassed other women, performing bothe moste excellentlie. For so industrious and good a houswife was she, according to the
36 lawes which Salomon prescribeth to such a stoute and

Their childrens patrimonie.

Orat: funeb: patris [Cap. 8.]

Wherein she was maister.

Her decking Gods Image.

Her esteemed nobilitie.

Her accounted riches.

She was both a good hi s- wife and a Sainte.

paynefull woman, as thoughe she had not knowen, what belonged to pietie and deuotion; On the other side, so whollie addicted she herself to God and diuine matters, as thoughe she had no medling with housholde busines. Neither did one of these studies hinder the other, but rather one was supported and holpen by the other. No time, no place failed her of prayer, for nothing all day did she more, neither was there any woman of so assured hope to obtayne presentlie what she should demand and begg of God, as she. None did so reuerence the hand and countenance of the Priests: none so honoured all kinde of Christian doctrine and wisedome. Who did so extenuate and waste her bodie by watching and fasting as she? who so fastened her self to prayer and singing of psalmes day and nighte like her? Who did more honour and admire virginitie than she, albeit herself was maried and bounde? Who was a greater help and comfort to orphans and widowes? who did so sustaine and lighten the calamities of the mournfull and afflicted? And this more, albeit to some these things may seeme small and of litle accounte, for that they are not manifest to their owne eye, thoroughe enuie not crediting what themselues can not witnesse; yet to me they are of greate worth, for that they proceede from faith and a spirituall feruour: as that in assemblies and holie places, you could not heare her euer speake worde, beside her prayers, and mysticall wordes, or what necessitie did enforce on her. And if in the olde law it was a glorie to the Altar, that neuer axe, or hatchett was seene or heard aboute it (which signified that things dedicated to god should be simple and naturall) why shall not she be commended for honouring holie things with reuerent silence, and for that she neuer tourned her backe towards the holie Table or Altar, and neuer would defile the holie grounde by spitting on it: And albeit she was a verie courteous and sweete woman, yet did she neuer reach her right hand to Gentile,[1] to take them by the hand, neither would she euer offer her lips to theirs to

margin notes:
- See how deuotion helpeth hus-wiferie and doth not hinder it.
- Her continuall prayer and rare hope to obtaine.
- Her reuerence of Priests and holie doctrine.
- Fastings;
- Her honoring of virginitie.
- Her charitie.
- Small workes greate proceeding from faith and spirituall feruour.
- Her silence.
- Her reuerence to holie places.
- Her alienation from Infidels. [1 r. Gentils or a Gentile woman.]

kisse them: by no meanes could she be persuaded, vrged or forged, to eate with those that were of an impure or profane table, Altar or religion: neither could her conscience endure
4 to beholde or passe by their wicked house or Temple. At no hand would she yield her eares or tongue, accustomed to heare, speake, and pronounce diuine things, once to be defiled by listening or rehearsing ethnicall tales or theatricall
8 songs: for she thought that no profane matter was meete for holie persons. And that which is more to be admired, neuer did she yield so to corporall sorrow (althoughe euen at strangers afflictions she tooke exceeding feeling and
12 griefe) that she vttered a worde or sounde of lamentation, without rendering God thankes also, neither did teares runne from her crossed eye-lidds, or [1] sadd cheere did euer seaze on her, but that she accepted the mishapp at Gods hands, and
16 this althoughe sondrie crosses and mischances befell her: For she thought it the dutie of a godlie and religious soule to submitte all humane things to Gods pleasure and holie prouidence. Other things of lesse euidence I ouerpasse,
20 whereof God is witnesse, and her faithfull handmaydes to whose knowledge she committed such matters.

And this was she before her husbands conuersion, how much she profitted after his retourne may well be imagined,
24 when by mutuall holie endeuour and emulation, each studied to surpasse other, as they excelled all others: And to coniecture other vertues by one, whereas her husband being moste bounteous to the poore, bestowing of [1] them
28 not onelie of their superfluities, but also of his necessaries, giuing to all and denying none, leste while he might seeme to denye the vnworthie, he might withholde releefe from the well deseruing, yet to auoide vaine glorie, and not to
32 be seene to doe that, which he did for the moste part, he left the care of bestowing, to his excellent and faithfull wife, who burned with so mightie and vnmeasurable loue of giuing, as [not] [1] the huge Atlantike sea, or whatsoeuer vast
36 thing, and not able to be exhausted would suffice her,

Whereto she denied her eares and tongue.

No profane matter meete for holie persons.

Her fortitude in tribulation. Crossing of eyes. [1 om. cum dies festus adesset.]

Note:

Holie emulation of man and wife. [patr. Cap. 20.] [1 r. on.]

[Cap. 21.] Nonnas vnmeasurable loue of giuing [1 om.]

<small>Pro: 20:</small>

<small>1 MS. thinking, thinking.]</small>

<small>Admirable charitie.</small>

<small>Orat: in laud: fratris Cæsarij [Cap. 15].</small>
<small>Burying at holie places.</small>
<small>She bare a light torche at her sonnes buriall.</small>

<small>Orat: funeb: patris [Cap. 30].</small>

<small>Her miraculous cure.'</small>

emulating by contrarie affection the horsleache or bloud-sucker mentioned by Salomon, ouergoing that vnsatiable greedynes of euill, with vnfillable desire of goodnes: And so readie was she and willing to deserue well of all, that she could neuer be satisfied herewith, thinking[1] her former wealth and what came after all to be too litle for that her liberall desire. Nay she would haue solde her self and her children if she mighte (as she often tolde me) and that moste gladlie, that the price mighte haue beene bestowed on poore folkes needes: to this woman did he remitte the raynes of giuing moste freelie and whollie.'/

Her yongest childe and holie youth CÆSARIUS a famous and admirable learned physicion, for which faculties he was honoured, vsed, and aduanced of the Emperours (CONSTANTIUS and VALENCE) being taken out of this worlde, when his precious ashes and laudable corps, was caried to the martyrs seate, with greate pompe and manifolde singing of hymnes, and honoured with the holie hands of his parents, she bare a lighte torche at his funerall, yielded deuotion in steede of sorrowe, made teares giue place to wisedome, and suppressed griefe with holie singing of psalmes./

He being taken from them, whome for his yong yeares and frailtie thereof, they moste feared to miscarie, then were his parents more free to runne their course towards heauen, with more tranquillitie, which then they did with all their house and familie./

GREGORIE her husband becomming Bishop as was foresignified, and therein conuersing with all pastorall vertue and vigilance, which God witnessed by miracle; 'the like miraculous cure did god worke on my mother not long after, which I thinke necessarie to relate, that we may honour her herewith as she is moste worthie./

She fell sicke, who otherwise by nature was a strong and courageous woman, and who all her life-time before, had neuer beene sicke: And amidst all her griefes, to be short, nothing so tormented her, as want of sustenance taking

accompanied with cruell hunger. Thus was she many
dayes vexed, and could finde no remedie : how then did
God nourish her and feede her? not with Manna rayned
4 from heauen as he fedd the Israelites, nor by bred sent by
a rauen, as he fedd ELIAS : how then? Forsooth she
thought she saw me, whome she loued moste dearelie, on a
sodaine to come to her in the nighte, with a baskett full of
8 white bred, and loues, blessed and signed with the Crosse   Loues
by me, and that I fedd her therewith, and that therewith   blessed and
  signed with
she was made whole : and indeede so came it to passe, as   the Crosse.
her nights vision shewed her, for therewith she recouered. /
12   One other miracle will I add, which was common to them   An other
  miracle.
bothe. When I sailed from ALEXANDRIA into Greece, by   [Cap. 31.]
the gulfe of PAMPHILIA retourning from my studies, the
time of yeare was then verie vnseasonable, albeit my mynde
16 was then to take my iournie. After I with others had
sailed a while, so cruell a tempest ouertooke vs, as the
passengers with me had hardlie remembered the like. And
all thereat fearing death, I was far more afeard of the
20 death of my soule, for I wretch was then in perill to dye,   See the
  danger of
without the renouation of baptisme : wherefore I wished   dying without Bap-
for that spirituall water, amidst those raging waters of the   tisme. Protestants are
sea threatening present destruction. Thereupon I cried out   not so
  minded.
24 vnto God, begged and besought of him a litle space of time
to obtayne that benefit; the others with me cried also for
me, albeit they were in common danger of corporall death,
and that did they more hartily than many a familiar or
28 neere friend would haue doone : For these men were of
greate benignitie and humane kindenes, by perills hauing
learnt to be moued with compassion at others calamities.
In this distresse of mine and ghostlie danger, my parents
32 by vision in the night, were made acquaynted therewith,   Strange
  helpe.
and succoured me, they comming from the land, bringing
helpe with them, and by their prayers (as it were) inchant-
ing the raging waues, as after by computation of the time
36 I vnderstood comming home to them : Which also a wholsome

A comfortable dreame or vision.

dreame declared, which I had, falling a sleepe, after the storme was somewhat aswaged. Methought I saw a cruell furie of hell, looking with gastlie countenance at me, and threatening me danger: At the same instant, an other of 4 the passengers, who was but a youth, yet loued me tenderlie, and had greate care and sorrowe for me being in that state, thoughte he saw my mother entering into the Sea, and that comming to our ship she layd hand on it, and drew it easilie 8 to the shore. This vision deserued credit, for presentlie the Sea became calme, and without trouble we arriued at RHODES:

S. Gregorie vowed to God to forsake the worlde if he escaped.

And my self was the gift offered to God for our safetie in this perill: for as I vowed my self to god and to forsake the 12 worlde, if I escaped that danger, so hauing my wished deliuerie, I yielded my self to his seruice, as I had promised.'/

She proceeding many yeares in that her holie course, and beholding aboundant fruit of her holie labours both in her 16 husband, lyuing fortie fiue yeares a holie Bishop, and in her holie children, neerlie imitating her holie stepps, like her husband, who liued allmoste an hundred yeares, comming

Orat: in Caesar.

to deepe olde age, yea equall to him in vertue and yeares, 20 full of stable and transitorie, eternall and temporall dayes, of principall renowne like her husband amongst mortall

Baron: in martyrolog.

men for vertue, left this life: Whose happie passage the Greeke and Latine Churche do venerablie recorde, and of 24 olde time haue donne, the fift of August.

An annotation touching her liuing with her husband being Bishop. /

Where we reade in this life that this holie woman liued 28 with her holie husband euer, yea after he was Bishop, some may thinke perhaps that like LUTHERAN or Protestant Bishops, Catholike Bishops did marie, or that like some later Greeke bishops (who would that Bishops might vse 32 their wiues before maried, when after they happened to be made bishops) he vsed her carnallie: But this example, helpeth neither: not the Protestants, for that GREGORIE

did not marie after he was made bishop,[1] but long before: [1 A later hand adds: as they do.] neither may we thinke that he kept company with NONNA his wife, after he was made bishop, or some looser Greekes
4 would persuade: For seeing, as S[t] EPIPHANIUS then lyuing affirmeth, that the Church receyued none to be deacon, sub- deacon, Priest, or Bishop, but either virgins or widowes, or who being maried was the husband of one wife, and euer lib: con: haeres; prope finem: et haeres: 69:
8 after abstayned from his wiues carnall companie, especiallie where the Ecclesiasticall Canons were sincerelie kept, and S[t] HIEROME auoucheth the same; and withall seeing that GREGORIE, was a vertuous Bishop by his holie sonnes testi- lib: contra Vigilantium.
12 monie, what may we reasonablie thinke, but that he obserued in this pointe the Churches law moste sincerely? Againe we see heero that he and his wife were allmoste threescore both of them, before he was made Bishop, whence there is no occasion
16 to suspect such leuitie, in so holie persons, at those yeares./

The life or passion of holie Iulitta a gentlewoman and martyr of Cæsarea, written by St Basill the Greeke Doctor[1] : She suffered in Diocletians persecution about
20 *the yeares of our Lorde: 304:* 30: Julie.

'**The** praise of this blessed woman martyr which now offereth it self to be sett forth, is the cause of this our assemblie and meeting: For we haue appointed this day to
24 be keptt solemne and festiuall by you, for that it reneweth the memorie of that greate conflict, which was fought in a womans bodie, but with noble and more than manlie courage, and which stroke all with admiration and astonish- A festiuall day ap- pointed in memorie of her.
28 ment, both them that beheld her combating, and those that heard thereof, by the relation of those that had experience of this her agonie: The moste blessed woman IULITTA (if we may with reasonable decencie terme her
32 a woman onelie, who with heroicall fortitude of mynde, hath ouergone the infirme condition of womans nature) by whose onelie magnanimitie and constancie of mightie spirite,

[1] Homil. in mart. Tul. ; in Migne, Scr. Gr. t. 31, p. 237. ff.

I doubte not but our common aduersarie was mightilie
amazed, and madded to see women to haue gotten such a
victorie on him, who throughe insolent and impotent pride
was wont to vaunt and with magnificall speeches to threaten
and bragge, that he would shake the whole earth to peeces,
and to destroye Citties and all the inhabitants, like a birds
neaste, and the eggs therein: in the meane tyme by this
worthie womans vertue, so much the more weaker proued he,
by how much more eagerlie, he vrged her to fall from Christ:
and as he laboured diuerslie to conuince her of inconstancie,
and that throughe her infirmitie of nature and sexe, she
was not able to defend her religion towards god, so by experience and triall founde he, that she was aboue her
naturall condition strong, and did deride and scorne the terrours, wherewith he hoped to haue frighted and daunted her./

This woman had a suite in law against a principall man
of the Cittie of Cæsarea, who by fraude and violent
handes, scraping all he could to him, and enriching himself
by preying on others wealth, had compassed a greate deale
Her iniurie and suite for her owne. of land to himself, and of Iulitta, had encroched on land,
houses, cattell and seruants; and more, after that he had
seised on all her other housholde stuffe which was verie
riche, by corrupting and suborning false witnesses and
Craft and might, ouercometh right. forged accusers, he preuenteth her of law and rightfull
iudgement, making his best title craftie inuention, base
briberie, and corruption of the Iudges. The day came
wherein this extortioner was to answer Iulittas suite, and
the cause to be decided, when the Crier calleth each partie,
before the bench, Iudges and aduocates in their places.
When Iulitta had begunne to tell her tale, and to informe
the Iudge of the vnmeasurable tyrannie of the man, and
to declare her tenure and title, whereby she had possessed
her goods taken away, from the beginning, and the long
time her possession and title had beene continued, and
thereupon besought iustice in pittifull manner against the
violence offered her, and the insatiable couetousnes of her

aduersarie, he then steppeth vp and sayeth; 'This action of
hers is such, as no long prescription can benefitt or auaile: *See a common sure,*
For there is no reason or law, that they should haue any *but Ethnik plea, against*
4 communitie or fellowship with vs, who doe not nor haue *religion.*
donne any worship to the gods, whome the Emperours
honour, vnlesse they reforming themselues, do first renounce
the faith of Christ.' The Pretor or Iudge thought that
8 proposition or pointe proposed by him to be verie agreeable to lawe, and greatlie to be regarded:/ Wherefore he
commandeth frankincense, and burning coles to be broughte,
and the Iudges aske her, whether she would deny Christ
12 or no: If she will, they say she might enioye the benefitt
of law, and the priuiledges thereof: but if she refused to *For her faith*
renounce him, and would stand stifflie to his faithe, then *she is denied all law and*
could she haue no vse of the barre, lawes, or common *iustice.*
16 wealth: for that according to the law and statute of the
Emperours then reigning, she had incurred the note of
infamie. But what did she then? thinke you she was
bowed or ouerweighed with the desire of sauing or recouer-
20 ing her goods? or did she neglect her cheefe profitt to be
reuenged on her aduersarie? or thinke you at this imminent
perill she was dismayed in mynde? nothing lesse. But
'rather (sayeth she) farewell life it self, and let all wealth *Her faithfull*
24 sinke, and my bodie perishe, than one impious worde shall *considera- tion.*
go from me against my creator and god.' And the more
she saw the Pretor to be moued to wrath at her speeches
so confidentlie spoken, the more, did she yield god more
28 aboundant thankes, for that while she lost her corruptible
riches, to an vniust rauener and robber, she thereby seemed
more to assure herself of the possession of heauenlie goods:
beholding this earth to be taken from her, that she might
32 receiue Paradise; her person to be made infamous, that
she may¹ be made worthie of the crowne of glorie; her [¹ r. might.]
bodie to be torne, reprochefullie with whipps, and to be
spoiled of this temporall life, that she might be partaker of
36 that happie hope, and blessed quires of all saints in the

THE MARTYRDOME OF JULITTA.

Her resolute answer.

ioye of heauenlie kingdome. She then being often demanded, and giuing no other wordes, but that she was the handmaide of Christ, and that she did detest them, that did prouoke and exhort her to renounce her faithe, thereat the wicked Iudge did not onelie bereaue her of that greate wealth, which was taken from her against all

Iudgement on her.

law and iustice, but also adiudged her to lose her life, and that cruellie by fire./ She herewith nothing daunted, as being nothing affected to any thing of this life, wherewith we are wont, much to be inamoured and delighted; but contrariwise, as we vse to runne and hasten to this lifes

Her courageous going to death.

delightes, so did she to the fire assigned for her; walking verie fast to the place of death, in face, gate, wordes which she spake, and moste cheerfull alacritie, witnessing forth the exceeding ioy which she possessed in mynde: And

Her wise exhortation to other women.

tourning to other christian women that were by, she besought them not to feare or quaile to suffer paynes for defence of christian religion, nor to excuse themselues thereof vnder pretext of womans weake nature, 'for that (sayd she) women are made of the same moulde that men are: wee were framed to the likenes or image of god, as

Women as capable of vertue as men, and therefore they may not excuse themselues as infirme.

well as men. Verilie women are created by God, like capable of vertue as men: for what meruail? are not we kinne, and of the same bloud with men in all poyntes? for not onelie flesh was taken to make the woman, but bone also of Adams bones, so that we also are no lesse bound to yield vnto god firmitie, strength and constancie of faith and patience in aduersitie than men.' Hauing sayd thus much, she leaped into the burning flame, which like vnto a shyning mariage bed embraced holie IULITTAS bodie, and sent the soule to heauen, and to the eternall rest thore,

The Saintes bodies dead are venerable.

which was agreeable to her merits; yet kept it her venerable bodie sounde, and no whitt hurte for her kinsfolke, which was buried in the comliest porche of the

They sanctifie the place and persons there.

principall Churche of all the Cittie, sanctifying both the place, and those that come to that place: And more, the

earth at this blessed womans bodilie presence gushed forth
a fine spring of moste gratefull water: so that this martyr
like a pittifull mother and nurse sweetlie feedeth all the
4 inhabitants of the Cittie, as it were with sweete milke
running forth plentifullie for the common vse of all
persons./ Herein dooth this martyr benignelie imparte
that fauour on vs, which of olde, holie ELIZEUS bestowed
8 on his people of IERICHO, changing by his blessing the
saltnes of the common waters of that place thereabouts
into a sweete taste and delicate./

A sweete fountaine springeth at her bodie.

O yee men, I beseeche you permitt not your selues to
12 be founde inferiour to women, in defending your religion:
and you women doe not leaue this example vnimitated,
which she hath shaped you, and withoute pretending any
impediment, sticke fast to your once embraced religion and
16 pietie, and indeede make triall, that this infirmitie of your
nature is no hinderance to any of you, why you may not
performe any good acte.'/ *Thus S. Basill./*

The admirable vertue of a Christian maide Captiue in
20 *Iberia; by whome that Nation was conuerted to Christ.*

That we may see how potent vertue is, wheresoeuer
and in whomesoeuer, that neither to be a slaue and captiue,
nor to liue remote from Christians amongst Pagans hin-
24 dereth a greate faith, and holie mynde to glorifie God
greatlie, by greate workes and worthie vertue; this storie
following will aboundantlie testifie; being of vndoubted
veritie, as witnessed by ᵃRUFFINUS, ᵇSOCRATES, ᶜTHEODORET,
28 and ᵈSOZOMENUS.

a: ll: 1: ca: 10
b: ll: x: c: 16
c: ll: 2: c: 24
d: ll; 3: ca: 6

'About that time,' sayth RUFFINUS (to weete in the yeare
327: as BARONIUS accounteth) 'the people of IBERIA, who
lye vnder the Pontike Pole, receyued the faith of Christ
32 and hope of heauen; But the cause of so greate a benefitt,
was a certayne Christian mayde, that was taken captiue by
them: who lyuing a faithfull and sober life amongst them,

Baron: to: 3:
Annal: Eccl:

Her holie life admirable to the Barbarians.

spending whole dayes and nightes in prayer, became thereby
in admiration to those barbarous people. They neuer
hauing beene acquainted with such manner of behauiour,
were verie curious and inquisitiue to know what it ment.
She simplie answered them, that in that manner she
worshipped Christ her god. The Barbarians meruailed at
that new and strange name, but conceyued nothing els:
notwithstanding her perseuerance in that manner of life,
made the women verie desirous to learne what commoditie
could come thereby. It was a fashion amongst them, that
if any childe were sicke, the mother carried it aboute from
house to house, to trie if any knew any remedie or medicine,
wherewith to cure it: and when one woman had thus
caried her childe aboute, seeking to finde some remedie, at
last she commeth to this captiue, demanding if she knew
how to help her litle one: Who answered that she knew no
humane remedie, yet sayd, that Christ her God, whome she
serued, could giue health beyond mans hope, albeit the case
seemed neuer so desperate: and after that she had layd the
childe on her hayre-cloth or Cilice, and had prayed ouer it
to her Lord, she restoreth the infant whole to the mother.
The fame hereof was caried to many, and withall came to
the Queenes eares, who was sicke of a moste grieuous
disease, whereof she had no hope of cure. Vpon this newes
she desireth, that the Captiue woman mighte be brought
vnto her: but she refused, fearing leste she might seeme to
vndertake presumptuouslie more than could be well expected
of one of her sexe. Whereupon the Queene causeth her
self to be caried to the captiues litle Cell. She as before,
layeth the queene on her cilice, and prayeth for her to
Christ, which donne she arose sounde and ioyfull. Then
teacheth she the Queene, that he who had made her wholle
was her god Christ, sonne of the supreme God, and withall
admonisheth her to call on him, for that it was he that
gaue kingdomes to Princes, and life to mortall men. She
then retourning home verie iocund, and her husband asking

how she was cured so soone, she tolde him. He then for
ioy commanding gifts to be sent to the woman that had
healed her, the queene answered: 'O king the captiue will *Her contempt of earthlie riches and delights.*
4 none of these things: she despiseth golde, contemneth siluer,
she maketh fasting her foode, delighting therewith as
others with eating: this onelie gift will be acceptable to *Her fasting and loue of her Sauiors glorie.*
her, if we will worship Christ her god, who healed me at
8 her request.' The king was not verie forward then to that
motion, and after also deferred the effecting thereof, albeit
he had beene often called on thereto by his wife: Vntill one
day it chanced that being in the woods hunting, many ac-
12 companying him, sodainlie so extreme darknes befell, as if *The kings admirable calling and conuersion*
it had beene midnighte, in so much as none could see which
way to goe: others wandering diuerse wayes, they knew
not whither, the king was left alone in greatest obscuritie,
16 not knowing which way to tourne him. Being in that
desperate case, this cogitation came to his mynde. 'If that
Christ which the captiue hath taughte my wife be trulie
god, and will now deliuer me out of this darknes, henceforth,
20 I will worship him, and forsake all other.' Presentlie when
he had vowed this in his hart, day-lighte was restored, and
he came safe to the Cittie, where forthwith he tolde his
Queene all that had past: And presentlie calling the
24 Captiue to them, he prayeth her to teache him how he
should worship Christ, promising that henceforward, he
would worship no God but Christ. The Captiue came, she *Her skill in religion. She instructeth the king.*
teacheth him Christ to be God, how to pray to him, and
28 how to worship him, and all els what a woman mighte
manifest: She willeth a Church to be built, and describeth *Christian churches of one vsuall forme.*
the forme thereof. The king therefore assembling all his
people, declareth vnto them all that had befallen to himself
32 and his Queene, and teacheth them the faith of Christ: so
that he, not being yet baptised, became notwithstanding
the Apostle of his nation. The men beleeue by the preach- *The king and Queene teache their people the faith.*
ing of the king, the women by the Queene; and all being
36 of one desire, a Churche is built out of hand, and the

walles being speedilie raised, the pillers came to be erected. And when the first and second had beene sett vp, the third comming to be reared, after it was one end in part eleuated, farder it could not be moued, by no engine nor force of men; albeit they had tried all meanes againe and againe. The people thereat were astonished, and the king much daunted, not knowing what to doe. / Nighte comming and all departing, the Captiue onelie watched there in prayer. Morning being come, and the king with those aboute him entering into the Churche, beholde the piller that had beene so immoueable, was reared vp straighte, and hong in the aire, aboue his base or foote, neere the space of a foote. Then the people beholding that admirable worke magnified God, and confessed that the kings faith and Captiues religion was true : when lo an other miracle, for as the people were so admiring, beholde the piller in the view of all, dooth faire and softlie descend vnto his base, none touching it, and there resteth verie streighte and sure: After that, the other pillers were with that celeritie raised and sett vp, as that day sufficed thereto for all. After that the Church was statelie built, and that the people thirsted more vehementlie after the faith of God, by the aduice of the Captiue an Embassage was sent to the Emperour Constantine in the name of the whole nation, all that had happened was declared to the Emperour, they besought him to send them Priests, who might perfect Gods worke begun in them. The Emperour with all ioy and honour, sent them Priests, as they requested, and tooke more comfort thereat, than if by conquest he had ioyned vnknowne nations and kingdomes to the Romane Empire.

That all things before related were donne, as is sett downe, the moste faithfull man BACURIUS, king of that NATION, and Earle of the Emperours housholde with vs, a man of exceeding zeale of religion and truthe, tolde vs at HIERUSALEM.'/ *Thus farre Ruffinus* / *lib: 1 cap: 10:*

Marginalia:
- Other miracles.
- The miraculous force of her watching in prayer.
- The Church is statelie built.
- By her aduice they send to the Emperour Constantine for priests.
- Constantines religious ioy.

The life of blessed Macrina Virgin, and sister to S. Gregorie Bishop of Nyssa, written by him in his Epistle to Olympius[1] a monck, at whose request he wrote it: somewhat abridged.

She died according to Baronius: anno Dñi 379: one yeare after S. Basill: tom: 4: Annalium. [19. Jul.]

'**This** worke (OLYMPIUS) which I terme an Epistle, for bulke hath the iust bignes of a booke, but the argument thereof will excuse me, seeing at your request I wrote it. You can not forgett our meeting and sweete conuersation, at the Cittie of ANTIOCHE, when you were trauailing to HIERUSALEM, to visite the monuments of Christs peregrination in flesh; there amongst other discourses and good communications, whereof your wisedome gaue manifolde occasion, we fell to make mention of an holie woman, if we may terme her a woman, who so surpassed the condition of her nature, of whome what I related, I had not learned of other mens reportes, but of my owne knowledge, neither was the virgin of whome we talked a stranger to me, that I had neede to learne of others the admirable things which I tolde of her, but she was my whole sister, and the first fruite of our mothers fertilitie: / Wherefore seeing you thought the historie of holie persons verie commodious, leste posteritie might be ignorant of this virgins life, who by the studie of wisedome arriued to the toppe of vertue, I thought conuenient to fullfill your desire, allbeit I haue sett downe her life in playne and vncomposed wordes, and with what breuitie I coulde. /

See the certain knowledge he had of this historie./

This virgin was called MACRINA, by her parents for loue and reuerence of our grandmother by the father, so called: who in time of persecutions, had suffered much for Christs confession: This was her vulgar name, yet she had an other secret name giuen her by vision before she was

An other name giuen her by vision.

[1] De vita S. Macrinæ virg. ; in Migne, Ser. Gr. t. 46, p. 959, ff.

borne into this worlde: For of such vertue was our
mother, that she gouerned her self in all things by the
counsell of God, and so much loued pure and chaste life,
that she was married in a manner against her will: For
both her parents being taken hence in the floure of her
youth, and the fame of her beautie drawing many to desire her to wife, if she had not matched herself to some
one, there was greate danger, leste some violence might
haue beene offered her: She therefore coupling herself
with a graue and renowned man, had this virgin for her
first childe: But her time of childe-birth being at hand,

Her vision. one day being oppressed with sleepe, she seemed to her
self to carrie in her armes, this virgin which then she had
in her bellie, and a glorious person standing by excelling
mans countenance in beautie, called the infant THECLA,
which is the name of that famous virgin and martyr,

S. Theclas renowne. moste renowned amongst all Christians: And when that
worthie person had thrice sayd, her name was THECLA, he
vanished awaye. Her mother therewith awaking, was also
withall soone deliuered of her, and that with greate ease.
This name seemeth to me to haue beene giuen her, rather
to signifie that she should be like her in vertue, and profession, than to giue her her name in the worlde. This
childe was brought vp, and thereto had her proper nurse,
notwithstanding was allmoste euer fedd, with her mothers
handes. She growing beyond infants age, was verie ingenious and wittie to learne, whatsoeuer belonged to her
yeares: her mother was verie carefull to haue her well
instructed, but would not permitt her to learne Poets,

See what authors are vnfitt for youth. and such authors as vsuallie children are taughte: For she
thought it vnseemelie, yea filthie to haue a yong mayd de-
filed with the discourses of furious tragedies, or wanton
comedies, or like argument or like vaine Authors. Wherefore she caused some choice partes of holie scriptures, as
of the wisedome of Salomon, and such like, which informeth to vertue and good life, to be readd vnto her.

She was taught the psalmes also, a parcell whereof euerie day at sett times she had to recite. For whether she arose out of her bed or did goe to her booke, or come thence; whether she went to the table, or came from the table, whether to her rest or to her prayers, euermore she was rehearsing some psalmes. She being thus bred, and her hands excellentlie exercised and taught to spinne, knitte and manage wooll, she was now twelue yeares olde; when the floure of her youth began meruailouslie to shine; and which was strange, her beautie was so rare, that albeit it was hidden what coulde be, yet it was not able to be concealed; no not in all the contrie, was there any thing so admirable as her beautie; no the paynters could not frame any peece comparable to her; such was the felicitie of her fayernes. Hereupon whole swarmes of yong men flocked to her parents, and sued to haue her to wife: but the father being wise, and of greate experience in discerning mens qualities, of them all chose one yong man, well borne and bred, and to him he betrothed his daughter, against that he [1] should be of ripe age: Who that while gaue greate arguments of singular hope, that he would proue worthy of that rare mayde: but all this expectation enuie made soone frustrate, for in that tender age, death tooke him awaye. / She knowing her fathers determination, that it was to match her to that yong man alone, hence she tooke occasion to refuse all other mariage: in which resolution she continued constant euer after. For when often motions had beene made her, by her parents, sundrie suing for her, she answered that there was no reason that she should not be permitted to sticke to that matche, which her father had before allotted her, and that she should not content herself with one mariage, as with one birth and one death. 'For (sayth she) he to whome my father despoused me is not dead, but liueth to God, by the assured hope of the Resurrection; so that I deeme him not to be dead, but to be gone to a far contrie: wherefore I iudge it an heynous

Her exorcises.

Her rare beautie.

[1 corr. from she.] *She was despoused but her husband died before-time.*

She thence chose neuer to marie other.

Her wise reason.

crime, if I should not keepe my faith to my husband, being onelie trauailed abrode:' With such reasons she repelled those that soughte to persuade her to mariage, and determyned to conserue her chaste purpose, and withall resolued neuer to depart from her mothers side. Whereupon her mother said to her often; 'My other children I bare onelie a certaine time in my wombe, but thee I must beare euer in my bowells.' Notwithstanding this daughters continuall liuing with her, was neuer either burdenous or incommodious; nay her officious diligence and dutifullnes towards her, was equall to the seruices of many maides: And yet withall the mother and daughter striued piouslie to requite others kindenes. The mother kept the daughters soule, the daughter kept the mothers bodie; seruing her in all needfull offices. And after she had satisfied her holie offices, thinking this also to belong to her profession, with her owne labours, she yielded her mother mayntenance, and not to her alone, but to three other principall persons, did she performe that humanitie. For her possession was dispersed in so many peoples. /

How greate a help she was to her mother.

Her mother being loaden with many cares, for her father was now dead, she still accompanied her, vnderwent part of her troubles, and eased her of a greate weight of her vexations: withall by her mothers vertuous gouernement, she conserued her life free from all reproofe, lyuing euer in her sighte, and hauing her euer witnesse of what she did. On the other side as she benefited herself by her mother, so by her holie conuersation, she was a guide to her mother to run with her the same course of pietie, which she had in purpose. /

Greate Basill her brother she persuadeth to the contempt of the worlde.

When her other sisters were honestlie placed by her mother, her brother BASILL called the greate, retourned from the common vniuersities where he had liued long: she fearing that he was become verie proude throughe his greate knowledge and eloquence, and that he thought himself to good for any dignities, and better than ordinarie magistrates; fell a persuading him to the studie of lasting

and true wisedome, to the contempt of transitorie and
vaine things. Which she effected so forceiblie, as forthwith despising the glorie of this worlde, and neglecting
the honour of Eloquence, he embraced the laborious and
hard kinde of life of seruing god in perfect pouertie, and
entered the redie way to excellent vertue; wherewith he
shyned after exceedinglie ouer the worlde, more than in
few wordes can be expressed. /

When she had shaken of all the matter of troublesome *She persua-*
ded her
life, she exhorteth her mother to leaue her former manner *mother with*
her maides,
of lyuing, and casting of the statelie and proude fashion *to forsake*
the world
of secular conuersation, her self and her maydes belonging *and be*
religious.
to her, all to goe lyue in the house of virgins in the same
manner as they did. But to leaue this speach for a while,
that the virgins sublime spirite may better appeare, I
must not passe ouer this narration following. /

Of foure brothers, the next after BASILL who was eldest, *Naucratius*
the seconde
was named NAUCRATIUS: who was a yong man of excellent *brothers*
vertue.
partes both of bodie and mynde: for he surpassed all the
rest in comelinesse, strength, swiftnes, and abilitie to all
things. He being two and twentie yeres olde, and hauing
in a publike speache shewed such skill as all his hearers
admired him, by Gods disposition, was carried with so
potent a spirit, that forsaking all present things, he
betooke himself to a solitarie and poore life, carying
nothing with him beside himself./ One of the house named *His poore.*
solitarie and
CHRYSAPHIUS followed him, for that he both loued him, and *laborious*
life.
that kinde of life: He hauing found an habitation neere
the floud IRIS (which rising in ARMENIA passeth thoroughe
PONTUS prouince, and falleth into the sea Euxinus) there
dooth this yong man liue in the thicke woodes, remote
from all secular noise, and townes tumultes; and withall
releeueth certaine olde and diseased men, who liued there
with him, thinking this holie worke nothing to dishonour
or hinder his profession. By hunting did he prouide foode
for those olde men (for he was verie experte in all such

kinde of hunting) and with this labour did he tame his yong and lustie bodie, yet euer was he readie to helpe and obey his mother, when she had neede of him. In this kind[1] of religious manner had he spent fiue yeares, when lo by the snares of a wicked woman[1] as was thoughte, he and his deere companion CHRYSAPHIUS, as they were a hunting for the releefe of the olde men, are slayne. His mother, albeit a perfect woman, in all vertues, hearing newes thereof, nature ouercoming in her she sounded, and lay some while as dead: for reason being conquered by the excesse of sorrowe shruncke, and like a strong souldior suddenlie wounded fell to the ground. Heere did the vertue of greate MACRINA shew it self; who at this newes kept herself vpright and vnconquered, and withall supported her mothers imbecillitie; with greate courage exhorting her to patience and fortitude: whence at last her mother withstood her sorow, and shewed no vndecent gesture or womannish passion of crying oute, renting her garments, howling, or other clamorous lamentation; but by reason she repressed the violence of nature, by her owne and daughters counsells healing her infirmitie. And then cheefelie did the virgins greate spirit shew it self: for how-beit nature failed not in her, she louing her brother greatlie, yet surmounting nature, she ouercame her owne naturall griefe, and was able to helpe an other. /

Her mother being then free from the care of bringing vp her children, and placing them in mariage, and her housholde troubles being for the moste parte diuided amongst her sonnes, this virgin wrought so with her mother by effectuall persuasion and her owne example, that she yielded to follow the studie of wisedome, and pure kinde of life, to forgoe her wonted course, and to betake herself to an humble and abiect manner of lyuing; to weete to liue with the multitude of virgins, after their manner, vsing the same table and diet, like bed, clothing and exercises as they did, withoute any difference or preheminence. Where-

fore such was their order of life, so excellent for deuotion,
grauitie and discipline, as can not be expressed with wordes.
For like as soules losed from the bands and troubles of   Their
4 their bodies, and freed from the prison of this life, so was   conuersa-tion
their life free from all the vanitie of humane things, next   vertues.
approching to the life of Angells. No ire, no enuie, no
hatred, no suspicions could be seene amongst them. All
8 desire of honour, glorie, and of like vaine things, all pride
and highe lookes, with the residue of such vices, were farre
from that place. Their deliciousnes was abstinence, their
glorie not to be knowne, their riches to possesse nothing,
12 and to despise earthlie wealth as dust which we shake from
our clothes and bodies. All studie they thought vaine,
which was employed on the care of this life: onelie did the
zeale of heauenlie things flourish in that place, perpetuall
16 exercise of prayer and contemplation, daylie singing of
Psalmes, which neuer ceased day[1] nor nighte, their labour   [¹MS. nay.]
and rest consisting therein. What speach then can dulie
commend this course of life? These virgins liues was
20 mixed of humane and heauenlie nature, partaking of bothe,
and neere to bothe. For as they were free from humane
perturbations, so it surpassed the condition of men; but
as it was exercised in the bodie, and conteyned in mans
24 shape, and vsed the instruments of corporall senses, so it
was inferiour to spirituall and Angelicall nature. Yet
some perhaps will dare affirme their life not to be inferiour
to Angells, seeing they liuing with flesh, like vnto the
28 Potestates who want bodies, are not oppressed with the
burden of their bodie, but eleuating their spirits, conuerse
in soule and behauiour with those celestiall powres./ They
had not lyued a small time in this kinde of profession, when
32 by daylie accesse of vertuous actes, growing in the loue and
taste of God, they approched to greate cleannes of harte./

But a greate helpe for attayning this excellent estate
had she of her brother PETER who was her mothers last
36 childe, and no sooner was he borne, but he lost his father

o 2

then deceasing. This brother, as soone as he was taken from his nurses brest, she being eldest brought him vp in excellent manner, teaching him vertue and holie knowledge euen from his childehoode, not permitting him any leisure for vaine studies. She shewed her self to him, as a father, maister, keeper, mother, and counseller to all excellent things, in so much as before he was past his childehoode, he had ascended to a highe degree of philosophie or Christian wisedome. He was of so pregnant witte, that he seemed to be borne to all kinde of artes, yea and manuall craftes. For withoute a teacher, he of himself became perfect cunning in those things which others obtayned not in long time with the help of maisters. He therefore despising externe studies and occupations, hauing a witt apt for all good learning, and euer imitating his sister, whome he proposed to himself, as the marke and paterne of all vertue, he made that progresse in vertue, that he was expected after to proue nothing inferiour to greate BASILL in excellent holynes. But then he was to his sister and mother worth all the rest, and with them ioyntlie did he aspire and striue to attaine the perfection of that Angelicall life. On a time when there was greate dearth and famine, many moued with the fame of their beneficence flocked from euerie quarter, to that oute-place, where they lyued so retired; where by his industrie such plentie of victualles was serued to the poore, that for the aboundant concourse of people thither, it seemed no solitarie place, but a Cittie. The mother then being verie olde, dying in the armes of her two children, went to God : But first blessing her children moste louinglie, as well absent as present, especiallie those that were present aboute her, offering them to God with prayer ; after she had touched them with her handes, one being at the one side of her bed, the other at the tother side, she spake these last wordes vnto God. ' *To thee Lord doe I dedicate the first and last, which is also the tenth fruite of my wombe: this daughter first begotten, is my first fruite, this sonne last borne is my tenth. To thee are bothe due, for both are thy gifts: On this first and last let thy holie blessing descend:*' and so ending her blessing, withall she ended her life, hauing before willed them to burie her in their fathers Sepulcher: Which when they had effected according to her will, the tyme after they employed in clyming higher towards perfect wisedome, allwayes strugling with their former life to goe forward, and to ouercome precedent vertuous actions with better./ *(Continuall studies to be better./)*

In the meane while the worthie Saint BASILL was chosen Bishop of CÆSAREA, when he consecrating his brother with his mysticall sacrifices made him Priest: And now againe did he aduance his course of life to grauer and holier exercises, ioyning to his present dignitie the studie of diuine knowledge and contemplation. The nynthe yeare after, BASILL that was renowned ouer the worlde died, leauing men, to goe to God; whereat his Contrie and Gods churche receyued greate occasion of griefe. But when MACRINA had intelligence thereof, she could not but be moued in her hart at so greate a losse; for how should not a sister feele that, which afflicted euen enemies? Notwithstanding as golde is fyned and tried by many furnaces, so that what escapeth the first may be discerned in the second, and what remayneth in those may whollie be purified in the third, and if passing all these it yield no drosse it is euident proofe of fine golde; so befell it in her, who being tried with diuerse calamities, as first with the death of our brother, secondlie with the losse of her mother, thirdlie with the departure of her cheefe brother BASILL the glorie of her house, and by none nay nor with all once daunted or yielding any base matter, she proued her self of excellent composition of mynde. *(S! Basill consecrated his brother Peter Priest. Her patient hearing of her brothers death.)*

After this some nyne moneths or thereabouts there was a Councell of Bishops assembled at ANTIOCH, wherein I also was present, which being perfectlie fynished before the yeare ended, I GREGORIE had a greate desire to go visite my sister; for it was now a greate while that we had beene *(Her brother Gregorie bishop of Nyssa visiteth her.)*

hindered of the sighte of ench other, I hauing (by sondrie troubles and tentations which I endured by being by the Princes of the Arrian heresie driuen out of my contrie) beene letted from comming to her. For whole eighte yeares was I in those molestations, so that this while I could not obtayne her presence. When I had now trauailed a greate way towards her, and was within one dayes iournie of her, a vision which I saw in my sleepe, foreshewed all that came after to passe, concerning her. For methought I caried the reliques of martyrs in my hands, whence a light issued, like vnto that which riseth of glasse sette against the sunne, wherewith my eyes were dymned. This sighte had I thrice the same nighte, yet could I not coniecture what it mighte signifie. I was notwithstanding verie carefull with my self to obserue if by the euent, I mighte gather the signification. When I approched neere to the solitarie place where she ledd her Angelicall and heauenlie life, L asked of one of my acquaintance, whether my brother were there: he answered me that he had gone thence foure dayes before to meete me, but taking an other way missed of me./ Then I demanded how this greate virgin did; who saying, sicke: I made more haste the sooner to be with her: for my mynde being terrified at that newes, it somewhat foresignified what followed. When I came to the place, vpon the fame of my comming, many were there attending me from places aboute, comming thither, as the fashion is, for honours sake to meete me: But at the churche the Quire of virgins modestlie expected my comming: When I had made an end of my prayer to God, and blessing of the companie, the virgins bowing their heads at the blessing, modestlie departed to their places all, none abyding with vs; whence I gathered that their head or captaine was not amongst them. Then a man going before and opening the dore I entered into the holie house, where that greate virgin was. She was then vehementlie sicke, yet lay not in bed or couch, but on the grounde, hauing a table or borde vnder her, with

a hayre or sackcloth vnder her on it. At her head she had
an other bord for her pillow which receiued her necke, and
vpheld her head verie handsomelie./ When she beheld me
4 at the doore, she raising her self vp on her elbow, and
putting her bodie forward what she was able, for reuerence
sake, did thus in steede of comming to meete me; which she
was not able, hauing lost all her forces by the feuer. But
8 I comming to her, and taking her in my handes, lifted her
vp, and restored her to her bed: Then lifting vp her hands
to God she sayd; 'I thanke thee my Lord God, that hast
vouchsafed me this benefitt, and granted me my hartes desire,
12 mouing this thy seruant to come visite me thy handmayd.'
And leste she might afflict me, dissembling her griefe, and
concealing her difficultie of fetching breath, she enforced
her self all she could to mirth, seeking occasion of pleasant
16 talke, and giuing vs occasion thereof by her demandes.
But when by inlarging of our speache, she had made
mention of BASILL, my hart was moued therewith, my *Her greate tranquillitie of spirit and rare skill of contemplating.*
countenance changed, and teares ran from my eyes: She
20 nothwithstanding was so far of from being deiected by my
perturbation and sorrow, that from the mentioning of
BASILL, she founde matter of highe contemplation, disputing thereupon of the cause and nature of humane things, of
24 Gods secret prouidence in sending aduersities, of the qualitie
of the life to come; whereof she discoursed with so diuine a
spirite, that by her speaches my minde seemed to be in
heauen, and transported out of my self: And as JOB (as the
28 scripture telleth) howbeit his bodie was all defaced and
broken with biles and botches, yet paine depriued him not
of reasons action, but when he was afflicted in bodie, he was
cheerfull in mynde, strong in spirit thoughe weake in bodie,
32 not intermitting or staying his talke of sublime things for
his bodies infirmitie, so mighte you beholde in this greate
woman. For allthoughe the ague had dried vp all her
forces, and her bodie waxing colde hastened towards death,
36 yet her mynde was so sounde and free, that she could

contemplate heauenlie things, in a manner withoute impediment: which I could easilie proue by setting you downe all her discourses of the soule of man, of mans life in this bodie, of the end why man was made, how he is mortall, and how immortall, and how he passeth hence to the next life : all which in the force of spirit she declared so wiselie and distinctlie, with so fluent copie, and so readie speache, as can hardlie be expressed : All this I say, I could readilie manifest, were it not that I feared my speache would grow ouer tedious. /

<small>As we call Bishops fathers, so she called him father.</small>

She hauing ended her talke ; 'It is time (sayth she) father that you goe rest awhile, and haue due care of your bodies needes, for you may well be werie of so long a iournie :' For my part albeit I tooke greate contentment to see her and heare her talke of so weightie matters, yet bicause it seemed good to her, and that I might obey her as my mystresse in all points, hauing gotten in the next gardens, a pleasing lodging, I rested me vnder the shadow of the trees. But I could take no delighte in any pleasant thing, my mynde being troubled with the feare of sorrow at hand. For now the signification of my former vision, seemed to be expressed in these present things : for the spectacle proposed of MACRINA resembled to me the reliques of a martyr, she in a manner like them being dead to sinne, and shyning with lighte throughe the grace of the holie Ghoste dwelling within her. And thus had I before expounded my dreame to one that had heard of it. She I know not how, coniecturing my sorrowfull cogitations, sent one to tell me more comfortable newes : willing me to be of good cheere and hope better of her, for that she felt her sicknes somewhat eased. She sayd so, not to deceiue vs, but sincerelie and trulie, albeit we were ignorant of her meaning. For indeede as one running in a race, hauing ouercome his aduersarie, and being presentlie to ariue at the goale, and to receiue his reward or victorious crowne, reioyceth and biddeth his friends aboute him to be merrie, as if he had

<small>He calleth her his mistresse.</small>

his desire; so she now expecting the reward of her heauenly calling, and with the Apostle pronouncing those wordes of her self: *Now remayneth there for me a crowne of*
4 *iustice, which is layd vp for me, and which the iust iudge will restore vnto me, seeing that I haue fought a good combate, I haue finished my course, and haue kept my faith*: she I say being thus affected, biddeth vs to be merrie, and to
8 hope better things of her. At the good tidings then, I arose, and hasten to goe and enioye them in presence. But when we came to her, there being no time to talke and spend vainelie, she began to recounte all things that had
12 befallen her, euen from her childehoode, relating all things so redilie as if she had read them out of a booke, not omitting what she remembered of her parents life, and what chanced before, and after my birth. The scope of that
16 speeche and narration was onelie to giue god thankes for all. She tolde me that her parents life was not so greate and renowned for riches, as increased and aduanced by Gods bountie, whereas for Christs confession her fathers
20 parents had beene much vexed, and persecuted, and her mothers grandfather had beene slayne by the Emperours, and all his goods giuen away to others for gods cause; notwithstanding that it had so prospered by Christs faith,
24 that at that time none was more worshipfull than they. And howbeit their substance was diuided into many partes, according to the number of their children, yet by Gods mercie, euerie one of their sonnes chance was such, that they
28 exceeded their parents welth: And for her self, that after she had made equall diuision to her brothers, she left nothing to her self, but by the handes of Priests, had according to Gods prescript giuen all away, and yet
32 throughe gods help she liued so, that she ceased not to labour with her handes, as gods will was, nor euer looked after any man, in whose liberalitie she reposed hope of mayntenance. And as she had neuer reiected those that
36 asked of her, so did she neuer looke that any should giue

Sidenotes:
She is merrie before her death; and why.

She recounteth all her course of life past: and why.

Her Progenitors noble sufferings for Christ, and Gods temporall blessing therefore.

She gaue all her goods away by the hands of Priests, and became voluntarilie poore according to the Euangelical counsell.

Nota. her; seeing as God of his goodnes by his secret powre, did so blesse her litle labours, that they like seede did bring forth manifolde increase. But when I did recounte my owne trauailes which I had passed, of banishment first for the faithe vnder VALENS the Emperour, then my conflicts and sweate endured in other troubles of the Churches; she replied: 'But see you be not ingratefull to Gods diuine benefitts: for if we esteeme it no small glorie to be borne of honest and honorable parents, and our father was of credit for his learning and law, amongst Cittisens, and in iudgements, yet his fame went not beyond PONTUS,

Gregories glorie. his glorie conteyned it self within his owne contrie, but thy glorie and fame stretcheth it self, vnto Citties, peoples, and sundrie nations: Churches send to thee for helpe, they call thee to order and determyne their matters; and doe you not consider therein Gods blessing? nor acknowledge the cause

The cause thereof his parents prayers. of so greate benefits? Thy parents prayers haue aduanced thee to this highth; thy owne desert litle or nothing auayling to attayne thither.'

When she did prosecute these things, I wished the day had beene longer, that our eares might haue beene longer delighted with her sweete discourses; but the voice of those

Euensong and praiers all nighte. that sang, called me away to Euensong. Wherefore when she had dismissed me to the Churche, the greate virgin did conuert her self to God by prayers, and so was the nighte spent: When day came by some signes I coniectured, that this would be her last day; but she to auert vs from such sad thoughtes, with other excellent speeches dooth imparte vnto vs the litle remnant of force which she had, albeit she tooke her breath with difficultie. I beholding her in that plighte, felt diuerse affections, fearing that I should neuer

Worthie religious women the glorie of their stocke. heare that voice of hers more, and that she the common glorie of our stocke would soone leaue this life; yet by those things which I beheld in her, my mynde was as it were diuinelie inspired and comforted, she seeming to me to

How she ouergoe the common nature of men. For at her last gaspe

allmoste, she seemed to feele no new pang, nor to haue any kinde of feare, but with a noble spirit to esteeme litle of this life, and while she had breth, still to talke and thinke *received death: with what behaviour and wordes.*
of heauenlie things, more like vnto an Angell than a woman; as if her spirit had no coniunction with her mortall bodie; in so much that shewing no vnseemelie gesture nor any perturbation, her flesh haled her not to bodilie passions. Then me thought did she declare to the standers-by, her pure and diuine loue to her heauenlie husband, which she harboured in her holie hart, manifesting her greate desire she had, speedilie to hasten vnto him: For whollie giuen to vertue, no delectable thing of this life, could call her eyes to beholde them. It did then draw neere sunne-sett, yet she remitted not her cheerefull mynde, but the neerer she did approche vnto her end, the cleerer did she descrie the beautie of her beloued, and so much the more did she long to be with him: not talking any more to vs that were aboute her, but to him, whome with fixed eyes, she did beholde with her mynde: For her bed looked towards the Easte: wherefore in prayer she spake to god, and with her handes did she beseeche him, murmuring with low voice words which we yet mighte reasonablie well heare, speaking in this manner. *The vse of praying toward the Easte.*

'*Thou O Lord* (sayth she) *hast taken from vs the feare of death: Thou hast made that the end of this life should be the beginning of true life: Thou doost deliuer our bodies to sleepe for a time, and againe by the last trumpett, wilt raise them vp from sleepe: Thou committest to the earth this earthlie bodie which thy self hast framed, and wilt require the same againe of her; and our mortalitie and deformitie, thou wilt deck with glorie and immortalitie. Thou hast freed vs from curse and sinne, by becoming for our sake accursed, and reputed sinfull. Thou hast crushed the dragons head, who swallowed man into the gulfe of pride. Thou breaking the gates of hell and weakening him that had powre to kille hast opened vs the gate to resurrection. Thou to the ouerthrowing of our enemie, and* *The powre of for safetie of our life, hast giuen a signe to those that feare thee, to weete, the marke of the holie Crosse.* Eternall God to whome I was dedicated from my mothers wombe, and whome I haue loued with all my forces, and to whome I haue consecrated my bodie and minde from my youth hetherto, send me I beseeche thee thy Angell, who may conduct me, to the place of rest, into the bosome of our holie fathers: Thou that hast broken the flaming swordes, and didst bestow Paradise on the theefe that was crucified with thee, and did flie vnto thy mercie; remember me also in thy kingdome: for I am also crucified with the pearcing thoroughe my flesh with thy feare, and dreading thy iudgements: let not that vast chaos and gastlie depth separate me from thy elect. Let not the enuious aduersarie hinder my iournie. Let not my sinnes, what I haue slipped by frailtie in thoughte, worde, or worke, be regarded of thy eyes, but pardon me whatsoeuer, O thou that hast powre to remitt sinnes, that I may be comforted at the deposition of my bodie; being founde in thy sight without spott in my soule, and appearing irreprehensible, my soule may be receiued at thy hands, as sweete incense moste acceptable to thee.'/ Saying thus she signed her eyes, mouthe, and harte, with the signe of the Crosse, and not able to speake any more throughe extreme drynesse, by opening her lyppes and mouing her handes, we perceiued that she did praye./ Euening came and lighte being broughte, she opening her eyes and looking towards the lighte, shewed her prompt mynde to euening-thankes giuing, but her voice fayling, with hart and handes she satisfyed her good desire: And when prayers were donne, she putt her hand to her face to crosse it, and fetching a greate sighe, ended her deuotion and life. She then neither breathing, nor once mouing, I remembering how that at our first meeting, she had willed, that my hands should shutte her eyes and mouth, I putt my hand trembling for griefe to her holie face, more to satisfie her desire, than that she had any neede thereof; for that as in ones naturall sleepe, her eyes were comelie close, her lips also ioyned, and her hands verie

Marginalia:
- the signe of the holie Crosse giuen by Christ.
- Soule without spott and irreprehensible.
- She signed her eyes, mouth and hand with the signe of the Crosse.
- Her composition of her bodie dying.

seemelie clasped together on her brest; yea all her bodie was so comelie composed, that it needed no hand to order it.

I was doublie greeued, partlie at that spectacle layd before me, partlie at the pittifull lamentations of the virgins, which sounded on euerie side of me: Vntill now they had carried themselues courageouslie, conteyning their inward griefe, close to themselues, and abstayning from teares, and this for reuerence of her lyuing, and vpon her example which they obserued, and fearing least she would reprooue them dooing otherwise, or might be molested with such behauiour. But when their mistresse was departed, ouercome with sorrowe, they burst out into incredible weeping, so that my self was scant my owne man, reason being putt from her purpose, and as one driuen and caried away by the violence of a strong brooke, it yielded to passion and gaue it self whollie to lamenting. And iust cause of such sorrow, did the virgins seeme to haue, when not for humane respects of familiaritie, comforte, good gouernement, and the like lost now, did they lament, but they grieued as if they had beene now spoiled of part of their hope to God, and health of their soules; for they wayling sayd. '*The light of our eyes is putt oute, the torche that shewed vs our way in our iournie is taken from vs; we are bereft of the healpe*[1] *of our life, the paterne of puritie, the chaine of concorde, the piller of the weake now haue we lost: Thou guiding vs, night was as good as day to vs; but now day is turned into night*': and they lamented moste, who called her their mother and nurse; who indeede were such who in the time of famine, lying in the wayes and pyning for want, she releeued, cherished and so instructed, that they chose to liue chaste and make that profession with her self./ But after that I had recollected my self, and had cast myne eyes on her holie countenance, being in a manner reproued by her for that vnseemelie noise and tumultuous demeanure, crying out with a loude voice I sayd; 'Cast your eyes, O virgins, on this bodie, and call to mynde her

She was Abbesse.

Her excellencies.

[1 MS. corr., orig. healthe.]

precepts, wherewith she taught you all seemelie and honest behauiour: That diuine spirite allowed vs one onelie time to weepe and shed teares, and that was when we prayed; which now you may performe, chaunging your lamentation into singing of psalmes': This spake I with as highe a voice as I coulde, to the end I might drowne the sounde of the lamenters. Then did I exhort them to withdraw themselues into the next house, reteyning onelie some few, which were those which she liuing most vsed./

Vestiana her worthines. Amongst which was one a moste noble woman, for riches, stocke, beautie, and all other good partes verie worthie, and besides for yeares yong. She had beene maried to a moste honest gentleman, but liued with him a verie short time. Wherefore being freed from mariage, she chose greate MACRINA for the keeper and guider of her widdowhood, and with the virgins she much conuersed, to the end she might learne of them, the perfect manner of lyuing vertuouslie: This womans name was VESTIANA, her father was called ARAXIUS, and was one of the Senators of

A consultation with what ornaments she should be buried. the highe Councell: To this woman, I sayd: 'I thinke none will now enuie, if I adorne the dead bodie, and clothe her pure and immaculate flesh with more riche and comelie garments.' She answered, 'I thinke, you were best first of all to know what was the will of the holie virgin touching this pointe: for we may not doo any thing contrarie to her lyking: for what shall best please God, that will be moste pleasing to her.' There was an other, who was Prefect or cheefe ouer the Quire of virgins; her

Lampadia. name was LAMPADIA; 'she (saith VESTIANA) vndoubtedlie knoweth MACRINAS mynde, touching the pomp of her funerall': I asking her opinion, for as it fortuned she was present at the consultation, she answered, but not withoute

Nota. teares, 'This holie virgin prepared her self an ornament, by lyuing chastelie and purelie, wherewith she mighte adorne both her life and her buriall; for touching her bodies garments and dressing, she recoiued none lyuing,

nor reserued any for the vse of her funerall; wherefore if
we would, we haue nothing, wherewith to decke her in this
manner.' 'Haue you nothing (sayd I) lying in store, where-
with her exequies may be sett forth?' 'What talke you, <small>See her rich clothing.</small>
sayth she, of lying in store, what she had you haue all
in your handes; beholde her cloke, and the couer of her
head, and an olde paire of shooes, this is all her riches,
this her housholde stuffe: nothing beside that you see, is
there in chest or chamber. Her onelie Cell of her riches,
was the heauenlie treasure, there did she lay vp all;
nothing left she on earth.'/ 'But what (sayd I) if of such
things as I haue, I produce somewhat to the adorning of
her buriall, will she, trow you, thinke it vnaduised?' 'I
thinke not (sayd LAMPADIA); for howbeit, sayd she, in her
life-time,[1] she refused not what honour you did her, partlie <small>[1 etsi vivo-ret, non
for the dignitie of your priesthoode, which she euer repudiaret.]</small>
honoured, and partlie for coniunction of bloud you being
her brother; no more will she being dead, seeing dying she
commanded her bodie to be buried by your handes.'
It being then concluded that her sacred bodie should be
seemelie trimmed, we diuiding the care betweene vs, I
commanded one of my seruants to bring a garment; but
VESTIANA decking her holie hed with her owne handes, as
she putt her hand vnder her necke, 'beholde (sayth she
looking on me), what a braue iewell the virgin hath hanging
at her necke,' and losing the knott behynde, she shewed me <small>A Crosse of iron and an
an iron crosse, and a ring of iron hanging at one string, iron ring, wherein was
which two she kept euer to her hart: Then sayd I, 'this a peece of the holie
treasure shall be diuided betwixt vs: take you the Crosse, Crosse, she had hanging
and my part shall be the ring'; for in the broade and flatt euer at her
part thereof was a Crosse grauen. She looking againe at harte.</small>
the ring, sayd; 'you were not deceiued in the choice; for
the ring is hollow, and in the brode parte, there is contayned a peece of the tree of life, which the Crosse grauen
without doth signifie.' When time came that the chaste
bodie was to be inuested, which by the greate virgins com-

mandement was to be donne by me, VESTIANA being present, who had shared with me in that greate inheritance, and assisting me to touch the holie bodie, said; 'doe not pretermitt to beholde a greate wonder, wrought by this holie woman,' and opening bare a litle of her brest, 'see you (sayd she) a litle small signe somewhat blacke vnder her necke,' (it was like a pointe made with a small needle) and putting the candle neere to shew it me playne, I sayd, 'what strange thing is it, to haue such a small thing?' 'This' sayd she 'is the monument of gods diuine helpe, shewed to MACRINA. For when on a time this part did swell vehementlie, and there was perill least shee should be forced to haue it cutte, or being incureable should spreade it self verie wide, her mother often requested her, that she would permitt the physicions hand and arte, to yielde what helpe he coulde, seeing that God had bestowed that skill for mans health: But she iudging it more grieuous, to lay open any parte of her bodie to mens eyes, than any infirmitie, at nighte after that she had serued her mother with her owne handes, as her custome was, she goeth into the moste holie chappell, where prostrating her self in prayer, she spendeth all the nighte in beseeching God for helpe, and mingling her teares aboundantlie flowing, with the earth, this remedie did she applie to her disease. Her mother being much grieued for her, and still exhorting her to vse the physicions helpe, she answered her that it would be sufficient medicine to cure her griefe, if she with her hand woulde on the place afflicted make the holie signe of the Crosse. When her mother had putt her hand into her bosome, to signe the sore parte, she made indede the Crosse thereon, but the disease was gone, and this onelie marke of that horrible swelling remayned to her end, that it mighte be, (as I coniecture) the token of gods helpe, whereby she might euer be moued, and putt in mynde to giue him thankes.' /

After that we had finished our worke, and had adorned the bodie with our domesticall store, the foresayd woman

A miracle wrought by her on her self.

Her chaste minde endureth not her bodie diseased to be layd open to men:

The Chappell moste holie.

Note her estimation of the Crosse.

sayd, that it was not decent, that the bodie should be *Her funerall attire.*
trimmed like a bride, in the sighte of the virgins, 'but there
is (sayth she) in my custodie a blacke cloke, of your mothers
4 garments, which as I thinke may well be cast ouer the
other attire, to the end that her holie beautie be not
beautified with the brauerie of strange attire': Which
opinion preuailing, the cloke was putt vpon the rest; she
8 notwithstanding in the blacke garment, did so shine, God I
imagine giuing this grace to her bodie aboue expectation,
that as it was shewed me in my sleepe, verie beames seemed
to issue from her beautie./
12   While these things were donne, and the place sounded
with the singing and lamentation of the virgins, the fame
hereof (I know not how) flying euerie way, all that dwelled
nighe, flocked to the funerall in such aboundance, that the
16 Courte could not conteyne them. When therefore the *Whole night vigills, and praying and singing, now and in the feaste of martyrs.*
vigills all nighte had beene spent in singing psalmes (as the
manner is in the feastes of Martyrs) and the breake of day
was come, so greate was the multitude of men and women
20 that came hither, that their weeping and wayling interrupted the singing of psalmes. And albeit I was not a
litle afflicted in mynde with others, yet did I so prouide,
that nothing what might be procured, was wanting in these
24 exequies. Wherefore destributing the people that were
assembled into companies, I ioyned the women with the
Quire of virgins, and the men with the multitude of *Multitude of monks present.*
monckes, that so good order might be kept, each ioyning
28 seemelie with their order of singers. But when the day
passed, and the place was too straight for the multitude,
Bishop ARAXIUS who was present with all his multitude of
priests, and was Bishop of this region or prouince, rising vp
32 commanded that the Tabernacle should faire and softlie goe
before, then that all that had to attend and assist him,
should with their presence wayte on the bodie. These *Two Bishops carrie the beare with other of the Cleargie.*
things being so donne, I and bishop ARAXIUS carried the
36 forepart of the beare, and two of the cheefe of the cleargie

FEMALE SAINTS.   P

carried the hinder part. Leisurelie went they before, and in like manner leisurelie did we follow: For whereas aboundant of people stoode about the beare, who could not be filled with that admirable and sacred sighte, we could with difficultie march on. On bothe sides did there a greate multitude of deacons, and other Churchmen go before, all in order, euerie one bearing a burning taper or wax candle in his hand: which pompe wanted not a mysterie, when as from the beginning to the end Psalmes were song of three orders of singers with one voice, like as the song of the three Children: and whereas betweene the monasterie and the Churche of the martyrs (where her parents bodies lay) there was seauen or eight furlongs (which is aboute a mile) we spent allmoste all the day in going thither: for the concourse of people still augmenting, euer hindered vs from going forward. When we came within the dores of the Temple, setting downe the beare we began to pray:. which prayer gaue to the people matter of lamentation. For the singers being made silent, when they had beheld the sacred face of the virgin, and the toombe of her parents was opened, into the which we determyned to putt her, one virgin crying oute sodainelie, that after that houre, they should neuer beholde againe that diuine head, and the rest of the virgins following with the same outcrie, the holie song of the Psalmes, was concluded, with this confused crie of lamentation. For the harts of all were wounded with the virgins crie and weeping, in so much as we commanding silence, and one beginning the vsuall prayers of the Churche, yet hardlie could the people compose and frame them selues to praye.

After we had ended our prayers, I began to be afeard remembering that precept of the lawe, where we are forbidden to reueale the turpitude of our father or mother. 'And how (sayd I to my self) shall I auoide this iudgement, if I shall beholde in my parents bodies, the common turpitude of mans nature; whereas by all likelyhood, their bodies being corrupted are brought to lothsome deformitie': My feare in this cogitation was augmented, by calling to mynde how NOE was offended, with a sonne of his sinning in this kynde. Before therefore the bodies were opened to our sight, they were couered ouer with a clene linnen clothe. For as the toombe was opened, forthwith was the cloth cast ouer them: Which donne, I and the Bishop of that region ARAXIUS, taking the holie bodie from the beare, layd it by her parents: wherein I fullfilled both the daughter and mothers desire. For they lyuing besought God euermore, that dying they might in bodie be ioyned, as in their life they had neuer beene separated. After we had performed all that belonged to this funerall, and I was to departe, prostrating my self at the toombe I kissed the dust, and so departed, sorrowfull and weeping, thinking with my self, what a benefitt we had lost. /

S. Gregorie honoreth the toomb, and kisseth the dust.

As I trauailed in that iournie backe, an honorable man of AUGUSTA a cittie of PONTUS, and Chiefetayne of the Armie there, hauing had intelligence of this dolefull chance, and grieuing himself thereat, accompanied with his subiects, went out curteouslie to meete me: He was allied to me both in friendship and bloud, and related vnto me a miracle wroughte by her, which hauing sett downe I will make an end of this historie. 'Consider I pray you (sayth he) how greate a commoditie ours hath left this life. My wife and I had once a greate desire, to goe see that Colledge or schoole of vertue; for so iudge I, that place is to be called, where that blessed soule did dwell. With vs was a litle daughter of ours, whose eye throughe a pestilent disease, was made verie deformed; a skynne being growne ouer the sight, and the white of the eye shrunk vp, so that it was an ouglie spectacle to looke at. We being entered into that diuine house, so was my wife and I parted in this place of religious women students of wisedome, that I went into that part where men dwelt, the

An other miracle.

Mark dis-

<small>tinct parts of the monasteries: one for men an other for the virgins.</small>

Ruler of whome was your brother PETER; my wife entered in where the virgins dwelt together with holie MACRINA: We hauing stayed there a prettie while, we thought it time to depart, and as we weare going away, on both sides, were we held perforce. Your brother Peter commanded me to staye and to take part of a Students dinner: Blessed MACRINA on the other side, would not lett my wife goe, but taking our daughter in her armes, tolde her, that she would not restore it,[1] before dinner was readie, and that she had tasted of philosophers or religious womens riches. She kissing the girle, and putting her mouth to the childes eyes, where her griefe was, she sayd; 'If you will lett her remayne with vs, I will requite this honour the best I can.' 'How (I pray)' saith the wenches mother. 'I haue (sayth greate MACRINA) a medicine which will cure her eye:' Which promise when one of the virgins had tolde me, we yielded verie willinglie to staye, albeit some vrgent busines called vs away. / When the feaste that Peter of his fauour and kyndenes had prepared for me was ended, and my wife had beene cheered of holie MACRINA, with all conuenient mirth, full of ioy and gladnes we went our way. / As we were in our iournie, we related to each other, what we had seene or heard, I amongst the men, and she amongst the virgins, omitting no litle thing that we could remember: When she had orderlie tolde all that past, and came to mention the promise that MACRINA made to cure the childes eye; there breaking of; 'But what ment we (sayth she) that did not accept of her offer, and require the oyntment and medicine which she profered vs!' I also blaming her for that negligence, and commanding one to hasten backe and to request her profered salue, the infant withall that was in her nurses armes, looked at her mother; the mother thereat looking also vpon her, sayd to her. 'Be not angrie with vs for our negligence, for beholde she hath trulie payd what she promised: by her prayers purchasing for vs the true medicine of all diseases, which

[¹ r. her,]

was of such force, that no signe of any hurt remayneth in thine eye, it being perfectlie healed by that diuine salue:' And saying so she tooke the girle and gaue her into my
4 handes. Then I calling to rememberance the incredible miracles, which are related in the gospell: 'What meruaile is it (sayd I) if blinde men receyued their sighte at the hands of god, when as his handmaide by her faith in him,
8 dooth doe the same cures: for this worke which we beholde, is litle inferiour to those miracles." While he tolde me these things sobs interrupted his talke, and teares in aboundance followed after. /
12 I haue heard many moe things related vnto me by them who lyued with her, and had perfect knowledge of all her life, but I iudge it not best to adioyne them to this historie: for many will beleeue no more than themselues
16 can doe: what things exceede the power of the hearer, they suspect them as far wide from truthe, and coyned by liers. / Wherefore I pretermitt that admirable tillage and crop in the time of penurie and famine: how corne
20 bestowed on the vse of the poore, neither diminished when it was in destributing, nor afterward, but remayned full the same measure and number. Many others far more admirable than these doe I passe vntouched, as well curings
24 of diseases, as expulsions of diuells, and true predictions of things to come; which all were founde moste true of those that made diligent triall of them; howbeit they seeme incredible and are iudged impossible of those who
28 are carnall and iudge according to the flesh, who are ignorant how the distribution of such gifts and graces is made according to the proportion of faith, and that small things are bestowed on them that haue litle faith, and greate
32 things to those that haue greate faith. Wherefore leste such as are weake to beleeue diuine gifts, may be offended, I lett goe in silence her greater and more sublime miracles, thinking it enoughe to end her historie, with that which
36 hath beene sayd.'/

Many moe and more admirable miracles did she, by curing diseases, expelling diuels and foretelling things to come. Why the holie Bishop will not relate those miracles, and who are vnworthie of such histories.

Of the acts of her Grandfathers: and an admirable miracle of them.

Because mention is made in S! MACRINAS life how her greate grandfathers suffered much for Christ, I thought it would be both pleasant and to the purpose to add out of S! GREGORIE NAZIANZENE somewhat thereof, with an admirable miracle wrought by god for their temporall comforte, that we may see his rare prouidence and benignitie he vseth to his patient louers. /

Orat: de laudibus Basilij.

He speaking in the life of greate BASILL [1] of the seuere persecution raised by MAXIMIANUS GALERIUS Emperour, and how many in PONTUS by their Christian valour ouercame that crueltie sayth. 'This tyrant did many of our valorous souldiors ouercome, some fighting vnto death, some almoste to death, yet liued that they might continue after their victorie, and be to others, examples of true vertues being lyue martyrs, and might be as quicke pillers and silent criers of faith and fortitude to their fellow Christians. Of this sort were the greate grandfathers of BASILL by the fathers side; who hauing before walked throughe all kynde of pietie and holines, by this tempest gaue this complement or consummation to their former life. For they being so resolued in mynde, willinglie to suffer whatsoeuer, that they might be crowned of Christ in his kingdome: notwithstanding they knowing withall that not fighters onelie are to be crowned, but such as fighte lawfullie: and the law of a martyr is, that neither we cast our selues into danger, nor yet giue euill example of dastardie, to the persecuter or weake brethren, but when we be brought into danger, and vrged to fighte, we flie not the combate: for that the first is a token of a rashe and precipitate spirite, the second of a fearfull, and sluggishe mynde; in this pointe therefore they determyne to obey the law giuer, and marke I

[1] Or. fun. in laudem Basilii, Cap. 5; in Migne, *Ser. Gr.* t. 36, p. 499.

pray you what counsell they tooke, or rather whether[1] [¹ r. whither]
Gods diuine prouidence, which gouerned all their counsells,
leadd them. /

4 They with a few companions and some seruants to
dresse their meate fledd into a certayn woode in the
mountaynes of PONTUS, where there are sondrie woods
wide and thicke. Some will admire the time which they
8 liued there; which was almoste seuen yeares: some rather
will meruaile how those tender and well-bred bodies, could
endure that hard, sharpe and vnwonted manner of life,
which it seemeth they leadd, lyuing vnder the open
12 heauens, in colde and heate, in the rayne and like wether;
especiallie as some may thinke, being in this desert
whollie bereft of the companie of men, who in former
times were wonte to haue many wayters and attenders
16 following them. But I will tell you a thing farre more
strange and admirable, which let none discredit vnlesse
perniciouslie and perillouslie he iudge it a lighte matter
and not worthie of greate commendation to suffer perse-
20 cutions and to vndergoe perills for Christs name. These
notable men one day wished for some more sauerie meates,
than long time they had tasted: for being worne and
wasted with that long hardnes, they began to feele some
24 sacietie of their ordinarie simple sustenance: yet did they
not like those murmuring Israelites in the desert, who
wished to be in Egypt againe, amongst their fleshpots,
and other commodities there abounding, not remembering
28 their heauie labours in clay and mire, but vsing wordes
sauoring of more holines and greater faith, sayd: 'Why
can not that God of miracles, who fedd his people wandering
in the desert so bountifullie, not onelie rayning bred vpon
32 them, but birds also, not feeding them with necessaries
onelie, but with delicates, who diuided the Sea, stayed the
sunne, stopped the floud Iordan for a while, and did
sondrie other meruailous benefits for his seruants (which
36 histories they then repeated, as ones mynde in such cases

will easilie recorde), *why I say can not he also this day feede vs his souldiors with more dayntie cates? So many wilde beastes are there in this woods, which haue escaped rich mens tables, whereof sometime we haue beene partaker: and so manie sorts of wholsome fouls flie ouer our heads, of all which there is nothing, but can easilie be taken, if it shall please their Lorde.*' They speaking thus, their wordes caught them daynties, and a new banquet came to them without paynes: for sodainlie came harts to them greate and fatte, yielding themselues to be taken, and killed by them, as if they had beene sorie that they were not called sooner: The good men tooke them by the heads[1]; they followed withoute drawing, withoute dryuing: there needed no horses to chace them, no houndes to take them, no men to intercept their wayes, as the lawes of hunting require; they being taken onelie by prayers, and held by iust mens petitions.

Who euer in our dayes, or in any former tyme heard of such hunting and such taking of deere! O admirable worke, they were their owne caruers[1]; what they pleased they held, what they let goe they reserued for an other feaste. Simple and extemporie cookes, made themselues a supper of some varietie, yet temperate: the guestes were gratefull, and not vnmyndefull of the benefitt. This admirable worke was a preparatiue to them of better hopes: By which also they were made more cheerefull to the combate in hande.'/

Thus there.

[1 gr. τοῖς νεύμασιν, capitum nuta.]

[1 gr. ταμίαι.]

FINIS:.

GLOSSARIAL, NOMINAL, AND GENERAL INDEX.

BY W. M. WOOD.

Aadan, King of Scots, 65/27.
Abiect, 74/10, subject.
Abound in his sense, 19/21, follow his inclination.
Aboundance, 23/22, abundance, quantity.
Aboundant, 210/3, abundance.
Aboundantlie, 79/6, abundantly.
Abrode, 57/12, 109/6, abroad, at large.
Abstracted, 115/7, absent-minded.
Acca, Bishop, 56/26.
Accomplish, 48/19, perform.
Accounte, 16/34, think, imagine, reckon up.
Aclitenis, a follower of St. Oswen, 100/22.
Actes, 76/6, doings, achievements.
Adamnanus, a monk, 66/20.
Addicted, 109/23, given to.
Adeodatus, son of St. Augustine, 139/9.
Adioyne, 213/14, subjoin, attach.
Adioyned, 79/20, united.
Admirable, 35/33, worthy of admiration.
Admiration, 33/7, astonishment.
Adored, 22/25, paid adoration, as a religious exercise.
Adriaticke (Adriatic) Sea, 33/30, its turbulence quelled by Helena casting one of the nails of the Cross of Christ into it.
Aduertised, 60/2, informed, made acquainted with.
Adulphe, King, 51/1, and father of the second St. Edburge.
Ægipt, 22/28, 78/27, Egypt.
Afeard, 107/14, afraid.
Afflictions, 63/21, tortures.
Agatha, mother of St. Margaret, 109/6.
Agnes, St., memoir of, 143 *et seq.*
Agreeable, 184/32, according.
Ailsburie, the church at, where St. Ositha was buried, 98.
Ake, 25/34, ache.
Alanus, father of Cradok, 89/35.
Alapion, the village of, 114/28.
Alexander, brother of St. Mechtilde, 113/29.
Alfin, son of Glunelach, 93/14.
Alfrede, King of the West Saxons, 105/2.
Alfride, King of Northumberland, husband of St. Cuthburge, 77/13.
Alftrude, Queen, 107/33.
Algar, Prince, 81/32.
Alien, 171/19, foreigner.
All, 37/31, any.
Allowing, 66/4, paying.
Allreadie, 9/22, 142/17, already.
Alnothe, the anchoret, 60/14.

Aloft, 74/8, lofty, high, mighty, powerful.
Alured, son of Ethelwold, 94/13.
Alypiana, a daughter of St. Gorgonia, 158/33.
Amazed, 27/31, dismayed.
Ambrose, St., 130/24; his life of St. Agnes, 143 *et seq.*
Amended, 25/25, corrected, reproved; 107/13, made good.
An other bodies, 24/7, somebody else's.
Anachoreticall, 21/21, living as anchorets; 73/31, like an anchoret.
Anchorets, there were women, as well as men, 21/16.
Andresia, the isle of, 96/16.
Angles and Saxons, 37/5, hired to assist the British against the Picts and Scots.
Anna, King of the East Angles, 54/14, 67/6.
Anna the Prophetess, 28, 29.
Antioch, the Council at, 197/33.
Antonie, St. (St. Anthony), 21/29.
Antwerp, 44/26 *et seq.*
Any, 111/12, any persons.
Aples, 41/22, apples.
Apostolike chaier, 20/24, the Pontificate.
Apparrell, 35/3, clothing.
Appertayneth, 19/29, appertains.
Applied, 25/12, performed.
Apprehended, 127/32, taken.
Araxius, father of Vestiana, 206/19.
Arbiterment, 122/11, arbitration.
Arius, 173/9, the heresy of.
Arme, *v.*, 18/25, mark, sign (in the heraldic sense of bearing arms).
Armies of monks, 22/28, monasteries, companies of monks.
Armorica, 36/33, the old name of Brittany.
Arnulphe, the Emperor, 84/18.
Arrian heresy, 133/35.
Arsenij, 22/29, a religious order.

Ascention, 34/21, ascension.
Aser, the tribe of, 28/19.
Ashwednsday, 110/26, Ash-Wednesday.
Aspasius, the viceregent, 150/36.
Assigned, 119/30, appointed, ordered.
Assumpted, 169/5, ascended, was borne aloft to heaven.
Assured, 67/17, true.
Astonied, 150/31, astonished.
Aswaged, 140/33, assuaged.
At, 80/33, by.
Athanasius, St., Bishop of Alexandria, 21.
Athea, cousin of St. Modwen, 92/8.
Attayning, 53/17, obtaining, gaining.
Audrie, the Abbess of Ely, 55/6.
Audrie, 67/6, another form of Etheldred.
Augmenting, 210/15, increasing.
Augustine, St., his memoir of St. Monica, 118 *et seq.*
Auncestors, 132/36, ancestors.
Aurelian, the Emperor, 30/10.
Austeritie, 95/35, severity.
Awfull, 13/3, full of awe, or dread.
Aydan, Bishop, 56/9.
Ayer, 9/31, air.

Bacurius, King of Iberia, 188/33.
Bad, 57/25, bade.
Badd, 63/32, wicked.
Bana, brother of St. Inthware, 80/5.
Band, 127/35, bondage.
Bandes, 157/1, bonds, union.
Bankett, 57/19, banquet.
Barbancius, a follower of St. Maxentia, 99.
Barbarian, by nation, 30/25, belonging to a race of barbarians.
Bare, 123/13, bore.
Barking, the Abbey or Monastery at, 52/31, 75/27; known as the treasury of saints, 76/26.

Barlie bredd, 80/28, bread made of barley, a coarse sort of bread.
Barne, 162/14, storehouse.
Baronius, the memoir of St. Helena taken from, 30.
Barre, 183/15, courts of law.
Burred, 25/20, shut out from.
Base, 30/24, of low extraction, not of gentle birth.
Baselie, 35/24, basely, in a poor manner.
Basenes, 158/2, ignobleness.
Basill the Great, St., his memoir of the holy Julitta, 181 *et seq.*; 192/31.
Baulme, 39/20, balm.
Beadd, 44/1, bed.
Beare, 108/22, bier.
Beare, 119/6, carry.
Beauuaise (Beauvais, in France), whither St. Maxentia secluded herself, 99.
Bede, the Venerable, 11/5, his testimony to the social intercourse between England and Ireland.
Beere, 130/6, bier.
Before, 167/11, until.
Bega, the first nun in Northumberland, 56/12.
Beheald, 81/12, beheld, took notice of.
Belke, 122/23, belch.
Bellie pleasures, 162/28, gluttony.
Belyed, 8/24, be called liars.
Benche, 146/5, judicial chair.
Bene, 122/3, been.
Benefit, 89/8, the grant of a piece of land.
Benefitt, 17/23, profit; 211/17, benefactor.
Benignitie, 9/11, goodness.
Berking, the monastery of, 107/18.
Berta, queen, mother of St. Edburge, 49/18.
Beseeching, 33/17, seeking, asking.
Bescemeth, 16/34; 161/16, becometh.
Besett, 153/8, bespotted.

Best, 48/30, chief, most notable, noble, or wealthy.
Bestower, 74/5, renderer.
Bestowing, 177/33, giving.
Bethleem, 22/35, Bethlehem.
Better, v., 155/11, improve, instruct.
Beuno, a holy man, 88/29.
Bewaring, 119/18, taking precaution.
Bewraying, 120/31, betraying, making known.
Bibbing, 131/6, imbibing, winebibbing.
Bicause, 2/1, because.
Biles, 199/29, boils (disease).
Bite, 25/23, injure.
Blacke Crosse of Scotland, 112/36.
Blacke or blew badge, 121/22, black eye, caused by violence.
Blockishnes, 126/6, stupidity.
Blyndnes, 32/5, blindness, evil belief; 126/12, foolishness, stupidity.
Boethius, 113/11.
Bolde, 95/27, emboldened, made bold.
Bonifacius, an English monk, 82/31.
Bosa, Bishop, 56/26.
Botches, 199/29, blotches, boils on the body.
Bote, 94/22, boat.
Bouncing, 63/34, beating, knocking about.
Bounde, 154/31, end.
Bowed, 183/19, bowed down, troubled, perplexed.
Bowella, 31/15, *here used in a forced manner for* issue, children.
Brable, 121/11, quarrel, strife, contention.
Braghane, 39/11, a king of the Britons, and father of St. Keyna.
Brake, 48/6, broke.
Branch, 80/21, child.
Braue, 35/12, good, fine, rich, handsome; 142/21, goodly, costly.

Braued, 23/27, adorned, made brave (to show a fine appearance).
Brauerie, 16/35, goodly appearance; 28/14, fine clothes and personal ornaments.
Braule, v., 26/6, brawl.
Brauling, 51/19, brawling, turmoil.
Bread of heauen, 44/18, the Holy Sacrament.
Breake, 162/33, subdue.
Brechnoch, 39/12, Brecknockshire.
Bredd, 3/14, bred, brought up.
Breguswide, mother of Hilda, her vision, 56/30.
Breuna, 91/11, the British name of St. Wenefride.
Briareus, 171/24.
Brickle, 160/34, brittle.
Bridle, 119/24, restrain.
Brieflie, 18/22, shortly.
Briga, the monastery of, 54/21.
Brigide, St., memoir of, 40 et seq.; 92/15.
Bring forth, 118/26, narrate, set out.
Britannie, 30/9, England.
Brithnote, Abbot, 79/23.
Brithwine, mother of St. Elflede, 101.
Britle, 105/30, fragile.
Brittanie (Brittany), the foundation of, 37/1.
Broken, 19/1, hurt, wounded, damaged.
Broone, Bishop, 41/35, unjustly accused.
Brosech, 40/23, the mother of St. Brigide.
Builded, 64/1, built.
Bulke, 189/8, size.
Bunches, 3/8, humps on the backs of camels.
Burdenous, 192/9, burdensome.
Buttrie, 119/22, buttery.
By grew, 99/11, did grow.

Cabbine, 148/22, room.
Cadoke, St., 39/16.
Cæsarius, brother of St. Gorgonia, 170/18.

Cale, 56/7, Calais.
Calum, the Abbey of, 63/6.
Calumniating, 102/23, traducing.
Canoch, St., 39/14.
Canute, King, 109/6.
Capicitie, 86/4, capacity, means of conjecture.
Carefull, 84/24, dutiful.
Carnall, 63/14, in the flesh.
Carnallie, 180/34, fleshly.
Carpe, 20/27, revile, blame, accuse.
Castre, the monastery at, 72/3.
Cates, 216/2, cakes, food.
Cathecumene, 152/6, catechumen.
Catherin, St., 82/22.
Cecilie, St., 82/22.
Cedmon, the poet, short notice of, 57/14 et seq.
Celliscline, the monastery at, 95/19.
Cerdike, King of the Britons, 56/32.
Certifying, 64/2, informing, causing to be made known.
Cesars, 32/18, lords, emperors.
Charges, 45/8, reckonings, bills.
Charles, King of France, 100/9.
Chastified, 121/14, chastened, made chaste.
Chaynes, 13/19, jewels and ornaments for the person.
Chebee and Senane, St., 91/30.
Cheuin, Bishop, 93/18.
Chiche, the place where was the monastery of St. Ositha, 98.
Choler, 44/4, 94/1, rage, anger.
Chollericke, 25/26, full of temper.
Choman, wife of Nangthee, 92/2.
Christian mynde, 74/6, knowledge of Christ.
Christine, aunt of St. Margaret, 109/20.
Chrysaphius, the follower of Naucratius, 193/27.
Cilice, 186/20, haircloth.
Cinifrid, the physician, 69/11.

GLOSSARIAL, NOMINAL, AND GENERAL INDEX. 221

Circumuented, 106/26, outwitted.
Cistertian, 113/26, Cistercian.
Cittie, 27/36, city, town, country.
Cittisens, 32/34, citizens.
Clappe, 5/4, instant, puff of wind.
Clare, the manor of, bestowed upon Romsey Abbey, 101.
Claritie, 38/16, 76/30, clearness, purity.
Cleargie, 47/23, clergy, churchmen.
Cloathing, 25/14, clothing, raiment.
Cloke, 90/32, cloak.
Cloying, 20/3, annoyance, weariness.
Clymbe, 105/5, climb.
Clyming, 197/6, climbing.
Coelus, a British Prince, father of St. Helena, 30/12.
Cofers, 102/16, coffers, treasure boxes.
Cogitation, 142/19, thought.
Cogitations, 18/27, inward thoughts, soul communings (in the religious sense of abnegation of self and devotion to the Almighty).
Cohabitation, 66/29, dwelling together under one roof.
Colde, 134/4, not having yet been made warm.
Coldingham, 65/29.
Colen Agrippina, 38/9, St. Ursula arrives at.
Coles, 183/10, coals, fire.
Collected, 18/22, collated, summarized.
Colledge, 38/34, convent.
Colour, 47/36, pretence, disguise.
Colude, Mount, 65/28.
Come runne, 137/28, came running.
Comlinesse, 38/12, Comelynes, 155/17, comeliness, handsome personal appearance.
Commodious, 189/23, advantageous.

Commoditie, 138/31, excellence; 186/9, advantage.
Common, v., 136/12, commune.
Common sort, 35/14, common people, lower orders.
Communication, 131/27, the Holy Sacrament.
Companie keeping, 61/33, consorting with, having connexion.
Compassing, 91/6, surrounding.
Compose, v., 30/10, settle, arrange, put in order; 210/29, quiet.
Composed, 109/32, calm.
Conagall, King of Scotland, 95/31.
Conanus, 36/32, the founder of the kingdom of Brittany.
Concourse, 51/32, company.
Concurring, 110/10, working.
Confirme, 145/16, make firm.
Congealing, 166/19, freezing.
Conioyned, 79/31, united.
Coniunction, 203/5, union.
Conserue, 15/8, 118/21, preserve, maintain, keep.
Conserued, 3/4, 67/14, conserved, preserved, put on record.
Considerate, 161/13, to the point, apt.
Consociate, 132/14, associate.
Consociation, 132/25, company, association.
Constantia, queen, 153/6.
Constantine the Great, 30 et seq.; 153/6.
Constantius Clorus, the father of Constantine the Great, 30/8.
Contemne, 59/2, eschew; 147/27, ignore.
Contemned, 17/15, ignored, put aside.
Conteyne, 111/8, confine.
Conteyned, 163/24, contained.
Conteyning, 174/13, confining, hiding; 205/6, restraining.
Contracted, 86/12, drawn up.
Contrarie, 50/23, wicked.
Contrie, 54/5, country.

Contrie monie, 45/9, the money of their own country.
Contrie soile, 88/30, native land.
Contumelie, 145/2, contempt.
Conuersed, 40/4, dwelt.
Conuert, 202/25, devote.
Conuerting, 77/25, subjecting.
Copie, 200/7, reproduction.
Corf, the river, 62/8.
Corporall, 14/10, 91/30, bodily.
Corporall natiuitie, 74/7, natural, bodily birth.
Corrupt, 33/25, become corrupt, or decay away.
Corse, 139/36, corpse, dead body.
Corses, 123/18, bodies.
Couent, 91/27, convent.
Counsaile, 5/22, 72/25, counsel.
Counterfett, 81/20, counterfeit, feigned.
Countie, 102/23, count, a title of honour.
Coupled, 109/16, joined.
Coyne, 45/10, coin, money.
Coyned, 213/17, coined, counterfeited.
Cradok, son of Alanus, 89/35.
Craue, 161/11, seek.
Credible, 113/18, trustworthy, truthful.
Criers, 214/17, heralds.
Crispus, the eldest son of Constantine the Great, 31/15.
Cross, the story of the miraculous discovery of the, 32 et seq.
Cunninglie, 57/27, cleverly, sweetly.
Curing, 96/27, healing; 172/27, remedying.
Curiouslie, 22/34, out of curiosity.
Cuthbert, St., 66/8.
Cuthburge, St., memoir of, 77 et seq.
Cyprian, St., his remarks on the dignity of virginity, 11 et seq.; 127/9.

Dastardie, 214/27, cowardliness.

Dauid, St., 39/17, Bishop of Menevia.
Dauid, son of St. Margaret, 113/10.
Daunted, 182/15, discouraged.
Dealt, 106/1, prevailed.
Decked, 161/27, decorated.
Deepe, 180/20, great.
Defalte, 37/26, nonpayment
Defiling, 22/17, deflowering.
Defyning, 174/30, affirming, declaring.
Deiected, 65/4, dejected, overcome with grief.
Deiecteth, 4/5, curbeth, keepeth under control.
Delectable, 118/12, choice.
Delicates, 215/33, delicacies.
Deliuered, 49/8, rendered free from; 77/21, surrendered, given over (as a wife).
Delphins, 35/21, dolphins, monsters of the sea.
Demanded, 184/2, questioned.
Demanding, 137/30, inquiry.
Demeanure, 18/13, demeanour, behaviour; 61/17, manner of living.
Demetrias, St. Jerome's epistle to, 18 et seq.
Demisd, 141/3, relieved.
Denise, St., the vision to St. Dunstan when consecrating the church built in honour of, by St. Edith, 103.
Denne, 34/7, den, cave (the place of our Lord's birth).
Departure, 69/12, death.
Derham, the monastery at, 79/8.
Deriued, 170/31, transmitted.
Descried, 115/27, discovered.
Desired, 167/31, sought after.
Desired to wife, 39/24, sought after in marriage.
Desolate, 62/24, deprived.
Despayer, 27/32, 129/28, despair.
Despoused, 47/7, 191/33, espoused, promised.
Detectest, 16/27, proveth, showeth forth.
Deuises, 129/1, tales, sayings.

Deyntilie, 3/14, daintily, nicely, in superior style.
Didane, Prince, 80/19.
Digested, 118/16, arranged, placed.
Diminished, 18/11, parted with, lost.
Diocletian, 30/19.
Diocletian's persecution, 181/19.
Dionothe, 37/10, a king of Great Britain, and father of St. Ursula.
Disburdened, 75/32, unburdened, set free from.
Discording, 122/20, disagreeing.
Discumber, 75/34, disencumber, cast off.
Discusse, 141/31, examine, dissect.
Disdayning, 62/10, not permitting.
Dispense, 35/32, deal with.
Dispute, 140/1, argue.
Dissolued, 128/2, loosened, melted; 148/14, unloosed; 169/4, parted.
Distressed, 64/2, persecuted.
Diuerse, 57/19, divers; 171/31, different, opposed.
Diuided to, 33/21, given to, divided amongst.
Diuination, 31/13, idolatrous worship.
Docill, 125/4, docile, prepared.
Documents, 66/11, 139/15, proofs.
Domesticall, 154/20, homely.
Dompneua, mother of St. Milburge, 60/33.
Donne vnto, 31/9, conferred upon.
Dores, 159/10, doors.
Dormunds, the monastery at, 72/2.
Dorram, the church of, 109/26.
Dorter, 83/18, dormitory, sleeping chamber.
Dorwent, the river, 66/3.
Drey, 48/17, dray, cart.
Drepanum in Bithinia, enlarged and enriched by St. Helena, 35/19.

Dressing, 15/31, clothing, garments.
Dronken, 64/14, drunk.
Drossie, 2/7, drossy.
Drousines, 3/6, drowsiness, slothfulness.
Drynesse, 204/23, parched up.
Dubtacus, 40/22, the father of St. Bridgit.
Dunstan, St., reproves King Edgar, 103.
Dunstane, Bishop, 76/9.
Durt, 50/4, dirt.
Dustie, 168/36, dark, dusky.
Dutifullnes, 192/10, performance of household duties.
Dymned, 148/24, dimmed.
Dympna, the holy, memoir of, 43 et seq.

Eadware, St., 79/29.
Eanswide, St., memoir of, 51 et seq.
Earthfull, 131/24, earthly, grown in the earth.
Easilie, 101/15, readily.
Ebba, the holy, memoir of, 65 et seq.
Ebbecestre, 66/4.
Ecgfride, second husband of St. Etheldred, 67/12.
Edbald, king, and father of St. Eanswide, 51/7.
Edburga, St., 64/35.
Edburge, St., memoir of, 49 et seq.
Edburge, another St., notice of, 50/36.
Edenburrow [Edinburgh], the monastery at, 95/33.
Ederanne, 84/23.
Edfride, a priest, 61/12.
Edgar, King, succours St. Elflede, 101/28; father of St. Edith, 102/32; wooes the holy Wulfhilde, 105/29.
Edgar, a son of St. Margaret, 112/31.
Edith, St., memoir of, 102 et seq.
Edith, another holy, mentioned, 104.

224 GLOSSARIAL, NOMINAL, AND GENERAL INDEX.

Editha, daughter of Ethelwolfe, 94/28.
Edmund Ironside, 109/3.
Edmund, son of Edmund Ironside, 109/4.
Edward, son of Edmund Ironside, 109/3.
Edward, son of St. Margaret, 112/27.
Edward the Martyr, King, brother of St. Edith, 103.
Edwine, king of Northumberland, 54/2.
Effected, 197/5, carried out.
Egbert, son of St. Sexburge, 54/16.
Egerlie, 38/15, eagerly, lustfully.
Egre, 100/29, eager.
Egrelie, 82/1, eagerly.
Eisteten, the Bishop of, 83/4.
Elerius, a holy man, 91/26.
Elenated, 69/22, taken from, translated.
Elflede, St., memoir of, 101 et seq.
Elge, 68/7, Ely.
Elie, the Abbey of, 55/4.
Elizeus, 185/7.
Ells, 28/25, else.
Elphegus, Bishop, 76/9.
Elwine, an abbess of Romsey, 102.
Embassadors, 37/9, ambassadors.
Embassage, 188/23, embassy.
Embeselled, 6/20, embezzled, diverted.
Embouldened, 81/21, made bold, encouraged.
Embracings, 77/12, worship.
Emerentiana, a holy virgin, 152/4.
Emma, mother of Edward the Confessor, 65/1.
Emme, queen, mother of St. Eanswide, 51/7.
Empayred, 45/20, impaired, damaged.
Emperiall, 31/1, Imperial.
Enamoured, 99/26, betrothed; 102/32, in love with.
Encroched, 182/20, encroached, trespassed.

Endeuour, 106/3, duty, adopt the best means.
Endewed, 146/30, endued.
Endure, 169/9, permit.
Enduring, 87/36, putting up with.
Enforced, 49/30, compelled.
Enforcing, 80/24, enforcement.
Englishe nation, 37/22, the tribe of the Angles hired by the British to assist them against the Picts.
Enricher, n., 30/17, endower.
Ensignes, 31/1, insignia.
Epiphanius, St., 181/4.
Ercombert, king of Kent, 54/15; father of St. Ermenilde, 58/23.
Erected, 136/29, stretched out.
Erkenbald, Bishop, 86/4.
Erkengoda, daughter of St. Sexburge, 54/19.
Erkenwald, St., Bishop of London, 52/6.
Ermelinde, daughter of St. Sexburge, 54/17.
Ermenilde, St., memoir of, 58 et seq.
Ernest, 72/20, earnest.
Estate, 64/3, condition.
Estates of the kingdome, 110/23, the ancient Scottish government.
Ester, 33/12, Easter.
Ethelard, cousin of King Ine, 75/14.
Ethelbert, King, father of St. Edburge, 49/17.
Ethelbert, King of Kent, 54/2.
Ethelburge, daughter of King Anna, 55/29.
Ethelburge, Queen, memoir of, 54.
Ethelburge, St., memoir of, 52 et seq.
Ethelburge, another St., memoir of, 74 et seq.
Etheldred, St., the abbess of Ely, 55/6; memoir of, 67 et seq.
Ethelfride, King of Northumberland, 65/13.
Ethelred, King of Mercia, 59/28; 107/33.

Ethelwold, King of the West Saxons, 94/12.
Ethelwold, father of St. Elflede, 101.
Ethelwolde, Bishop, 76/9, 79/18.
Ethelwolfe, king of the West Saxons, 94/27.
Ethnicall, 177/7, national.
Ethnicks, 100/15, autochthones.
Euent, 198/15, fulfilment.
Euer, 190/25, always.
Eugenia, a daughter of St. Gorgonia, 158/33.
Eunuches, 13/30, recommended as examples for virgins.
Euodius, 132/15.
Exactlie, 163/25, rigidly.
Exceeding, 62/14, large, great.
Excellentlie, 52/29, exceedingly.
Excercised, 124/34, exercised, fully acquainted with.
Exemplar, 139/16, exemplary.
Exhaled, 89/29, inhaled.
Exhaust, 102/16, exhausted.
Exequies, 207/4, obsequies.
Experience, 181/30, observation.
Explicating, 61/28, explaining, expounding.
Exprobating, 149/7, reprobating.
Expulsions, 213/24, expellings.
Extemporie, 216/22, temporary.
Extenuate, 176/12, attenuate, waste away.
Externe, 30/25, belonging to another country (colonial); 196/14, external.
Externes, 169/14, outsiders, persons not on great terms of intimacy.
Extrinsecall, 6/31, useless.

Fainte, v., 18/8, relapse, depart from.
False play, 41/33, wrong doing.
Falte, 23/23, 31/27, 70/14, fault, sin, wickedness.
Familiars, 161/10, familiar, every-day friends and companions.
Famine, 84/27, hunger.
Farder, 7/23, farther.
Fardered, 35/30, furthered, gave more scope to.

Fastened, 145/4, joined.
Fayernes, 155/16, fairness.
Fayned, 31/27, fastened, fixed (by counterfeiting).
Fayned, 81/10, 102/24, feigned, counterfeit.
Feared, 164/7, put in terror.
Featnesse, 25/36, trimness, nice appearance.
Fellow, 37/12, companion, helpmate, wife.
Fennes, 67/10, the fenland country.
Ferme, 151/34, farm.
Festiuitie, 143/25, feast.
Fetcheth his winde verie short, 145/24, becomes short of wind, is taken seriously ill.
Fewell, 144/21, fuel, fire.
Feyning, 74/34, faining, making excuse.
Fierie, 61/6, fierce.
Filthie, 90/13, 190/31, wicked, vile.
Finane, Bishop of Lindisfarne, 65/25.
Fined, 2/6, refined.
Firme, 37/14, strong, of good foundation.
Firmitie, 184/27, firmness.
Fitt, 43/23, worthy; 161/1, proper, apt.
Fitted and feated, 90/5, bedecked and trimmed.
Fitter, 169/4, more properly.
Flien, Hermannus, D.D., his account of St. Ursula, 36 *et seq.*
Flouds, 49/33, floods, tempests.
Floure, 5/31, 190/5, flower, springtime.
Flowre, 170/32, flour.
Fluds, 164/3, floods.
Flying, 171/10, separating from.
Folkam, the church of St. Peter at, 51/31.
Fond, 171/9, foolish.
Fone, the Cistercian monastery at, 114/13.
Foote, 188/12, base, bottom; 188/13, measure.
Forbidd, 32/14, forbidden.

FEMALE SAINTS. Q

Forces, 204/4, power, ability; 197/7, senses.
Foresaid, 64/19, aforesaid.
Foresignified, 39/19, foretokened.
Forged, 177/2, forced.
Forgoe, 3/19, 63/19, forego, give up.
Forgoing, 155/32, renouncing.
Forme, 139/16, style, fashion.
Former, 111/18, first.
Forren, 155/7, foreign.
Fortuned, 112/12, happened; 206/31, chanced.
Foulenesse, 120/21, fault.
Foules, 47/15, birds.
Foundresse, 108/5, founder, originator.
Fountaine, 161/7, origin.
Foxe, 106/13, fox (not here used in a literal sense, but so denominating a crafty woman).
Fowlenes, 125/16, iniquity.
Fower, 28/21, Fowre, 79/7, four.
Fraight, 131/8, freighted.
Fraighted, 102/26, freighted, laid in store.
Fraile, 3/12, weak; 19/8, fragile, weak, liable to temptation.
Francklie, 7/9, freely.
Fraude, 106/12, treachery.
Fraught, 55/16, laden, clothed.
Freelie, 39/28, at ease.
Fresh water passengers, 129/33, persons going to sea for the first time.
Frideride, the miracle happening to, 84/22.
Frideswide, St., memoir of, 80 et seq.
Frighte, 53/30, frighten.
Frighted, 182/15, frightened.
Friselled, 160/15, frizzled, curled.
Frithwald, Prince, father of St. Ositha, 97.
Friuolous, 57/27, vain, unworthy.
Fructifie, 89/26, 154/14, ripen.
Fruite, 158/31, children.
Fruitlesse silence, 154/9, without bearing fruit.

Fundament, 50/28, base.
Furia, St. Jerome's epistle to, 28.
Furious forhead, 126/4, violent boldness or insolence, angry impetuosity.
Furnitures, 35/12, church upholstery.
Fyled, 23/26, defiled, bewrayed.
Fyned, 197/21, refined.
Fyning, 1/13, fining, refining.
Fynished, 197/34, ended.

Gadding, 159/10, parading.
Gainfull, 9/5, more than usual, i.e. compound.
Gallwey, the monastery at, 95/34.
Garnish, 19/19, decorate, beautify.
Garnishing, 50/2, nourishing.
Gaspes, 169/13, sighs.
Gate, 23/15, gait, way, manner, fashion; 161/35, gait, walking; 162/4, house.
Gaye shewes, 92/3, delights, pleasures.
Gayned, 83/7, persuaded, converted.
Gentilitie, 153/26, the Gentiles, paganism.
Gentill, 96/18, gentile, pagan.
Gentills, 31/7, gentiles (as opposed to Christianity).
Gentrie, 157/20, noble birth.
Gerebern, the priest, 44/14.
Gerusius, St., 134/13.
Ghastlie, 61/6, terrible.
Ghele, 44/31, the burial-place of the Virgin Dympna.
Ghoste, 82/25, 139/9, spirit.
Ghostlie, 66/17, holy; 172/26, spiritual.
Girded, 92/24, placed a girdle on.
Giruij. 67/11.
Glade, 39/15, the mother of St. Cadoke.
Glastenburie (Glastonbury), the founder of, 74/4.
Glittered, 33/10, was made bright, shined.
Gloric, 83/9, pride.
Glunelach, first a thief, then a bishop, 93/4.

God inuisible, 138/9, invisible God.
Goe, 213/34, pass.
Goe liue, 20/29, go *and* live.
Good liking, 18/16, great satisfaction.
Good man, 159/15, husband.
Goods, 17/9, possessions, riches.
Gorgonia, St., memoir of, 154 *et seq*.
Gotha, the sacking of Rome by the, 22.
Gouernesse, 102/8, ruler (*i.e.* Abbess).
Grace, 96/27, gift, power.
Grandecester, the city of, 69/1.
Gratefull, 185/2, soothing, refreshing.
Grauest, 55/19, most saintly.
Grauitie, 19/7, graveness, modesty, decorousness.
Greate grandfathers, 170/28, forefathers.
Gregorie, father of St. Gregorie, 155/24.
Gregorie of Nazianzum, husband of St. Nonna, 171/5.
Gregorie Nazianzene, St., his life of St. Gorgonia, 154 *et seq.*; his life of St. Nonna, 170 *et seq.*
Gregorie of Nyssa, St., his memoir of St. Macrina, 189 *et seq*.
Gregorie of Tours, St., 34/2.
Greeue at, 22/20, made grief for.
Greeued, 83/29, grieved.
Grew into greate desire, 105/30, became enamoured.
Grieued, 70/13, caused pain.
Guider, 206/15, instructor.
Guild, 19/18, gild, adorn, cover with gold.
Guilded, 33/10, gilded.
Gunwald, the custodian, 83/16.
Gushed forth, 185/1, yielded.
Gushing oute, 112/19, weeping, overflowing.

Had, 36/6, possessed; 112/35, held.
Had of their coyne, 45/10, possessed some of their foreign money.
Hale, 75/35, pull, convince.
Haled, 37/21, led, driven.
Hamburge, the Abbey of, 60/17.
Handwrittes, 129/13, handwritings, laws.
Happ, 94/36, mischance.
Happe, 61/15, chance.
Happie, 80/21, goodly.
Harbourlesse, 19/24, without habitation or dwelling-place.
Hardlie, 20/28, harshly, disrespectfully.
Hardlie, 179/18, scarcely.
Hardnes, 215/23, hard, poor living.
Harken, 45/7, make inquiry.
Harkeneth, 144/8, hasteneth.
Harte, 4/7, heart.
Hartilie, 58/18, heartily.
Hasten, 201/9, hastened.
Haught, 4/6, high, mighty.
Hauing, 173/1, obtaining.
Haye, 135/6, man is 'grass': when dying dried grass or hay.
Hayre, 40/7, 92/22, 148/13, hair.
Head, 172/2, husband.
Headines, 140/8, rashness.
Heale, 120/28, correct.
Hebrues, 32/15, Hebrews.
Heereuppon, 7/34, hereupon.
Helena, St., memoir of, 30 *et seq*.
Helenopolis, 35/29, the new name of the town of Drepanum.
Her, 166/36, its.
Hererike, father of holy Hilda, 56/3.
Hereswide, sister of Hilda, 56/7.
Hertheie, the nunnery of, 56/12.
Hesiodus, the poet, 174/19.
Heynous, 90/24, heinous.
Hierome, St. (St. Jerome), his epistle to Demetrius, 18 *et seq.*; his advice to a Virgin, 20-21; the companion and guide of St. Paula, 22 *et seq.*; 181/10.
Highe crie, 150/20, loud voice.
Highth, 202/18, height.

Q 2

Hilda, Abbess, daughter to Hererike, memoir of, 56 *et seq.*
Hildelitha, 52/28, a learned woman and preceptor of St. Ethelburge.
Hildelitha, St., memoir of, 76 *et seq.*
Hinge, 127/15, pivot.
His, 137/13, 188/12, its.
His, 61/1, 's [*i.e.* Penda his = Penda's].
Hoaste, 152/27, host, company.
Hoate, 100/1, hot, lustful.
Holde, 106/21, held as a prisoner.
Holie Crosse, the Church of the, 36/3.
Holie Viaticum or voiage foode, 78/32, consecrated wafer, &c., the Eucharist given to folk in their dying moments.
Holofernes, the destruction of, 27.
Holy Virgins, the church of the, at Cologne, 38.
Homicide, 88/6, manslayer.
Hong, 188/12, hung.
Honorius, St., 54/7.
Hoped, 172/16, expected.
Horton, the monastery at, 107/21.
Hoste, 142/24, the consecrated wafer offered as a sacrifice in the Mass.
Howres, 119/15, hours.
Hubila, Abbess, 84/36.
Humane, 19/10, 32/2, human, natural.
Humanitie, 162/8, kindness, tender dealing.
Humber, the river, 67/12.
Hunnes, 38/10, the Huns.
Hurte, 153/22, disease.
Hushe, 136/21, hushed, silenced.
Huswife, 159/10, housewife.
Hydenherin [Heidenheim], 83/6.
Hymnes, 48/10, chants, praises, religious services.
Hypsistary, the heresy of, 156/2, 171/17.

Iarred, 25/30, quarrelled.
Iberia, memoir of a Christian maid captive in, 185 *et seq.*
Iester, 44/24, jester.
Iewes, 32/28, Jewish.
Iles, 30/3, isles.
Immarcessible, 81/14, unwitherable.
Immoderatlie, 43/20, excessively, more than moderate; 83/28, overmuch.
Imperiouslie, 53/31, impetuously, without opposition.
Impes, 11/30, scions, buds, youths.
Impietie, 43/32, wickedness, lewdness.
Impudencie, 167/5, insistence.
Impure, 62/8, inflamed.
In fine, 38/8, finally, at last.
In hand, 74/14, in dealing, persuading.
In steede, 170/16, instead.
Inamoured, 184/10, in love with.
Incense, 29/23, provoke.
Incensed, 61/31, imbued.
Incertayntie, 7/6, uncertainty.
Incommodious, 192/10, troublesome.
Incommodities, 158/11, inconveniences.
Inconsumptible, 33/23, not capable of being consumed or exhausted (spoken of the Cross of Christ, which, although distributed in small pieces to pilgrims, still remained intact).
Incorrupt, 55/27, undecayed, whole, intact.
Incredible, 112/6, excessive; 112/17, scarcely believable.
Incredit, 32/1, in credit, in esteem.
Indamage, 62/16, do damage, mischief.
Indeficient, 136/5, never deficient.
Ine, or Inas, King of the West Saxons, 74/3.
Infame, 44/2, make infamous.
Infamed, 50/20, made infamous, wicked.

GLOSSARIAL, NOMINAL, AND GENERAL INDEX. 229

Infancie, 147/1, childhood, innocency.
Infectious, 55/27, wicked.
Infirmed, 91/32, made ill or weak.
Infirmitie, 58/13, illness.
Inflamed, 63/11, inspired, imbued; 110/11, inspired, prompted.
Informed, 94/11, reformed.
Informeth, 190/35, relateth.
Ingratefull, 202/7, ungratefuL
Iniurie, 24/27, abasement.
Iniurie, v., 73/9, injure.
Iniuried, 35/6, injured, oppressed.
Iniurying, 73/9, injuring.
Inquisitiue, 186/4, inquisitive, making inquiries.
Inspired, 33/1, endued, endowed, imparted the privilege.
Instructed, 22/11, informed, made acquainted with.
Instruments, 121/27, indentures.
Insultation, 149/18, insults.
Integritie, 15/30, 16/9, preservation from defilement.
Intermitting, 199/32, stopping.
Intertayned, 30/11, entertained, received as a guest.
Intertayning, 80/2, entertaining, making welcome.
Interteyning, 21/26, entertaining, receiving as guests.
Inthralled, 163/2, in subjection.
Inthware [Juthware], St., memoir of, 79.
Intire, 11/30, entire.
Intollerable, 104/24, not to be endured.
Intreate, 17/25, entreated.
Intruded, 18/24, obtruded, suggested.
Inuade, 53/27, run upon.
Inuested, 207/36, dressed, prepared for burial.
Inuested with, 80/33, received the order of.
Inuiolable, 161/13, not to be broken.
Inuironed, 47/20, environed.

Iocund, 186/36, gay, joyful, cheerful.
Iohn, Bishop, 56/27.
Irreprehensible, 204/19, not reprehensible.
Isodorus, 22/30, the religious followers of.
Issue, 51/18, progeny.
It, 212/9, her.
Iustina, mother of Valentinian, 133/33.

Jerome's epistle to Furia, 28.
Judith, the widow, short account of, 27 et seq.
Julitta, martyr, memoir of, 181 et seq.

Keepe company againe, 105/20, resume cohabitation.
Kenred, King of Mercia, 73/21.
Kenrede, of the blood royal of the West Saxons, 77/8.
Key colde, 131/15, cold as a key.
Keyna, St., memoir of, 39 et seq.
Keynwire, 39/27 = ' Keyn the virgin.'
Kicking, 25/31, rising.
Kinesburge, St., memoir of, 71 et seq.
Kineswide, St., memoir of, 71 et seq.
Kinne, 72/33, 161/10, kinsmen.
Knew not, 121/16, knew better than.
Knowen, 23/17, known; 134/24, knowing.

Laboured, 51/12, 54/23, wrought upon.
Lamenting, 107/36, complaining, bewailing.
Lampadia, 206/29.
Lanfrank, St., Archbishop of Canterbury, 50/32.
Lastlie, 75/13, at last.
Later, 138/36, latter, last.
Laudable, 141/30, praiseworthy.
Laude, 34/4, 112/33, praise, give thanks to.
Lauding, 19/29, praising.

Lauer, 14/6, washing, cleansing by the rite of baptism.
Layeth on, 146/7, threateneth.
Lazara, the companion of St. Modwen in her pilgrimage to Rome, 96/13.
Leadd, 148/9, led.
Leadd, 56/4, led (lived).
Leapers, 41/20, lepers.
Leaproua, 41/22, 103/12, leperous.
Learne, 123/32, inform.
Learnedest, 32/10, most learned.
Lease, v., 114/33, glean.
Leese, 114/4, lose.
Leisurelie, 210/1, slowly, reverently.
Lent, 106/12, given for a set period.
Lentfast, 54/33, the fast during the season of Lent.
Leontius, Bishop, 173/15.
Letted, 198/4, hindered.
Letter of diuorce, 30/23, divorcement.
Leuitie, 181/16, carnal-mindedness.
Libertie vniuersallie, 30/16, universal liberty, toleration.
Licentius, 132/29.
Lien, 104/22, lain.
Liers, 213/18, liars.
Lighte, 178/19, lighted.
Lightes, 48/11, tapers, candles blessed by priests.
Lightsome, 152/36, joyful.
Like, 194/35, the same.
Like liers, 81/8, liars like himself.
Liked, 30/30, pleased; 77/28, loved.
Liming, 54/9, the monastery at.
Linage, 74/3, lineage, family.
Lindan, Bishop, 39/7, apparently the author of the memoir of St. Ursula.
Lindseie, the province of, 52/8.
List, 53/32, desired.
Listed, 141/7, wished.
Liuelie, 64/11, apparently.
Liuing, 108/21, when alive.
Loaden, 192/21, loaded, laden.

Lodge, v., 19/24, prepare housecovering.
Lonfrontin, the monastery at 95/34.
Longed, 168/7, longed for.
Looser, 181/3, less strict.
Lose, 60/8, 160/18, loose.
Losed, 42/33, loosed (said of a mute, whose tongue was miraculously loosened).
Lotharie, son of St. Sexburge, 54/16.
Lothe, 75/3, cause to heave; 131/6, loathe.
Lothing, 74/7, loathing.
Loues, 179/8, loaves.
Louinglie, 196/29, with great love.
Lucian, St., and martyr, 35/19.
Lurking, 85/19, hidden.
Lutheran or Protestant Bishops, 180/30.
Lynnen, 68/12, linen.
Lyppes, 204/23, lips.
Lyuing, 19/28, living.
Lyulie, 80/13, living, flowing.

Macarij, 22/29, a religious order.
Machilla, Bishop, 41/10.
Macrina, St., memoir of, 180 et seq.
Mad, 173/9, wicked.
Madded, 182/2, made mad, maddened.
Made lie, 162/6, made to lie.
Magnificall, 163/18, 189/4, high, mighty, bragging.
Maister, 13/4, 40/24, master, lord.
Make, 137/23, do.
Malcolme, King of Scotland, 109/12.
Malepertlie, 125/36, malapertly, disorderly.
Mammocks, 3/18, trifles, fragments.
Manage, 109/27, perform; 191/8, work.
Manchilde, 105/6, baby boy.
Manichees, 123/16, Manichæun heresy.
Mannor place, 74/17, manorhouse.

Mans companie, 98/4, being corrupted by man.
Marcella, a lady of Rome, commended by St. Jerome, 21 ; the first noble woman of Rome to take on the monastical profession, 22.
Marcolane, King of Scots, father of St. Maxentia, 99.
Mard, 5/32, marred, spoilt, destroyed.
Margaret, St., Queen of Scotland, 109 et seq.
Margarites, 8/3, 144/30, pearls.
Marie, 77/18, marry.
Marking, 120/36, noting.
Martyred, 60/16, slain.
Matched, 121/5, 190/7, mated, married.
Matches, 156/35, mates, equals.
Matter, 210/18, cause.
Mattocke, 92/13, pickaxe.
Mature, 109/33, wise.
'Maude the goode,' queen of Henry I., 113/5.
Mawmets, 47/6, false gods.
Maxentia, St., memoir of, 99, 100.
Maximianus Galerius, 30/21, 214/10.
Maximianus Herculeus, 30/19.
May, 183/33, might.
Mayme, 91/8, maim, hurt.
Maynlie, 126/32, greatly, heartily.
Meane, 58/28, way, method ; 167/27, set term, proportion.
Mechtilde, St., memoir of, 113 et seq.
Medicine, v., 162/34, doctor.
Meede, 114/16, reward.
Melarius, 39/16, father of St. David.
Men rulers, 120/10, men in authority.
Ment, 186/4, meant.
Menz, the diocese of, 82/33.
Merchandised, 7/1, acted as merchants.
Mere, 124/13, open, apparent.
Merefin, brother of St. Mildred, 63/5.

Merilie, 121/24, merrily, cheerfully.
Meruailous, 26/12, marvellously.
Meruailouslie, 53/23, marvellously.
Merwenne, the Abbess of Romsey, receives and looks after St. Elflede, 101 ; 102/7.
Meynie, 149/22, multitude.
Milane, the church at, 133/30.
Milburge, St., memoir of, 60 et seq.
Mildred, St., niece of St. Edburge, 49/25 ; memoir of, 63 et seq.
Milgith, sister of St. Milburge, 61/3.
Militarie orders, 34/35, soldiers.
Mineruina, the first wife of Constantine the Great, 31/17.
Mislike, 19/20, dislike, disapprove of.
Missused, 46/12, dealt harshly.
Moderate, 19/9, keep under, govern, rule.
Modwen, St., memoir of, 92 et seq.
Moe, 75/24, more.
Molestations, 198/5, troubles.
Molested, 85/36, troubled.
Mollified, 172/8, made tender.
Momentaneall, 4/13, transitory, momentary, lasting but a moment.
Momentaneous, 78/11, momentary.
Monasticall weede, 79/9, monastic uniform.
Mone, 102/19, moan.
Moneths, 45/2, months.
Monheime, the monastery of, 86/11.
Monica, St., memoir of, 118 et seq.
Monie, 45/12, Monnye, 24/6, 35/3, money.
More, 33/27, 56/5, greater, better.
More, 105/11, moreover.
More comfort, 28/4, greater comfort.
More white, 47/27, whiter.

Morwald, father of St. Milburge, 60/34.
Moste rare, 56/22, most wise.
Moste white, 107/28, very white, pure white.
Mother, 25/11, superior, the lady superintendent of a religious house.
Moulde, 184/20, fashion, manner.
Moulten, 77/3, molten, heated.
Mounting, 130/24, spouting forth.
Mournfull, 176/18, those in sorrow.
Moyling, 35/5, moiling, toiling.
Multitudine, 48/5, multitude, number of people.
Munday, 110/27, Monday.
Mundus, a priest, 85/11.
Mutable, 4/9, 129/6, Muteable, 174/36, changeable.
Mute, 42/29, dumb.
My owne man, 205/13, my own self.
Mylde, 141/5, mild.
Mysticall wordes, 176/26, words relating to the mysteries of religion.

Nangthee, an Irish Prince, 92/2.
Natiuitie, 42/30, birth.
Naucratius, a brother of St. Macrina, 193/18.
Naught, 31/18, wickedness (adultery is here meant).
Naughtie, 94/6, wicked, evil.
Nauie, 38/5, navy, ships.
Neaste, 105/6, nest.
Necessitie, 24/9, neediness.
Neece, 49/25, niece.
Neere, 67/11, near.
Neerlie, 180/18, nearly, closely.
Nesting, 105/11, the origin of his name.
Nicea, 173/8 (the first Council at).
Nicobulus, a nephew of St. Gorgonia, 158/34.
Nobilitie, 25/15, noble family.
Nodd, 111/26, nap.
None like, 67/22, as a nun.

Nonna, a daughter of St. Gorgonia, 158/33.
Nonna, mother of St. Gregory, 155/24.
Nonna, St., memoir of, 170 *et seq.*
Nonnerie, 55/7, nunnery.
Nonrie, 56/12, 103/4, nunnery.
Northfolke, 79/18, the county of Norfolk.
Notable, 47/3, noteworthy, esteemed.
Note of infamie, 183/17, mark of disgrace as an outcast.
Nouiceship, 102/12, novitiate, first becoming a novice.
Number, 164/18, count.
Numnesse, 166/19, numbness.
Nurtured, 30/14, brought up, educated.
Nutriment, 144/22, nourishment.

Obite, 103/36, death.
Oblation, 75/27, sacrifice.
Obscuritie, 187/15, darkness.
Obsecrations, 26/23, beseechings.
Obtayne, 198/6, gain to.
Obtayned, 42/17, procured.
Obtaynedst, 170/1, didst obtain, gain.
Occasion, 20/15, cause.
Of, 8/24, 74/6, 212/18, by.
Of, 8/13, from.
Of, 3/8, 28/13, off.
Of, 177/27, on.
Of purpose, 70/29, on purpose.
Offa, King of the East Angles, becomes a monk, 73/22.
Offa, Prince, father of St. Ethelburge, 52/7.
Officiousnes, 55/15, performing menial duties.
Oldenes, 136/17, becoming old.
Olympius, a monk, 189/3.
Omnipotent, 171/18, most high.
On, 112/29, upon, to.
On a time, 74/17, such a time.
One milke, 152/5, the same milk (meaning that the two children had been suckled by the same nurse).
Onelie, 9/22, 19/33, only; 77/27, singly.

Oportunitie, 44/23, chance, occasion.
Oppressed, 190/12, overcome.
Oratorie, 96/14, house of prayer.
Orbila, abbess, 92/15.
Ordayned, 93/32, predestinated.
Order, 24/30, management, government, rule.
Order, v., 30/10, set in order, arrange.
Ordered, 109/30, put in order.
Orders, 210/10, bodies, companies.
Ordure, 74/28, filth.
Orgarius [Otgar], Bishop, 84/14.
Ornamentes, 13/20, good mental qualities.
Ositha, 94/35.
Ositha, St., memoir of, 97, 98.
Ostforus, Bishop, 56/27.
Ostia, where St. Monica died, 132/22.
Oswald, St., 65/14.
Osway, King, 66/4.
Oswen or Osman, St., memoir of, 100, 101.
Oswie, King, 65/14.
Other-where, 92/19, elsewhere.
Otherwhiles, 105/33, other times.
Ouche, 56/34, ornament or jewel.
Ouergoe, 202/36, surpass.
Ouersoft, 140/7, soft beyond reason.
Ouerpasse, 177/19, pass over.
Ouerweighe, 142/12, overbalance.
Ouerwent, 163/23, surpassed.
Ouglie, 103/14, 126/27, ugly, deformed.
Out of, 22/8, outside.
Out of hand, 187/36, forthwith, instantly.
Oute-place, 196/24, by-place, out-of-the-way spot.

Pachumius, the monasteries of, 21.
Palme, 77/4, reward.
Pantrie, 119/21, pantry.
Papps, 39/21, paps, breasts.
Parasite, 145/36, sycophant.
Parcell, 191/1, portion.
Partie, 60/4, person, man.

Past, 34/34, passed.
Patheticall, 57/28, pathetic.
Patricius, husband of St. Monica, 121/31.
Patricke, St., 41/10.
Paula, St., St. Jerome's account of, 23.
Paula, St., 22 et seq.
Pauleworth [Pollesworth], the monastery at, 94/33.
Payed, 82/17, spotted.
Payne, 47/1, pain, pangs, torture.
Paynfull, 103/10, diligent.
Paynting, 155/7, painting, sketching.
Pearce, 100/31, pierce.
Pearcing, 164/5, piercing.
Peepe, 57/4, look.
Pend, 60/6, confined.
Penda, king of Mercia, father of St. Kinesburge and Kineswide, 71/17.
Pende, 57/11, confine.
Peregrination, 189/12, journeying.
Perfect, 196/12, perfectly.
Perfect, 118/27, finish.
Perfecter, 9/36, more perfect, superior (i.e. male sex).
Perforce, 37/21, by force.
Perill, 16/13, disgrace.
Perillouslie, 215/18, at his peril.
Persecuter, 52/12, persecutor, enemy.
Perseuer, 154/4, persevere.
Personage, 4/15, personal appearance.
Perturbation, 168/9, trouble, distress; Perturbations, 127/26, troubles, disturbances.
Perturbed, 79/15, disturbed.
Peter, a brother of St. Macrina, 195/35.
Peter, a son of St. Gorgonia, 158/32.
Peter, bishop of Alexandria, 21.
Peter of Cambray's account of the holy Dympna, 43 et seq.
Peter pence, 74/5, Peter's pence (when first sent from this country to Rome).
Pettie, 80/19, mean, of low degree.

Phanuel, the father of Anna the Prophetess, 28/18.
Philosophia, the meaning of, 133/2.
Phocas, a son of St. Gorgonia, 158/32.
Physicions, 1/12, physicians.
Pictes and Scottes, 36/25, Picts and Scots.
Pillers, 19/17, pillars, monuments.
Pittifull, 33/30, 72/22, full of pity, compassionate.
Place of rest, 83/18, sleeping apartment.
Placed, 100/19, given.
Plaine, 115/2, ground.
Pointe, 208/7, spot.
Pole, 140/36, world.
Pontike Pole, 185/31, Black Sea district. Iberia was near the Euxine.
Poore, 44/22, poor.
Possessed persons, 49/7, persons possessed with evil spirits.
Posted, 45/17, made haste to return.
Posterne gate, 90/9, back entrance.
Potent, 89/5, great, mighty.
Potestates, 195/28, superiors in authority over them.
Poulled, 61/9, polled, arranged.
Powre, 88/18, power.
Powre, 77/31, pour.
Powred, 34/29, poured.
Pranked profers, 92/4, trickt out, showy.
Precedent, 197/8, preceding.
Predestinated, 129/9, preordained.
Prefect, 206/28, head, chief.
Preheminence, 194/36, preeminence.
Premised, 110/23, laid down, addressed.
Prepared, 168/9, ready.
Preparatiue, 216/25, preparation.
Preposterous, 171/8, absurd.
Prescript, 201/31, advice.
Prescription, 183/2, occupation.
Presentlie, 25/1, 46/35, 95/5, 200/34, instantly, at once.

Presentlie, 19/1, shortly, by-and-bye, soon afterwards.
Pretendeth, 146/14, makes pretence.
Pretermitt, 208/3, Pretermitte, 167/26, omit, overlook.
Prettie while, 212/3, long time.
Preuented, 144/23, forestalled.
Preuenteth her of, 182/24, prevented her from obtaining.
Prime, 52/10, first, earliest.
Princelie, 43/14, royally; 97/34, princely, necessary, sumptuous.
Principall, 163/6, the greatest, noblest.
Principia, a disciple of St. Marcella, 22.
Probation, 52/12, 63/13, exercise, discipline.
Proclayme, 31/2, proclaim, announce, substitute.
Procurement, 79/22, recommendation.
Profane, 174/18, non-Christian.
Profered, 212/31, offered, promised.
Profering, 13/34, offering.
Profunditie, 124/21, depth of ignorance.
Propose, 33/13, exhibit, show.
Proposed, 77/15, informed, showed, made acquainted with; 200/22, foreshadowed.
Prosecute, 202/20, rehearse.
Protasius, St., 134/13.
Prouoked, 81/1, constrained.
Psalmodie, 24/34, the time for psalm-singing.
Publicklie, 21/33, Publikelie, 58/16, publicly, openly.
Punishable, 126/11, worthy of punishment.
Purchase, 122/14, procure.
Purgation, 168/10, purging, cleansing.
Purge, 112/34, purify.
Purging, 175/15, cleansing
Purifying waters, 168/19, the water used at baptism.
Purposes, 18/28, pursuits, occupations.
Putt by, 65/33, stopped from.

Qnaile, 33/35, give way, abate.
Quash, 173/6, nullify.
Quicke, 214/16, alive.
Quiers, 170/6, choirs.
Queane, 46/35, bad woman; 147/23, harlot, whore.

Rabbines, 32/29, Rabbinical scholars.
Rage, 33/33, violence (of winds and storms).
Raging, 46/33, enraged; 63/23, waxing angry.
Raging a new, 31/29, becoming again enraged.
Rare, 26/32, rich, great.
Rase, 82/11, burn down.
Rased, 95/19, destroyed.
Raynes, 178/11, reins.
Reared, 188/3, erected.
Reasons why the Scotch and Irish Saints are included amongst those of England, 10, 11.
Reassume, 105/23, revert to.
Receyued, 197/17, received, had.
Receyuers, 33/22, receivers, partakers.
Recluse, 111/16, secluded.
Recommended, 98/2, commended.
Recompenced, 23/31, made equal with, set off against.
Reconcilement, 122/27, reconciliation.
Redeeme, 111/12, free.
Reduce, 110/20, reform.
Refell, 124/36, repel, refute, expose.
Refrayning sleepe, 80/23, refraining from sleep.
Regarded, 183/9, commended.
Regenerated, 168/13, born again.
Regiment, 49/31, regulation, governance.
Regular habit, 51/53, religious dress.
Religion, 57/18, religion (the profession of).
Religious, 21/31, 111/15, professed followers of religion.

Religious purpose, 19/31, vow of religion.
Religious weede, 98/13, the clothing of a religious.
Religiouslie, 36/2, piously, in the name of religion.
Religiouslie visited, 22/25, visited professionally as a matter of religion.
Reliques, 36/2, 127/27, 130/31, sacred relics.
Remitte, 178/11, commit.
Remitted, 84/26, abated.
Remittest, 129/16, pardonest.
Remitting, 166/36, abating.
Renewer, 174/12, regenerator, one who performed the baptismal rite.
Renouation, 168/12, renewing; 179/21, rebirth.
Renting, 194/18, rending.
Repelleth, 140/29, putteth away.
Reprobate, 150/7, vile, miserable.
Reproche, 120/14, weapon.
Reprochefull, 26/29, full of reproach.
Reprochefullie, 183/34, shamefully.
Reproofe, 192/25, reproach.
Reproue, 19/20, criticize, object to.
Repugning, 140/25, repugnant.
Repute, 121/27, consider.
Request, 21/5, repute, sought after.
Resolue, 111/2, melt.
Reteyning, 206/8, retaining, keeping.
Retinew, 81/20, retinue.
Reuerence, 161/29, pay due respect.
Reuerend, 76/13, reverential, revered.
Reynes, 29/6, reins.
Rhene, the river, 87/33.
Rifled, 22/7, ransacked, pillaged.
Rigged, 22/9, rifled, ransacked.
Riot, 43/16, luxurious mode of life.
Rioting, 55/3, vanity (of the world).

Ripenesse, 105/14, maturity.
Romsey, the Abbey of, 101/23.
Ronane, brother of St. Modwen, 92/8.
Rosobea, a follower of St. Maxentia, 99.
Rottennes, 120/16, sin.
Rowllinge, 90/20, rolling.
Ruddiness, 160/30, redness, colour.
Rudelie arayed, 90/2, not sufficiently well dressed.
Ruffinus' account of the captive maid in Iberia, 185 *et seq.*
Rule, 123/28, strip, band; *Regula ferrea*, iron rod or bar. Cp. our "ruler."
Runne, 100/27, running.

Sabaoth, 171/14, Saboth, 156/5, Sabbath.
Sacietie, 215/24, satiety.
Sacrifice, 140/18, the Mass.
Safe, 22/14, kept in custody, imprisoned.
Safride, mother of St. Frideswide, 80/20.
Sage, 120/5, wise.
Saile, 49/32, progress, go.
Saintlike, 96/26, like a saint, saintly.
Salington, the village of, 52/9.
Santen, 47/35, a town on the Rhine.
Satersday, 93/7, Saturday.
Saturnus, 91/24.
Sauegard, 27/36, 51/14, safeguard, safety.
Sauerie, 215/21, savoury, choice.
Sayed, 50/24, said.
Scalecliffe, the oratory at, 96/14.
Scant, 95/11, scarcely.
Schollers, 43/1, scholars, followers, in religion.
Scrapen, 64/13, scraped.
Scurrill, 19/4, scurrilous, wicked, profane.
Sea, 64/20, see, diocese.
Sea Apostolike, 74/5, the Apostolic See (i.e. Rome).
Seauen, 52/32, 210/13, seven.
Seaze, 177/14, seize.
Secular, 19/6, not professing religion; 26/25 (as opposed to religious); 111/3, worldly.
Secular greatnes, 50/9, worldly pomp.
Securelie, 147/27, safely.
Seeldome, 68/12, 159/28, seldom.
Seeme, 162/17, appear.
Seene, 195/7, perceived.
Semphronius the prefect, 146/11.
Sensible solace, 6/5, enjoyment of the senses.
Sequele, 172/12, sequel.
Serapions, 22/30, a religious order.
Serch, 43/23, search.
Serpentine, 40/3, said of stones that present a serpent-like appearance.
Seruila, 'a litle seruant,' Orbila's name changed to, 92/30.
Seruile workes, 110/31, daily occupations (which should be omitted on holy days).
Sethrith, 55/28 (? step-daughter of King Anna).
Sett forth, 207/4, performed.
Sett out, 35/4, set free, let out.
Seuere, 92/26, severe, austere.
Sexburge, St., memoir of, 54.
Shadowing, 160/16, covering.
Shaped, 185/14, fashioned.
Sharp of witt, 161/9, witty, wise.
Shee mules, 164/32, vicious animals.
Sheppheard, 156/21, shepherd.
Shined, 54/21, shone, displayed light.
Shipmen, 129/32, sailors.
Shipwracke, 38/5, shipwreck.
Shodd, 102/9, shed (tears).
Short, 80/27, meagre, small.
Shott vp, 80/22, grown up.
Showres, 164/7, rain, storms.
Shrewdlie, 57/10, keenly, cunningly.
Shrowded, 24/6, clad in a shroud.
Shruncke, 194/11, gave way.
Sider, 85/22, cider.
Sidewlla, St., 79/30.
Sieldome, 68/16, seldom.
Sighere, a prince of the East Saxons, husband of St Ositha, 97.

GLOSSARIAL, NOMINAL, AND GENERAL INDEX.   237

Signe, 208/30, mark.
Silvester, Pope, 31/33.
Singular, 76/10, particular, concise.
Slacke, 3/6, inattentive.
Sleeping on both eares, 66/21, fast asleep.
Slight, 64/4, sleight, cunning device.
Sloncke, 57/23, slunk.
Smell, 145/15, odour.
Smelling, 78/14, becoming acquainted.
Smocke, 27/24, garment.
So, 38/18, 112/35, such.
Soale, 153/10, sole (of the foot).
Societie, 62/4, company, followers.
Sockes, 96/6, foot clothing.
Socrates, 185/27.
Sodaine, 139/19, sudden.
Sodainlie, 69/19, suddenly.
Some impe or member, 81/31, one of his fraternity.
Sondrie, 3/27, 26/33, sundry.
Songues, 55/23, songs, hymns, psalms.
Sophronia, 21/34.
Sort, 91/32, manner.
Souldiors, 32/33, Souldiours, 115/28, soldiers.
Sounde, 166/5, resound.
Sounded, 209/12, resounded.
Sounded, 194/9, swooned.
Sounding, 35/23, resounding, being made known.
Southsayers, 150/24, soothsayers.
Sower, 25/35, sour.
Sowre, 122/24, sour, angry, bitter.
Sowre, 45/27, unwholesome.
Sozomenus, 185/28.
Spake, 50/27, spoken.
Sparenes, 164/15, scantiness.
Spoiled, 65/3, despoiled; 94/18, bereft.
Spoyling, 53/25, despoiling.
Sprong, 80/13, sprang, sprung up.
Spying, 121/18, observing.
Stable, 51/17, firm, abiding; 37/14, endurable.

Stanching, 80/28, quenching, satisfying.
Stale, 48/2, 90/9, stole.
Starrie gemme, 103/26, heavenly visitor.
Stay, 106/5, stop.
Staye, 115/2, support.
Stayed, 109/32, staid, demure.
Stayed, 215/33, delayed.
Staying, 199/32, stopping.
Staynes, 55/8, stains.
Stemme, 80/22, parentage.
Stewes, 147/17, brothels.
Stilled, 139/31, made still, quieted.
Stipends, 37/26, wages, reward, hire.
Stirre, 108/24, move; 150/26, stir up.
Stocke, 36/32, family, *stirpes*; 44/2, progeny.
Store, 24/15, plenty.
Store of dwellers, 47/22, population.
Stoute, 175/36, strong, able.
Straight, 84/10, strict.
Straight, 209/29, narrow.
Straite, 20/31, strict, virtuous.
Strake, 100/29, struck.
Streneshalch, the monastery of, 56/18.
Strenshalen, the monastery at, 94/34.
Striken, 82/14, 120/21, struck, stricken.
Striuelin, the monastery at, 95/33.
Stroke, 181/27, struck.
Stroken, 128/24, struck.
Strowing, 141/10, strewing.
Studious, 35/9, diligent.
Studiouslie, 53/10, steadfastly, zealously.
Sturres, 108/19, stirs, disturbances.
Suauitie, 55/25, suavity, flavour, odour.
Substance, 173/11, dignity.
Sucked vp, 89/29, partook of, imbibed.
Suckling meates, 111/30, food for infants.
Suite, 73/10, suit, quest.

238 GLOSSARIAL, NOMINAL, AND GENERAL INDEX.

Suite in law, 182/16, lawsuit.
Supernall, 43/15, 70/13, 162/21, heavenly.
Suppe, 120/4, imbibe, swallow.
Supplant, 81/7, overcome.
Sure, 145/2, true.
Surgeons iron, 120/15, sharp instrument used by surgeons.
Suteable, 4/10, suitable.
Swarmes, 191/15, multitudes.
Sweate, 202/6, sweating.
Sweate out, 140/31, cast out.
Sweete, 176/34, gracious, distinguished for suavity.
Swounde, 137/27, swoon.

Tabernacle, 209/32, canopied bier for the corpse.
Tables, 121/26, indentures, conditions.
Tablet, 56/34, flat ornament of gold or jewelry.
Take in hand, 22/6, undertake, do.
Tale-carrying, 122/4, tale-bearing.
Tasted, 138/2, hankered after.
Tatling, 66/18, evil speech.
Tearmed, 77/30, termed, called.
Temporall, 132/18, earthly.
Tend, 175/21, go.
Tenet Isle, 49/26, the Isle of Thanet.
Tentations, 50/4, 198/2, misfortunes.
Termes, 76/16, statements, details.
Terrene, 111/4, earthly.
That, 161/22, that which.
That while, 57/13, at that time.
The morrow, 48/20, on the morrow, next day.
Thecla, the spiritual name of St. Macrina, 190/15.
Theeues, 9/6, thieves.
Theiltild, a nun, 85/10.
Their, 120/9, here used for *'s*.
Them, 37/33, those.
Thence, 57/24, therefrom.
Thenith, the father of St. Wenefride, 89/6.

Theodora, the daughter of Maximianus Herculeus, 30/27.
Theodore, Archbishop, 64/20.
Theodoret, 185/27.
They for, 70/12, therefore.
Thicke, 130/20, frequent.
Thirteth, 49/7, ? thirteenth or thirtieth.
Thoroughe, 58/25, through.
Threatened, 167/10, declared.
Threed, 91/6, thread.
Thridd, 20/5, thread.
Tibbe, St., 73/31.
To, 19/2, of.
To, 164/30, too.
To, 168/28, for.
To her head, 158/23, as her lord.
To weete, 118/17, to wit.
Tonbert, Prince, husband of St. Etheldred, 67/10.
Tooke such griefe, 31/21, became so grieved.
Toppe, 133/23, climax.
Torgitha, 53/14, one of the sisters of the monastery at Barking.
Torment of stomacke, 112/8, stomach-ache.
Tossings, 49/33, troubles, vexations.
Towardlie, 11/30, promising, likely.
Trafike, 157/6, traffic.
Translated, 48/34, transferred.
Translation, 49/4, transfer.
Trauailing, 189/11, travelling.
Trayne, 74/20, train, followers, servants.
Trie, 33/2, make trial of.
Trigetus, 132/29.
Trikingham, the church of, 60/19.
Trimme and tricked, 16/11, well dressed and adorned with trinkets.
Triumphed to her of his preye, 107/2, making joy of her as his prey.
Troble, 138/5, trouble.
Troth, 87/16, truth.
Trow, 75/29, think.
Tuffes, 160/16, tufts.
Tumultes, 193/32, noises.

Turgotte, the confessor of St. Margaret, 112/17.
Turpitude, 148/17, wickedness.
Twoes, 166/11, us two, twain.
Tye, v., 4/12, tie, ally.

Vaine, 57/33, vein, strain, style, manner.
Vaine, 129/1, empty.
Vanting, 145/36, vaunting, bravado.
Valens, the Emperor, 202/5.
Valentinian, 133/33.
Vehementlie, 198/35, grievously.
Veiled, 97/22, wore the veil.
Venemous, 20/22, venomous, heretical.
Venerable, 118/10, venerated; 184/33, worthy of veneration.
Veneration, 102/6, worship.
Verie forward, 187/9, eager to embrace.
Vesta, the goddess, 146/26.
Vestiana, 206/18.
Vesture, 40/10, garment, raiment.
Vetrude, a variant of Wilfride, 104/2.
Vexed, 36/24, troubled.
Vicar, 150/34, vice-regent.
Vile, 119/22, odious, untasteful.
Vile weede, 108/6, sorry, old garments.
Violaters, 55/1, violators, wrong-doers.
Violentlie, 40/25, ruthlessly, unlawfully.
Virgin lost, 95/4, lost virgin.
Virginall veile, 98/14, a nun's veil.
Vitalianus, husband of St. Gorgonia, 158/28.
Vocall prayer, 163/10, psalms or hymns of praise.
Voices, 145/9, musical notes.
Voide, 111/28, destitute.
Vouchsafed, 30/15, sought, requested.
Vnaccustomed, 172/35, unusual.
Vnamiable 4/17, unattractive.

Vnburden, 83/29, disburden, cast away sorrow.
Vncomposed, 189/27, simple, not elaborated.
Vndecent, 194/17, indecent.
Vnderstanding, 106/32, hearing, knowing, being made acquainted.
Vnderstood of, 45/3, knew of.
Vndiuided, 95/10, indivisible.
Vndoubted, 118/5, 161/12, not to be doubted.
Vndoubtednes, 104/10, truthfulness, trustworthiness.
Vnfillable, 178/3, not to be filled.
Vnitie, 79/31, consanguinity.
Vnknowne, 188/30, undiscovered.
Vnmeasurable, 78/12, 144/35, 177/34, immeasurable, not to be measured.
Vnmoueable, 64/1, not to be moved.
Vnsatiable, 178/2, insatiable.
Vnualuable, 144/30, not to be valued.
Vnwares, 5/34, unawares, without any notice.
Vpreared, 163/15, upright.
Vrsula, St., memoir of, 36 et seq.
Vses, 17/27, purposes, objects.
Vsurped on, 104/19, unlawfully taken.
Vulgar, 189/32, common.

Walburge, St., memoir of, 82 et seq.
Warding, 53/29, taking ward of.
Ware, v., 27/24, wore; 121/22, carried.
Warilie, 78/23, cautiously.
Warmthe, 151/27, heat.
Waste, 152/7, worthless.
Wasted, 28/5, thinned.
Wasted, 36/24, harassed, troubled, laid waste to, destroyed.
Water-meates, 28/16, gruel, broth, &c.
Waues, 120/35, turnings, fashions.
Wax, 32/1, increase.

Waxed, 92/25, became, grew.
Wayling, 23/30, wailing, lamentation.
Wayte on, 172/21, serve.
Wayting, 34/27, waiting, serving.
Weart, 128/14, wert, wast.
Wedune, the monastery at, 59/34.
Weede, 28/15, the dress of a religious.
Weede, 59/25, clothing.
Weete, 34/23, wit.
Weighing, 158/4, counting.
Well-bred, 215/9, well-nurtured.
Wen, 91/10, Welsh for 'scar.'
Wench, 70/11, girl.
Wenefride, St., memoir of, 88 et seq.
Wenflede, aunt of St. Wulfhilde, 106/2.
Werburge, St., grand-daughter of St. Sexburge, 54/19.
Werewell, 106/3.
Werynes, 163/3, weariness.
Westerle, 45/7, a place near Antwerp.
Wether, 215/12, weather.
What, 115/28, who.
What, 106/19, which.
What a one, 118/32, what sort of a person.
What throughe, 36/19, 57/2, because of.
Whether, 24/18, 215/1, whither.
Which, 75/22, 130/15, what.
Which, 33 / 14, what, that which.
Whitby, the monastery of, 56/18.
Whiteliuered, 149/8, cowardly.
Whole, 189/21, full.
Whole, 153/21, perfect, healed.
Whole, 84/5, recovered from sickness.
Whollie frustrate, 172/23, frustrated.
Wholsom, 66/11, wholesome.
Wholsome, 32/36, true (spoken of the Cross on which Christ was crucified).
Whyspering, 94/4, whisper.

Widows, St. Paul's and St. Chrysostom's definitions of true, 26.
Widowes (widows) living in monasteries, 21 et seq.
Wier, the river, 59/11.
Wilburge, Princess, mother of St. Ositha, 97.
Wilfrid, mother of St. Edith, 102.
Wilfride, Bishop, 56/27, 67/15.
Wilgith, St., 79/29.
Willebrord, brother of St. Walburge, 83/1.
Willeth, 146/16, causeth.
William the Conqueror, 100/9.
Wilton, the nunnery of, 103/4, 106/32.
Winburne, the monastery at, 78/17.
Winebibber, 120/20, here used in an upbraiding manner.
Winnebold, brother of St. Walburge, 83/1.
Wisards, 8/24, wiseacres, wise men.
Wished, 168/26, 180/13, desired.
Withburding, 105/13.
Withburge, St., memoir of, 79.
Witheriack, 91/25.
Within, 140/21, inwardly.
Wittie, 190/27, ready, quick.
Witting, 66/27, knowing.
Wolle, 20/4, wool.
Wollen, 68/12, woollen.
Womanish, 134/17, 194/18, womanly.
Wooddie, 44/30, forest-like.
Woodnes, 126/27, madness.
Worke, 89/16, prevail upon with words or entreaties.
Workes of maturitie, 80/23, works fit to be performed by those of mature age.
Worthie, 22/35, sacred, worshipful.
Worthines, 107/21, greatness.
Wrapped, 163 / 2, wrapped up.
Wryting tables, 133/27, tablets for writing on.

Wulfere, King of Middle England, 54/18, 59/21, 58/27.
Wulfhelme, father of St. Wulfhilde, 105/15.
Wulfhilde, St., memoir of, 105 *et seq.*

Yeare compleate, 68/5, whole year.
Yearne, 20/5, yarn.
Yeares fitt, 39/23, fit age, ripe, apt.

Yield, 170/19, give, make.
Yield, 64/15, give way.
Yong, 30/14, 77/9, young, youthful.
Yonger far, 49/27, much the younger.
Youthfull blouds, 92/21, young gallants.

Zammale, 44/34, a place near Antwerp.
Zenobius, 132/29.

RICHARD CLAY & SONS,
BREAD STREET HILL, LONDON,
Bungay, Suffolk.

The Publications for 1872-85 (one guinea each year) are :—

49. An Old English Miscellany, containing a Bestiary, Kentish Sermons, Proverbs of Alfred, and Religious Poems of the 13th cent., ed. from the MSS. by the Rev. R. Morris, LL.D. 10s. 1872
50. King Alfred's West-Saxon Version of Gregory's Pastoral Care, ed. H. Sweet, M.A. Part II. 10s. ,,
51. The Life of St Juliana, 2 versions, A.D. 1230, with translations; ed. T. O. Cockayne & E. Brock. 2s. ,,
52. Palladius on Husbondrie, englisht (ab. 1420 A.D.), ed. Rev. Barton Lodge, M.A. Part I. 10s. ,,
53. Old-English Homilies, Series II., and three Hymns to the Virgin and God, 13th-century, with the music to two of them, in old and modern notation ; ed. Rev. R. Morris, LL.D. 8s. 1873
54. The Vision of Piers Plowman, Text C : Richard the Redeles (by William, the author of the Vision) and The Crowned King; Part III., ed. Rev. W. W. Skeat, M.A. 18s. ,,
55. Generydes, a Romance, ed. ab. 1440 A.D., W. Aldis Wright, M.A. Part I. 3s. ,,
56. The Gest Hystoriale of the Destruction of Troy, in alliterative verse; ed. by D. Donaldson, Esq., and the late Rev. G. A. Panton. Part II. 10s. 6d. 1874
57. The Early English Version of the "Cursor Mundi"; in four Texts, edited by the Rev. R. Morris, M.A., LL.D. Part I, with 2 photolithographic facsimiles. 10s. 6d. ,,
58. The Blickling Homilies, 971 A.D., ed. Rev. Dr. R. Morris, LL.D. Part I. 8s. ,,
59. The "Cursor Mundi," in four Texts, ed. Rev. Dr. R. Morris. Part II. 15s. 1875
60. Meditacyuns on the Soper of Our Lorde (by Robert of Brunne), edited by J. M. Cowper. 2s. 6d. ,,
61. The Romance and Prophecies of Thomas of Erceldoune, from 5 MSS.; ed. Dr. J. A. H. Murray. 10s. 6d. ,,
62. The "Cursor Mundi," in four Texts, ed. Rev. Dr. R. Morris. Part III. 15s. 1876
63. The Blickling Homilies, 971 A.D., ed. Rev. Dr. R. Morris. Part II. 7s. ,,
64. Francis Thynne's Emblemes and Epigrams, A.D. 1600, ed. F. J. Furnivall. 7s. ,,
65. Be Domes Dæge (Bede's De Die Judicii), &c., ed. J. R. Lumby, B.D. 2s. 1879
66. The "Cursor Mundi," in four Texts, ed. Rev. Dr. R. Morris. Part IV, with 2 autotypes. 10s. 1877
67. Notes on Piers Plowman, by the Rev. W. W. Skeat, M.A. Part I. 21s. ,,
68. The "Cursor Mundi," in 4 Texts, ed. Rev. Dr. R. Morris. Part V. 25s. 1878
69. Adam Davie's 5 Dreams about Edward II., &c., ed. F. J. Furnivall, M.A. 5s. ,,
70. Generydes, a Romance, ed. W. Aldis Wright, M.A. Part II. 4s. ,,
71. The Lay Folks Mass-Book, four texts, ed. Rev. Canon Simmons. 25s. 1879
72. Palladius on Husbondrie, englisht (ab. 1420 A.D.). Part II. Ed. S. J. Herrtage, B.A. 15s. ,,
73. The Blickling Homilies, 971 A.D., ed. Rev. Dr. R. Morris. Part III. 10s. 1880
74. English Works of Wyclif, hitherto unprinted, ed. F. D. Matthew, Esq. 20s. ,,
75. Catholicon Anglicum, an early English Dictionary, from Lord Monson's MS. A.D. 1483, ed., with Introduction & Notes, by S. J. Herrtage, B.A. ; and with a Preface by H. B. Wheatley. 20s. 1881
76. Aelfric's Metrical Lives of Saints, in MS. Cott. Jul. E 7.. ed. Rev. Prof. Skeat. M.A. Part I. 10s. ,,
77. Beowulf, the unique MS. autotyped and transliterated, edited by Prof. Zupitza, Ph.D. 25s. 1882
78. The Fifty Earliest English Wills in the Court of Probate, 1387-1439, ed. by F. J. Furnivall M.A. 7s. ,,
79. King Alfred's Orosius, from Lord Tollemache's 9th century MS., Part I, ed. H. Sweet, M.A. 13s. 1883
Extra Volume. Facsimile of the Epinal Glossary, 8th cent., ed. H. Sweet, M.A. 15s. ,,
80. The Early-English Life of St. Katherine and its Latin Original, ed. Dr. Einenkel. 12s. 1884
81. Piers Plowman : Notes, Glossary, &c. Part IV, completing the work, ed. Rev. Prof. Skeat, M.A. 18s. ,,
82. Aelfric's Metrical Lives of Saints. MS. Cott. Jul. E 7., ed. Rev. Prof. Skeat, M.A., LL.D. Part II. 12s. 1885
83. The Oldest English Texts, Charters, &c., ed. H. Sweet, M.A. 20s. ,,

EXTRA SERIES.

The Publications for 1867-1878 (one guinea each year) are :—

I. William of Palerne; or, William and the Werwolf. Re-edited by Prof. Skeat, Lit.D. 13s. 1867
II. Early English Pronunciation, with especial Reference to Shakspere and Chaucer, by A. J. Ellis, F.R.S. Part I. 10s. ,,
III. Caxton's Book of Curtesye, in Three Versions. Ed. F. J. Furnivall. 5s. 1868
IV. Havelok the Dane. Re-edited by the Rev. W. Skeat. M.A. 10s. ,,
V. Chaucer's Boethius. Edited from the two best MSS. by Rev. Dr. R. Morris. 12s. ,,
VI. Chevelere Assigne. Re-edited from the unique MS. by H. H. Gibbs, Esq., M.A. 3s ,,
VII. Early English Pronunciation, by A. J. Ellis, F.R.S. Part II. 10s. 1869
VIII. Queene Elizabethes Achademy, &c. Ed. F. J. Furnivall. Essays on early Italian and German Books of Courtesy, by W. M. Rossetti and Dr. E. Oswald. 13s. ,,
IX. Awdeley's Fraternitye of Vacabondes, Harman's Caveat, &c. Ed. E. Viles & F. J. Furnivall. 7s. 6d. ,,
X. Andrew Boorde's Introduction of Knowledge, 1547, Dyetary of Helth, 1542, Barnes in Defence of the Berde, 1542-3. Ed. F. J. Furnivall. 18s. 1870
XI. Barbour's Bruce, Part I. Ed. from MSS. and editions, by Rev. W. W. Skeat, M.A. 12s. ,,
XII. England in Henry VIII.'s Time : a Dialogue between Cardinal Pole & Lupset, by Thom. Starkey, Chaplain to Henry VIII. Ed. J. M. Cowper. Part II. 12s. (Part I. is No. XXXII. 1878, 8s.) 1871
XIII. A Supplicacyon of the Beggers, by Simon Fish, 1528-9 A.D., ed. F. J. Furnivall: with A Supplication to our Moste Souereigne Lorde ; A Supplication of the Poore Commons ; and The Decaye of England by the Great Multitude of Sheep. ed. by J. M. Cowper, Esq. 6s. ,,
XIV. Early English Pronunciation, by A. J. Ellis, Esq., F.R.S. Part III. 10s. ,,
XV. Robert Crowley's Thirty-One Epigrams, Voyce of the Last Trumpet, Way to Wealth, &c., 1550-1 A.D., edited by J. M. Cowper, Esq. 12s. 1872
XVI. Chaucer's Treatise on the Astrolabe. Ed. Rev. W. W. Skeat. M.A., LL.D. 6s. ,,
XVII. The Complaynt of Scotlande, 1549 A.D., with 4 Tracts (1542-48), ed. Dr. Murray. Part I. 10s. ,,

Early English Text Society.

The Subscription, which constitutes membership, is £1 1s. a year [and £1 1s. (Large Paper, £2 12s. 6d.) additional for the EXTRA SERIES], due in advance on the 1st of JANUARY, and should be paid either to the Society's Account at the Head Office of the Union Bank, Princes Street, London, E.C., or by Cheque, Postal Order, or Money-Order (made payable at the Chief Office, London) to the Hon. Secretary, W. A. DALZIEL, Esq., 67, Victoria Rd., Finsbury Park, London, N., and cross 'Union Bank.' (United-States Subscribers must pay for postage 1s. 4d. a year, extra for the Original Series, and 1s. a year for the Extra Series.) The Society's Texts are also sold separately at the prices put after them in the Lists.

ORIGINAL SERIES.

The Publications for 1886 are:—

84. Additional Analogs to 'The Wright's Chaste Wife,' No. 12, by W. A. Clouston. 1s.
85. The Three Kings of Cologne. 2 English Texts, and 1 Latin, ed. Dr. C. Horstmann. 17s.
86. Prose Lives of Women Saints, ab. 1610 A.D., edited from the unique MS. by Dr. C. Horstmann. 12s.

The Publications for 1887 will be chosen from—

88. Early English Verse Lives of Saints (earliest version), Laud MS., ed. Dr. C. Horstmann. [*At Press.*
Cursor Mundi. Part VI. Introduction. Notes, and Glossary, ed. Rev. Dr. R. Morris. [*Part printed.*
The Lay Folks' Catechism, by Archbp. Thoresby, ed. Canon Simmons and F. D. Matthew. [*Text printed.*
Early English Verse Lives of Saints, Standard Collection, from the Harl. MS., ed. Dr. C. Horstmann.
Supplementary Early English Lives of Saints, ed. Dr. C. Horstmann.
The Early and Later Festialls, ab. 1400 and 1440 A.D., ed. Dr. C. Horstmann.
Sir David Lyndesay's Works. Part VI. [*At Press.*
Some more Early English Wills from Somerset House, ed. W. H. S. Utley, B.A.
Thomas Robinson's Life and Death of Mary Magdalene, ab. 1620 A.D., ed. O. Sommer. [*At Press.*
Q. Elizabeth's Translations, from Boethius, &c., edited from the unique MS. by Walford D. Selby. [*At Press.*
Treatise on the Virtues, from a Stowe MS., ab. 1200 A.D., edited from the unique MS.
Early English Deeds and Documents, from unique MSS., ed. Dr. Lorenz Morsbach.
Merlin, Part IV., containing Preface, Index, and Glossary. Edited by H. B. Wheatley.
Beowulf, a critical Text, &c., ed. Prof. Zupitza, with Dissertations by Prof. Müllenhoff.
Pilgrimage of the Lyf of Manhode, in the Northern Dialect, ed. S. J. Herrtage, B.A.
Anglo-Saxon and Early English Psalters, ed. W. Aldis Wright, M.A., Ph.D.
Early English Homilies, 13th century, ed. Rev. Dr. R. Morris.
The Rule of St. Benet: 5 Texts, Anglo-Saxon, Early English, Caxton, &c., ed. Rev. Dr. R. Morris.

EXTRA SERIES.

The Publications for 1886 and 1887 will be chosen from—

The Wars of Alexander, ed. Prof. Skeat, Litt. Doc. [*At Press.*
Charlemagne Romances:—Huon of Burdeux, by Lord Berners, ed. S. L. Lee, B.A. Part IV. [*At Press.*
Torrent of Portyngale, from the unique MS. in the Chetham Library, ed. E. Adam, Ph.D. [*At Press.*
Bp. Fisher's English Works, Pt. II, with his Life and Letters, ed. Rev. Ronald Bayne, B.A. [*At Press.*
A Dialogue against the Fever Pestilence, 1573. By W. Bullein. Ed. A. H. & Mark Bullen. [*At Press.*
Sir Bevis of Hamton, ed. Prof. E. Kölbing. Part II. [*At Press.*
Guy of Warwick, Part II, ed. Prof. J. Zupitza, Ph.D. [*At Press.*
Hoccleve's Minor Poems, ed. F. J. Furnivall, M.A., Ph.D. [*At Press.*
Hoccleve's Complaint, ed. F. J. Furnivall, M.A., Ph.D.

Preparing:—

Barbour's Bruce, ed. Rev. Prof. W. W. Skeat. Part IV.
Lonelich's Holy Grail, ed. F. J. Furnivall, M.A., Ph.D. Part V.
The Destruction of Jerusalem, Text A, edited from the MSS. by Dr. F. Kopka.
Robert of Brunne's Handlyng Synne, A.D. 1303, re-edited by Dr. Furnivall.

The Publications for the years 1879 to 1885 (one guinea each year) are:—

XXXIII. Gesta Romanorum (englisht ab. 1440), ed. S. J. Herrtage, B.A. 15s.   1879
XXXIV. The Charlemagne Romances:—1. Sir Ferumbras, from Ashm. MS. 33, ed. S. J. Herrtage. 15s.   ,,
XXXV. Charlemagne Romances:—2. The Sege off Melayne, Sir Otuell, &c., ed. S. J. Herrtage. 12s.   1880
XXXVI. Charlemagne Romances:—3. Lyf of Charles the Grete, Pt. I., ed. S. J. Herrtage. 16s.   ,,
XXXVII. Charlemagne Romances:—4. Lyf of Charles the Grete, Pt. II., ed. S. J. Herrtage. 15s.   1881
XXXVIII. Charlemagne Romances:—5. The Sowdone of Babylone, ed. Dr. Hausknecht. 15s.   ,,
XXXIX. Charlemagne Romances:—6. Rauf Colyear, Roland, Otuel, &c., ed. S. J. Herrtage, B.A. 15s.   1882
XL. Charlemagne Romances:—7. Huon of Burdeux, by Lord Berners, ed. S. L. Lee, B.A. Part I. 15s.   ,,
XLI. Charlemagne Romances:—8. Huon of Burdeux, by Lord Berners, ed. S. L. Lee, B.A. Pt II. 15s.   1883
XLII. Guy of Warwick: 2 texts (Auchinleck MS. and Caius MS.), ed. Prof. Zupitza. Part I. 15s.   ,,
XLIII. Charlemagne Romances:—9. Huon of Burdeux, by Lord Berners, ed. S. L. Lee, B.A. Pt III. 15s.   1884
XLIV. Charlemagne Romances:—10. The Four Sons of Aymon, ed. Miss Octavia Richardson. Pt I. 15s.   ,,
XLV. Charlemagne Romances:—11. The Four Sons of Aymon, ed. Miss O. Richardson. Part II. 20s.   1885
XLVI. Sir Bevis of Hamton, from the Auchinleck and other MSS., ed. Prof. E. Kölbing. Part I. 10s.   ,,

LONDON: N. TRÜBNER & CO., 57 & 59, LUDGATE HILL.
BERLIN: ASHER & CO., 53 MOHRENSTRASSE.

www.ingramcontent.com/pod-product-compliance
Lightning Source LLC
Chambersburg PA
CBHW021401230426
43666CB00006B/597